The Christian Family

BEE WORLD

BIBLICAL EDUCATION BY EXTENSION

The Christian Family

BEE World

First Edition

Current Printing—June 2012

© 2018 BEE World.

Revision 5/2018: Removed article on Repentance in Lesson 10.

Every attempt has been made to provide correct information. However, the publisher does not guarantee the accuracy of the book and does not assume responsibility for information included in or omitted from it.

Printed in the United States of America.

For information regarding permissions or special orders, please contact:

BEE World
International Headquarters
990 Pinon Ranch View, Ste. 100
Colorado Springs, CO 80907

ISBN: 978-1-937324-16-2

Contents

Christian Family

Welcome to the course on raising children! We are embarking on a great journey together. This course is written by parents, for parents, and to parents. We have had toddlers and teenagers and have personally experienced the things about which we are writing.

Even though we all are committed believers and all of us have tried diligently to raise our children according to biblical principles, we have had our discouragements, successes, and failures. We do not offer this course as the ultimate answer to the wonderful world of raising godly children. We know that no matter how hard we try, the results are sometimes not what we hope for. We do believe, based on our experiences, that applying the biblical principles in this course can increase the chances that your prayers for godly children who want to serve the Lord will come to fruition.

Our overriding principle in this course is:

> Success in raising children means prayerfully modeling and teaching Christian principles and trusting God with the results.

Think with us for a moment about the process of growth. The giant redwood tree grows from a seed merely 1.6 millimeters in diameter to become a tree that exceeds ninety meters in height. Scientists must use a microscope to see a whale egg, but a full-grown whale reaches a length of over thirty meters and a weight of over seventy-two thousand kilograms.

The mysterious and magnificent process of growth has been God-ordained since the creation of the world. The physical growth of plants and animals follows predictable patterns of cell division, multiplication, and differentiation. Certain basic requirements are necessary for growth, such as the presence of light and proper nutrients. Those basic requirements can foster or encourage growth, or factors like disease can hinder growth.

In a sense, many concepts that are true of physical growth are also true of spiritual growth. This course is our guide that we hope will help you accomplish your desire of raising your children to become mature and responsible Christians. We deal with some of the essential "nutrients" for growth to maturity, as well as some of the major hindrances that can cause a precious seedling to be uprooted before it has a chance to see maturity.

Our desire is to see the seedling become a well-rooted plant, capable of flowering and bearing fruit. This course is designed to give you some guidelines on how to undertake the process of nurturing your children toward spiritual maturity. We will look at the biblical teaching on child-rearing and suggest some practical ways to apply the ideas we find in Scripture. We hope that you enjoy this course and that you are given a deeper commitment to family values, a stronger relationship with your child, and a better understanding of how to grow a child for God.

Course Outline

Unit 1: Growing a Child for God

Lesson 1: Train a Child in the Way He Should Go

Lesson 2: Building the Temple of Wisdom

Lesson 3: Patterns of Parenting

Unit 2: Understanding Your Child

Lesson 4: Dealing with Children From Birth to Age Six

Lesson 5: Dealing with Children Ages Seven to Twelve

Lesson 6: Dealing with Adolescents

Unit 3: Disciplining in Love

Lesson 7: Discipline

Lesson 8: The Strong-Willed Child

Lesson 9: The Rebellious Adolescent

Unit 4: Teaching Your Child to Walk with God

Lesson 10: Beginning with Christ

Lesson 11: Teaching Our Children to Commit to God's Way of Life

Lesson 12: Releasing Your Child to God

As you plan your study schedule, decide on what dates you want to finish each unit. You can then divide this time into study periods for each lesson. We suggest that you try to do one lesson per week or three lessons per month. The lessons vary in length, but you should allocate about four hours per lesson. You can do this if you study about one hour each day. At this rate, it will take you approximately eight months to complete the course. If you desire to finish this course more quickly, you may do two or three lessons per week.

Author

This course was written by the BEE World team. Sandy Schaffer (with Entrust International) and Jody Dillow were the principle writers.

Bibliography

Arp, David and Claudia. *Almost 13*. Nashville: Thomas Nelson, 1986.

Bailey, Kenneth. *Poet and Peasant; and Through Peasant eyes: A Literary-cultural Approach to the Parables in Luke*. Grand Rapids: Wm. B. Eerdmans Publishing Company, 1983.

Botel, Helen. *Parents' Survival Kit*. Garden City, NY: Doubleday, 1979.

Campbell, Ross. *How to Really Love Your Teen*. Colorado Springs, CO: David C. Cook, 2004.

Chess, Stella and Alexander Thomas. *Know Your Child: An Authoritative Guide for Today's Parents*. New York: Basic Books, 1987.

Crabb, Lawrence J., Jr., *The Marriage Builder*. Grand Rapids: Zondervan, 1982.

Dobson, James. *Dr. Dobson Answers Your Questions*. Carol Stream, IL: Tyndale, 1982.

———. *Parenting Isn't for Cowards*. Carol Stream, IL: Tyndale, 2007.

———. *The New Dare to Discipline*. Carol Stream, IL: Tyndale, 1992.

———. *The New Strong-Willed Child*. Carol Stream, IL: Tyndale, 2004.

Edersheim, Alfred. *Sketches of Jewish Social Life in the Days of Christ*. New York: James Pott & Co., 1881.

European Child Evangelism Fellowship. *The Responsibility of Christian Parents.* Langenbruck, Switzerland: Child Evangelism Fellowship Europe, 1980.

Fox, John. *Fox's Book of Martyrs.* Public Domain, 1563.

Getz, Gene. "The Myth about Spoiling Your Baby." In *Parents & Children*, edited by Jay Kessler, Ron Beers, and LaVonne Neff. Wheaton, IL: Victor, 1986.

Goldberg, Lois. "ewil" and "iwwelet." In *Theological Wordbook of the Old Testament*, edited by. R. Laird Harris, Gleason L. Archer, Jr., and Bruce K. Waltke, 2 vols. Chicago, IL: Moody Press, 1980.

Gothard, Bill. *Institute of Basic Youth Conflicts Life Notebook.* Oak Brook, IL: Institute of Basic Youth Conflicts, 1972.

Greenfield, Guy. *The Wounded Parent: Coping with Parental Discouragement.* Grand Rapids: Baker Books, 1982.

Kelfer, Russel. *Wait: God's Encouragement for Uncertain Times.* Minneapolis, MN: Richmond Studios, 2003.

Kesler, Jay and Ronald A. Beers. *Parents and Teenagers.* Wheaton, IL: Victor, 1984.

Lybrand, Fred. *The Absolute Quickest Way to Help Your Child Change.* Kauffman Burgess Press, 1997.

Narramore, Bruce. *Help! I'm a Parent.* Grand Rapids: Zondervan, 1972.

Ortlund, Anne. *Children are Wet Cement.* Grand Rapids: Revell, 1981.

Short, Thomas. "Christian Marriage" in *Pulpit Digest.* Great Neck, NY: The Pulpit Digest Publishing Company.

Swindoll, Charles R. *You and Your Child.* Nashville: Thomas Nelson, 1977.

————. *You and Your Child Bible Study Guide.* Nashville: Thomas Nelson, 1993.

Schaeffer, Edith. *The Tapestry: The Life and Times of Francis and Edith Schaeffer.* Nashville: W. Publishing Group, 1985.

Soderholm, Marjorie. *Explaining Salvation to Children.* Minneapolis, MN: Free Church Publications, 1979.

White, John. *Parents in Pain.* Downers Grove, IL: InterVarsity, 1979.

Unit 1: Growing a Child for God

Many ideas about child-rearing exist in different cultures, and child-rearing practices vary from one extreme to another. Well-meaning parents in many countries believe that they are doing the best they can to raise their children. Christian parents, in particular, have a desire to do what is right in child-rearing, yet many of us acknowledge our own shortcomings. The Bible is our guide for life, and we can find much help within its pages. It provides both a general philosophy of Christian child-rearing and some practical suggestions on how to train our children.

In Unit 1 we will focus on the many Scripture passages that discuss children and how to raise them. Our purpose will be to lay a biblical foundation for child-rearing from which the rest of the course will flow and on which it must be based. We will also examine some negative patterns of child-rearing parents tend to practice and contrast them with a more biblical pattern of parenting that teaches a child to walk with God.

Unit Outline

Lesson 1: Train a Child in the Way He Should Go

Lesson 2: Building the Temple of Wisdom

Lesson 3: Patterns of Parenting

Unit Objectives

By the end of this unit, you will be able to do the following:

- Demonstrate an understanding of the major passages of Scripture that deal directly with the subject of child-rearing

- Explain the primary responsibility of the parents to take an active role in the spiritual training of their children

- Outline a plan to develop and deepen the spiritual training of your children both by means of personal example and by the use of prepared and spontaneous teaching

- Delineate some negative patterns of parenting and the problems that can result from these patterns

Lesson 1: Train a Child in the Way He Should Go

Lesson Introduction

Most occupations demand many years of education as preparation. Teachers complete numerous requirements to teach in the public schools. In some countries, medical doctors must have twenty years of schooling. Carpenters and plumbers go through several years of apprenticeship and training before reaching full efficiency in their fields. Yet for the work of rearing a child from the crib, we give almost no formal training (Narramore, 11).

Perhaps we assume that if conception, pregnancy, and childbearing are all natural body functions that move along without any special training, then child-rearing should come naturally, too. However, it has become painfully apparent that this is not so. We hear many accounts of unhappy homes and the alienation of parents from their children, as well as the increasing problems of young people who use drugs and alcohol. All these problems point to a glaring shortcoming in child-rearing and a need to return to an approach that is grounded in the teaching of the Bible.

In this lesson we want to look at the training process and see what it entails. We will examine some of the Scripture passages that deal with child-rearing and the practical application of these passages.

Lesson Outline

Topic 1: A Biblical View of Children

Topic 2: A Look at Proverbs 22:6

    Who Is To Train Your Child?

    Training Requires Commitment

    What Is Training?

    The Goal of Training

    Training Involves Teaching

    The Length and Character of Training

    There Are No Guarantees

Topic 3: God's Classic Passage for Training Children

    When to Teach

    Formal and Informal Teaching

Topic 4: The Balanced Home Training of Jesus

Topic 5: Conclusion

Lesson Objectives

By the end of this lesson, you will be able to do the following:

- Explain the primary responsibility of the parents in the spiritual training of their children and accept the challenge of assuming spiritual leadership in your home

- Examine your relationship with the Lord, which is the point where all effective training begins

- Discuss the characteristics of training outlined in Deuteronomy 6:4-9

Topic 1: A Biblical View of Children

Imagine when your child trustingly puts his little hand into yours. That hand may be sticky from the candy it has just held, dirty from playing outside, or have a bandage on the little finger, but as a parent, this does not matter. What matters is that his hand is placed in yours. God placed each of your children in your home, giving you the responsibility to take their hands and guide them along the path which leads to Christian maturity. (Adapted from European Child Evangelism Fellowship, 3.)

Training is Leading

The kind of home you provide for your children is very important. In some ways we may compare the home to an incubator, whose environment fosters the growth of the child who otherwise would not survive. A home can do great damage to the child or can be a source of great blessing to him. The effect of the home environment is dramatically presented in a popular poem.

> If a child lives with criticism, he learns to condemn.
>
> If a child lives with hostility, he learns to fight.
>
> If a child lives with ridicule, he learns to be shy.
>
> If a child lives with shame, he learns to feel guilty.
>
> If a child lives with tolerance, he learns to be patient.
>
> If a child lives with encouragement, he learns to have confidence.
>
> If a child lives with praise, he learns appreciation.
>
> If a child lives with fairness, he learns justice.
>
> If a child lives with security, he learns to have faith.
>
> If a child lives with approval, he learns to like himself.
>
> If a child lives with acceptance and friendship, he learns to find love in the world.
>
> —Dorothy Law Nolte, as quoted by Ortlund, 58.

Your child will learn most of his fundamental values at home. Many of his attitudes, ideas, and habits will be established on the basis of what he learns at home. As one pastor phrased it, "the parents' fingerprints are smeared all over their offspring."

This is not to say that the child is merely a lump of wet clay to be shaped solely by the parents and the environment. Each child has an inborn temperament and will. Thus, he can choose to accept or reject your teaching and your values. He will ultimately stand before God alone, responsible for his own actions.

For now he is yours to guide; his hand is in yours. Your responsibility is to train him with the goal of Christian maturity in mind. One day, when he leaves home, he will take many things with him—not necessarily physical objects, but the ideas, values, and habits he has accumulated under your roof. He will carry many of those things, both good and bad, into the family he establishes. Thus, the training that takes place in your home now may carry on for generations to come. That may give us a new perspective on our responsibility to train our children, knowing that our actions now will have an effect on future generations.

In this lesson, we will discuss the subject of training, looking at some key Scriptures to guide us in our thinking. Let us look first at a few Scriptures that speak about the child, the recipient of training.

QUESTION 1

Before you go further with this lesson, open your Life Notebook and write down general child raising practices in your culture. Do those practices vary within the Christian community? Or do people generally raise children the same, regardless of religious beliefs?

How the Scriptures View Children

Assignment

- Please read the following article:

How the Scriptures View Children

A child defies description at times, especially when you have seen one in his high chair just dump a bowl of spaghetti over his head for the pure joy of feeling it ooze down his face. No wonder people often use metaphors to describe the wonder that is a child.

Psalm 127, attributed to Solomon, uses several metaphors to describe children. For example, verse 3 says, *"Children are a gift of the Lord."* When your child is born, you are entrusted with God's property; the Hebrew word translated "gift" means "property, inheritance, portion."

God gives you the children He wants you to have because of His love. Conversely, it may be in God's plan to withhold children, as in the case of Hannah, whose womb the Lord had closed (1 Sam 1:3-6). Hannah was a godly woman; Scripture does not say that her barrenness was a punishment from God. It does say that children are a gift, a gift that is not given to everyone and not given in equal proportions.

It would be foolish to judge a person's spirituality based on the number of children he has. Many ungodly men in the Bible had numerous children. Children are God's property which He chooses to assign to a family.

All husbands and wives borrow their children. Our children are not our own. Our children belong to God. He has loaned them to us for a season. …They are not ours to keep but to rear. …They are not given to us so that we can force them to fulfill our lives and thus, in some way, cancel our failures. They are not tools to be used, but souls to be loved. (Short)

Our response should be to appreciate the gift God has given us.

If you really see your children as a gift from the Lord, **it should completely change your attitudes** about them. The attitudes should include **awe**—that God would think enough of you to give you this gift in the first place—and **appreciation** for the gift itself. Are those your attitudes? Do your children see satisfaction in your eyes when you look at them? Do you honor them by listening to them and valuing what they think and say and feel? Does your conversation reflect that they are prized?

Psalm 127:4 says that children are "like arrows in the hand of a warrior." Not everyone has the same size quiver. There are those who would prescribe the proper size of the family, claiming that a quiver had five arrows. Yet we see many godly men in Scripture who had fewer arrows or more in their quivers. There is nothing in Scripture to support a prescribed family size for every Christian.

When the psalmist compared children to arrows in the hands of a warrior, he was speaking of the strength and pride that a man can rightly feel in his family. From a practical viewpoint, children in the Old Testament played a valuable part in the family, working to aid in the financial support of the family and fighting when necessary to preserve the very life of the family.

In Psalm 128:3 children are compared to olive branches, or seedlings. During the period of gestation, God designs each seedling, putting together a distinct personality. When you become a parent, you receive that little seedling and can nurture it, water it, and watch it grow until it becomes a strong and productive olive tree.

Psalm 128 depicts the blessedness of the man who fears the Lord and walks in His ways: his wife is like a fruitful vine in his house and his children like olive plants around the table. The scene is one of domestic peace and harmony, as mother and father delight in watching their young seedlings grow. It is clear that God considers children a gift and a blessing for the family. We need to nurture and prune our young olive plants, encouraging and disciplining and giving tender, loving care that will help our children to bear fruit.

Jesus held children in high regard, even calling a child into the midst of the disciples and saying to them, "Unless you…become like children, you shall not enter the kingdom of heaven" (Mt 18:3). Then, with the child still standing there, He said, "Whoever then humbles himself as this child, he is the greatest in the kingdom of heaven. And whoever receives one such child in My name receives Me" (Mt 18:4-5). The word "receives" is the Greek word meaning "to accept, or welcome." Those of us who have been given the gift of children should accept and welcome them.

QUESTION 2

Based on your reading of the article, match the Scriptures with the related view of children.

Scripture	View of Children
Psalm 127:3	Arrows in a quiver
1 Samuel 1:5	Children to be received as Christ is received
Psalm 127:4	Seedlings growing into olive branches
Psalm 128:3	Gift of the Lord
Matthew 18:4-5	Gift not given to all

QUESTION 3

Take some time to discuss with your spouse what it would mean if you viewed your children the way Scripture does as described in the above article. Record notes from your conversation in your Life Notebook.

Topic 2: A Look at Proverbs 22:6

Probably the most familiar of all verses on child-rearing is Proverbs 22:6:

> *Train a child in the way he should go and when he is old he will not turn from it.*

Even though this passage is often quoted, we shall see in this topic that it is often misunderstood. Properly understood, however, it is loaded with practical insight.

Who Is To Train Your Child?

Scripture generally assumes that the parents are held responsible by God to be the primary trainers of their children. While the Scriptures recognize a corporate responsibility in the body of Christ for one another and for our children, the primary task of leading a child to maturity is the parents' obligation. This task may be delegated to others, such as grandparents or other care-givers, when both parents must work, but the responsibility and the authority remain with the parents.

You as a parent are a partner with God in making disciples of your children. Does this process come naturally and easily? Probably not. That is why Scripture gives you instructions on how to train your children and warnings to be careful about how you do it.

When we think of training, we usually think of planned, purposeful activity, such as an athlete training for the Olympics or a soldier training for war. Yet Scripture shows that there is another kind of training process that is going on all the time: learning by association. Proverbs 22:24-25 gives us an example.

These verses warn us that we can learn anger by associating with a hot-tempered person. In other words, learning by association is when you and your child learn by simply watching other people and gradually assimilating their habits.

Your children certainly do this. They see your actions and begin to act the way they see you act. Of course, your child's peers will also affect him, but who ultimately spends the most time with your child?

QUESTION 4

Children are at home the majority of their time, even when you take into account the time at church and in school. Therefore, children's experiences at home impact them for life. In your Life Notebook, reflect on that statement. Record some ways that you can make the most of the time you have with your child at home.

While there are outside influences on a child's life, the home has the most influence in shaping a child's character. What happens in the home plays a part in developing a child's personality and the kind of adult he will become. Were you aware that much of your child's life is spent in the home? And each day in our home, in the midst of our family, we as parents are sending our children unspoken messages on how to act and live. We can teach a child how to be angry, how to complain, or how to have a critical spirit. We can also communicate how to be patient, how to be gentle, and or how to have a thankful spirit. We need to recognize what it is that we are communicating through our actions as well as our words and ask God to help us to exemplify Christ-like character.

QUESTION 5

In your Life Notebook, reflect on what behaviors, either positive or negative, your child has learned from you that you did not directly teach. List the names of your children separately, and then write down several of those items for each child. Note which behaviors are common to all, and record your response to the results. You may also want to take a moment to pray for each child.

> God wants you to lead and nurture your children. Whether you are consciously teaching your child or not, he will learn from you.

Training Requires Commitment

Assignment

- Please read the following article:

Four Commitments for Successful Training

God wants parents to be active overseers, fathers or mothers who openly and lovingly guide and instruct the child entrusted to them.

Commitment to Christ

Training must begin in the parents' lives with their personal commitment to God. If you do not know Christ in an intimate way, it will be very difficult for you to impart a spiritual walk to your children. Most of child training is caught, not taught.

Commitment to God's Word

Read Deuteronomy 6:6-7.

As the writer of Psalm 119 discovered, God's Word needs to be central to our lives as parents. We need to become saturated in the Word of God, which transforms our perspective from the earthly to the eternal. As we live in the very presence of God from day to day, we can know that we are in His will and know that we have assurance of His support in our tasks.

There is no formula guaranteed to produce success in rearing children. If we try to follow such a formula, we will always run into some situation that does not fit or is not covered by the formula. Children are all different; they are not all poured from the same mold. Thus, we need godly wisdom, and our best source of such wisdom is the Scripture. There must always be a primary place in our lives for reading and meditating on His Word.

Commitment to Teach

In addition to our commitment to God and to His Word, we must be committed to teach (Deut 6:7-9). Many Christians feel inadequate when it comes to being a spiritual leader in the home. With God's help, as we ask Him for wisdom, there is no reason we cannot begin to lead, based on our own Christian experience. While there will always be new obstacles and circumstances demanding an increase in our faith, we have no excuse if we fail to pass on to our children what the Lord has already taught us through our own relationship with Him.

Commitment to Correct

Read Deuteronomy 6:10-12. Just as we need correction, so do our children. Read Hebrews 12:7-13. These verses remind us that the loving father is not one who never chastises or corrects but one who cares enough to do just that. It would be nice if children just accepted all of our instruction without any defiance or rebellion, but the sin nature in a child makes it inevitable that we will need to correct and chastise.

Proverbs 29:15 warns us that a child left to himself brings shame to his mother. On the other extreme, a parent can provoke a child to anger and exasperation by too much correction and nagging (Eph 6:4). Between these two rocky extremes the parent must chart a course of loving discipline, avoiding the cliffs that could destroy the child.

Taking the leadership within our family is a choice. Either we choose to actively cooperate with God and His Word or by default we choose to disobey, allowing our children to be disciplined by the influences and cultural fads of their day.

QUESTION 6

Most of what you teach your children is through your example, not your words. *True or False?*

QUESTION 7

Based on the article "Four Commitments" (refer to this article above), which of the following statements are valid perspectives on child training? *(Select all that apply.)*

A. Disciplining our children is an indicator of our love for them.

B. A child left to make his own decisions will probably turn out well if he is not disciplined.

C. Loving discipline is the best path to take in the discipline of our children.

D. To better exercise wisdom in our training, we must be saturated with the Word of God.

What Is Training?

The Hebrew word translated "train" in Proverbs 22:6 is the word *chanak*. In biblical usage, it is usually translated *dedicate*, but *begin*, *initiate*, or *inaugurate* are considered better translations. A vivid picture of this initiating process comes from a related verb which means "to rub the palate." In order to encourage a newborn baby to nurse, the Hebrew midwife commonly dipped her finger in honey or the juice of crushed dates and then rubbed it vigorously on the gums and palate of the suckling's mouth until the baby puckered and began to suck. After this the child was immediately placed on his mother's breast to feed.

In contemporary language, the idea expressed in Proverbs 22:6 is that parents should motivate a child in the right direction. You can begin in the earliest days of your child's life the process of training him in the right, wise way to live.

QUESTION 8

Think for a moment about the Hebrew word *chanak* in Proverbs 22:6. How would you *chanak* your child?

The Goal of Training

Your objective in training your child is to gradually mold your child's will so that his character and conduct become aligned with the truth or instruction you provide. Thus, your training ultimately has both biblical conduct and biblical character as its goals.

Mere outward compliance to parental requirements is not biblical training, for this can be obtained without inner transformation of the child. A child may go to Sunday School, memorize the Ten Commandments, read his Bible, and periodically pray, yet persist in lying, cheating, stealing, dishonoring his parents, and rebelling against God.

Does this describe your child? Essentially, such a child is not "trained," for the goal of training is not this kind of mere outward obedience. Nor is the goal to produce a child who can recite an endless number of Scripture verses, but is unable to apply them. Remember, your goal in training is to build Christian character that will enable your child to stand firm in the Lord as he matures. The child needs to be trained in many areas: he must learn obedience, respect, kindness, generosity, and patience. He needs to learn to get along with others, as well as to appreciate the gifts and talents that God has given to him. Proper training gradually directs your child toward a saving faith in Christ and then continues toward the goal of maturity in the Lord.

QUESTION 9

Look up the following passages. Match the Scripture with the corresponding goal of training.

Scripture	Training Goal
Ephesians 3:14-19	We should take every opportunity to train our children.
Ephesians 5:16	Our children should experientially know the love of God.
1 Timothy 1:5	We must thoroughly teach the Scriptures to our children.
2 Timothy 3:14-17	The goal of training is love from a pure heart and a clean conscience.

QUESTION 10

Do the goals discussed in the Scriptures above correspond with what you and your spouse have considered to be your goals? If you were to adopt these goals, what would change in your approach to training your children? Record your thoughts in your Life Notebook.

Training Involves Teaching

In the Old Testament, there are ten words used for the concept of teaching. The meanings of these ten words can be summarized as follows:

1. *alaph* - To cause familiarity with; the one who teaches causes the child to become familiar with a variety of subjects

2. *bin* - To increase perception and discernment

3. *dabar* - To give verbal instruction, which can be both positive and negative

4. *zahar* - To admonish, warn

5. *yada* - To impart knowledge with a purpose, to help to observe

6. *yasar* - To correct, chasten, and admonish

7. *yara* - To guide while allowing for failure

8. *lamad* - To bring about skillfulness and instill obedience

9. *sakal* - To give insight, to cause to be prudent

10. *shanan* - To teach diligently (repetitively)

The point of listing all of these verbs is to show the many facets involved in the training process which parents are to carry out. Parents generally practice most of them without thinking about it. This list shows us the comprehensive nature of our job description!

The Length and Character of Training

Assignment

- Please read the following article:

Training
How Long Does the Training Last?

Perhaps you think of a child as being between infancy and maybe ten or twelve years of age. The Hebrew word for child is used with a much broader meaning, however, ranging from a newborn (as in 1 Sam 1:22-23; 4:20-21) to a person of marriageable age (Joseph in Gen 37:2).

In the second half of Proverbs 22:6 Solomon uses a verb which probably comes from the noun meaning "beard." This verb form "denotes the aging of persons." Thus, the phrase "when he is old" probably means when he is old enough to grow a beard or when he reaches adulthood. Solomon appears to be envisioning a training responsibility that carries the child into adulthood. When the child is small, we are to create in him a thirst for godly knowledge and encourage him to submit to God and His Word. Our teaching culminates in maturity, when the child is a man or woman, old enough to marry, ready to take on the responsibility of a family. From this point on, parental training in Scripture is generally limited to counseling, exhortation, and rebuke.

Should All Children Be Trained the Same Way?

Proverbs 22:6 commands us to train a child "in the way he should go." The literal rendering in this verse is "according to his way." The meaning of this phrase is not understood the same way by all scholars.

Traditionally, this has been taken to mean "according to God's way." Others have suggested that this phrase can be interpreted to mean "according to the child's habits and interests." The instruction must take into account his individuality and inclinations, and be in keeping with his degree of physical and mental development. According to this interpretation, Proverbs 22:6 suggests that one set plan may not work with every child but that we should take into consideration the child's personality as we seek to train him to maturity.

The literal meaning of "way" is "road" or "path," but used in a metaphorical sense it may refer to a characteristic, mode, or manner. With this latter interpretation the verse would suggest that we are to train a child "in accordance with his characteristics or traits."

What does this mean? Essentially, it means that we should tailor our training to suit our child's personality. Children were not created on an assembly line and cannot all be handled the same way. Each child's characteristics are different, and what helps develop character with one child may not always work with a second.

Parents commonly make two mistakes.

1. They try to use the same approach with all their children.

2. They compare one child with another, whether consciously or unconsciously.

Both faults stem from failing to see and appreciate each child's individual characteristics. When this happens, conflict invariably begins.

QUESTION 11

Based on the article, how long does the parents' training of the children continue?

    A. Old age

    B. The child becomes an adult, that is, a male child is old enough to grow a beard

    C. Age five to ten

    D. The child is married

QUESTION 12

Discuss with your spouse the implications of this article for your training methods with your children. In your Life Notebook, attempt to evaluate whether you have used the same approach with all of them or if you have compared them with their siblings. What effects can these practices have? If you have no children, evaluate how your parents related to you and your siblings.

There Are No Guarantees

The conclusion of Proverbs 22:6 says that, when a child is old, he will not depart from "it." This is often understood as a guarantee that the children of dedicated Christian parents will never be lost or a promise that wandering offspring will return sooner or later to the fold. Is this really what the passage teaches?

Assignment

- Please read the following article:

Are The Results Guaranteed?

The conclusion of Proverbs 22:6 says that, when a child is old, he will not depart from "it." This is often understood as a guarantee that the children of dedicated Christian parents will never be lost or a promise that wandering offspring will return sooner or later to the fold.

Some believe it teaches that, after a man has lived a life of sin, he will return to the teaching of his youth. If, as we discussed, the word "old" is understood as "grown up," or mature, this latter interpretation loses its force.

We must ask, *what is the antecedent of "it"*? "It" refers back to the training; when the child is mature, he will not depart from his training. A gradual transformation of character, either positive or negative, takes place over the years as the child internalizes values and reacts in a particular way to his training. It will be difficult for him, as an adult, to change or to go a different direction. If the training has been good, if he has been rooted in the proper soil of the Word, he will not likely be uprooted easily.

The verse, however, is not an unconditional promise that a child who is properly raised will never reject training or refuse it. Proverbs are not unconditional promises but observations on what generally holds true in life. Generally speaking, children will not forsake their childhood training. But some children do reject the training of their parents. When this happens, the parents must depend upon God in His mercy and grace to keep working in the child's life.

Training is a two-sided coin. It involves:

- The parents' responsibility

- The child's response

The parent is responsible to train his child; the child is responsible to respond. As an adult he will become responsible for his own actions. Those who believe that Proverbs 22:6 offers a guarantee of

---

salvation for the children of dedicated Christian parents have assumed, in essence, that a child can be programmed so thoroughly as to determine his course.

Some parents believe that, if they do their part in bringing the child up in the way that he should go, if they provide the right environment for spiritual growth, a good outcome is guaranteed by the Lord. Yet many dedicated and sincere Christians have grown sons or daughters who have rebelled against God and their own families. These mothers and fathers did the best they could to raise their children properly, but their children chose to reject Christian teaching.

When a child goes astray, it can produce enormous guilt in the parents. If they view Proverbs 22:6 as an absolute guarantee that children whose parents trained them up properly will turn out well, they can only conclude that the child's rebellion is their own fault. They have failed to keep their half of the bargain and have sent their beloved child to hell by their parenting failures.

When we look at the entire Bible, however, we find no support for the view that the total responsibility for sin in the next generation falls on the backs of parents. Many godly men in Scripture had offspring who turned away from the Lord, yet few are blamed directly for parental failure.

The case of Eli is often used to warn parents of their responsibility (1 Sam 2:12-36). The wrath of God did fall on Eli because he failed to restrain his grown sons and remove them from the priestly office. Some theologians believe that God was not holding Eli accountable for the rebellious nature of his grown sons, Hophni and Phinehas, who were old enough to be responsible for their own actions. As the high priest, Eli was responsible to remove his sons from the priestly position they were desecrating, and he apparently could not bring himself to do it.

Ephesians 6:1-4 makes it clear that the issue of child-rearing is two-sided. Parents are admonished to bring up their children in the training and instruction of the Lord, in such a way as not to exasperate them. Children are instructed to obey their parents, which is the right thing to do, and to honor them. Thus, the parents' responsibility is proper and loving instruction and example, and the child's responsibility is to respond to the instruction with obedience and respect.

There are cases where the parents have been diligent in the training of their children and have been examples of godly character, yet a child chooses not to respond with obedience and respect. In such a situation God does not intend for parents to grovel in guilt for circumstances beyond their control.

Ezekiel 18:1-4 is helpful to us in assessing blame for the sinful behavior of grown children:

Then the word of the Lord came to me saying, "What do you mean by using this proverb concerning the land of Israel saying,

'The fathers eat the sour grapes,

But the children's teeth are set on edge'?

"As I live," declares the Lord God, "you are surely not going to use this proverb in Israel anymore. Behold, all souls are Mine; the soul of the father as well as the soul of the son is Mine. The soul who sins will die."

Ezekiel 18:20 concludes:

The son will not bear the punishment for the father's iniquity, nor will the father bear the punishment for the son's iniquity; the righteousness of the righteous will be upon himself, and the wickedness of the wicked will be upon himself.

These words from the Lord make it clear that each adult is responsible for his own behavior.

QUESTION 12

Please read the following proverbs. Each of them make statements that might seem like absolute promises, just like Proverbs 22:6. Think about each of them. Which of the statements made in these proverbs are likelihoods rather than absolute promises? *(Select all that apply.)*

    A. Proverbs 10:4

    B. Proverbs 10:22

    C. Proverbs 10:27

    D. Proverbs 28:16

    E. Proverbs 12:21

QUESTION 13

In the reading "Are the Results Guaranteed?", what do you understand the author's main idea to be? How would you summarize his conclusion? Do you agree or disagree and why? Record your answers in your Life Notebook.

QUESTION 14

Do you know someone who is tormented by guilt over a grown child who has gone astray? What encouragement could you give to such a person? Outline what you might say to him or her. Why not put his name into your Life Notebook now and pray for him, asking God to give you an opportunity to share with him?

Topic 3: God's Classic Passage for Training Children

Read Deuteronomy 6:4-9, a classic passage about training children. These six verses are known to the Jews as the *Shema*, from the Hebrew word translated "hear" in verse 4.

To this day Orthodox Jews recite the *Shema* daily and teach their children to recite it when they are old enough to talk. This passage contains one of the clearest statements in Scripture regarding parents' responsibility to train their children. In verses 4-5 we find the basis for effective parenting: knowing and loving the Lord. If we love the Lord with all our heart, then His words will be inscribed there:

> And these words, which I am commanding you today, shall be on your heart (Deut 6:6; see also Lk 6:45).

Thus, training is founded on the example of parents' lives and their own personal walk with God. This is the primary teaching of this passage: the heart of God's desire for us is devotion to Him; faith and total allegiance is to be given to the one true God. He requires from His people nothing less than to love Him with all their heart, soul, and might.

QUESTION 15

The major thrust of the *Shema* is that effective child training begins with the parents' personal relationship with the Lord. Open your Life Notebook and reflect on these questions. First, ask yourself how you would answer the four questions below and secondly, turn your answers into written prayers asking God to help you be the man or woman of God your child needs as a parent.

    1. How vital is your relationship with the Lord?

    2. Is it **with all your heart**—or is it hollow?

3. Is it **with all your soul**—or is it superficial?

4. Is it **with all your might**—or is it a half-hearted attempt?

Without this close relationship of love for the Lord, "Whatever instruction we give our children is like a noisy gong. And the longer and louder we clang our cymbals, the more our children will just cover their ears."

> It is out of the overflow of a vital, loving relationship with God that parents are to instruct their children. The teaching should be conducted diligently, continually, and with a view to preparing the child for life.

(Questions and quotes in this topic from Swindoll, *You and Your Child Bible Study Guide,* 40-42.)

Spend some time in prayer and meditation today as you reflect on the depth of your own walk with the Lord.

When to Teach

In Deuteronomy 6:7 God describes when we should teach our children His Word. These verses say that we are to teach:

- When you sit in your house

- When you walk by the way

- When you lie down and when you rise up

Assignment

- Please read the following article:

The Old Testament Model for Child Raising
When To Teach

In Deuteronomy 6:7 God talks about when we should teach our children His Word. These verses say that we are to teach:

When you sit in your house and when you walk by the way and when you lie down and when you rise up.

This verse covers almost every activity of a normal day. Thus, family life is a "classroom" in which parents should daily communicate the truths about God to their children in a positive way. The passage uses both the words "teach" and "talk." God is telling us that parents should saturate the routine of normal living with the very presence of God in their homes.

Moses recorded these verses of Deuteronomy at a time when the Israelites were preparing to enter the land of Canaan. At such a time the Lord emphasized the spiritual training of children. The spiritual dangers facing the Israelites, and especially their children, were formidable. Ahead of them lay not only physical battles but spiritual battles against powerful forces. Is it any different today? Sadly, the Israelites of Moses' day failed to heed the warning of Deuteronomy. They neglected to teach their children, who became easy prey to the false religions of Canaan, as we see in Judges 2:10-13. Read the passage before continuing.

Modern parents can learn from this example. What did the Lord ask parents to do to prepare their children? When should they teach their children?

QUESTION 16

If the Israelites are our guide, we can conclude that there is little spiritual danger to our children in neglecting the classroom of life (see Judg 2:10-13). *True or False?*

Formal and Informal Teaching

Assignment

- Please read the following article:

Formal and Informal Teaching

Formal Times

By using two verbs, *teach* and *talk*, Moses may have been indicating that there are to be certain formal teaching times in the life of a family, when parents would impart Bible knowledge to their children, and certain informal times of teaching. Formal teaching takes place, for example, during a period of family devotions together.

Other formal teaching times at home may be planned throughout the year. On special holidays or occasions for celebration, such as Christmas, Easter, birthdays, births, marriages, funerals, and family reunions, parents have the opportunity to teach spiritual truths. We can let these opportunities go by too easily. Yet these are occasions when children are more sensitive, more vulnerable to receive what we have to say.

Talk is what takes place in the normal context of family living. Moses is asking parents to impart spiritual truth to their children on a daily basis, as they simply talk to them. Parents can explain to a child why they do or do not do certain things in their family life. For example, we can explain why we pray before meals, help a neighbor, go to church, show love and concern for others, or why we do not lie or never watch certain films. As you offer simple explanations to your children, you are communicating values and encouraging a child's discernment. These explanations should not be lengthy lectures but simple statements of what you believe God's Word teaches.

Informal Times

Nature provides many wonderful opportunities to talk to a child about the beauty, order, design, and intricacy of God's creation. In so doing, you can communicate your faith in God's goodness, strength, and omnipresence. Each day is filled with opportunities to talk with our children about the Lord.

Children may be especially open to parents' instruction at certain times. Special "teachable moments" occur spontaneously, and parents need to learn to recognize them. A child may be giving you a signal that he is open to this kind of teaching: perhaps he asks a thoughtful question or has an inquiring look on his face or has just gone through an emotional experience that leaves him vulnerable. At such times the child may be more open to receive spiritual truths, and he will readily receive biblical explanations on a level he can understand.

Be aware when these teachable moments occur; it is easy to miss the opportunity for spontaneous teaching. Some common teachable times are:

1. When a parent prays with a child at bedtime

2. At times of special need: sickness, injury

3. When the child is facing some unusual pressure at school

4. When a death in the family occurs

5. When the child is struggling with feelings of guilt

An important factor in taking advantage of teachable moments is that we remain "approachable." Are you willing to listen to your children and patiently answer their many questions day by day? If you are, your child will know you care. Then when that the child has a question that is bothering him, he will not think, "Oh, Dad (or Mom) does not care. He (or she) never listens to anything I say anyway!" Instead, he will feel free to come and ask you that important question, and you will have a special opportunity to help him spiritually.

Why is it that sometimes we hesitate to "teach" and "talk" to our children about the things of the Lord the way Moses urges us to in Deuteronomy? Perhaps the price is too high—a lot of time and interest must be devoted to the child. Many parents are simply unwilling to pay this price. Sometimes we devote our time and interest to other things that seem to be more important and neglect the priority of training our children. These other things may be good and profitable, but the training of a child toward spiritual maturity should unquestionably be among the highest of our priorities.

If parents are unwilling to pay this price in time and interest when the children are small, they may have to pay a much higher price later—the price of heartbreak or regret... or worse.

God's Word contains wondrous things for us to communicate to our children, especially the message of the gospel of our Lord Jesus Christ. It is a privilege to bring up children in the Christian faith and a joy to see our children grow to become mature in the Lord. Let us not neglect the primary responsibility God has given us as parents to train our children in God's Word.

QUESTION 17

Reflect on Deuteronomy 6:4-9. Think of some practical ways to apply the admonition to teach when you walk by the way, when you lie down or rise up.

- Write down your ideas in your Life Notebook and set some goals for yourself in the area of teaching.

- Memorize these verses. You may want to write out the verses on small pieces of paper to memorize by reading them aloud repeatedly. As you continue to read the verses, you will soon be reading less and reciting from memory more.

Topic 4: The Balanced Home Training of Jesus

Assignment

- Please read the following article:

The Balanced Home Training of Jesus

The early life of Jesus provides an example of how the Hebrew model of education was faithfully adhered to and carried out by Jesus' earthly parents. Read Luke 2:39-40, 52.

The album we have of Jesus as a boy contains only two photographs: one of His childhood (Lk 2:39-40); the other as He stands on the threshold of His teenage years (Lk 2:41-52). Neither are fully developed, but enough of the lines are present to give resolution to those early, formative years. Let's pick up the first snapshot.

In verse 39 we see Mary and Joseph during those early years of Jesus' infancy. Pictured here are two committed parents—committed to the Lord and committed to their child. And their commitment is meticulous, "[performing] everything according to the Law of the Lord" (Swindoll, *Your and Your Child*, 44).

Not only did Mary and Joseph attend to the spiritual training of the young Jesus, but they also emphasized the practical. Jesus learned the trade of carpentry, so that He was able to help support Himself and provide for His family (Jn 19:26-27). He was known as the carpenter or carpenter's son (Mk 6:3).

Four areas of growth are mentioned in verses Luke 2:40 and Luke 2:52. We are told that Jesus grew in wisdom (mental growth), in stature (physical growth), in favor with God (spiritual growth), and in favor with man (social growth). These verses show us the humanity of Christ and the aspects of His development, aspects which we should also consider in raising our children. Some parents would emphasize only the spiritual aspect of a child's development. Yet spiritual development does not take place in a vacuum. A child needs to grow socially, mentally, and emotionally, as well.

Jesus' life is depicted as balanced. The phrase "in favor with God and men" indicates that both His relationship to God and to man were in harmony. In His everyday contact with people it is evident that His contact with the heavenly Father never suffered.

QUESTION 18

What are the four ways in which Jesus matured?

Topic 5: Conclusion

It is appropriate that we looked at the life of Christ as the final emphasis in this lesson. For as we consider the task of training, our goal is that our children might conform more and more to the image of Christ. Not surprisingly, this is a goal we need to set for ourselves as well—not once a year, as a New Year's resolution, but daily. Let us seek to be like Him, to model Christ-like character before our children. Our lives will speak louder than all our words.

The task of training is an awesome one, as we have seen. Yet God calls us to commit ourselves to this task over and over again, each new morning when our children hop out of bed to start another day. As we renew our commitment to the task of training, we need to look afresh to Jesus, keeping our eyes on Him, leaning on Him, and letting Him show us, by His matchless example, how to be wise and godly parents.

QUESTION 19

It is time to sum up what we have been studying. Open your Life Notebook and write out answers to the following questions.

1. What have been your greatest joys in raising children? Your greatest struggles in the training process and why?

2. How can you deepen your training commitment in light of your study on the four commitments?

3. How do you evaluate yourself in terms of the example you set for your child?

4. What are some specific examples of teaching and talking with your children?

5. Has your training been the same with every child? In what ways have you tended to compare your child with his siblings? What are the results of your training?

6. What ways have you tried to train a child according to his character traits, abilities, and interests?

7. What was the most significant for you in this study? Discuss your answers with your spouse.

Note: If you have no children, evaluate your own parents in some of these areas. If your children are grown, also answer this question: If you could redo your parenting, what would you do differently?

Lesson 1 Self Check

QUESTION 1

Proverbs were not intended to be absolute promises from God but are general principles and guidelines which may have exceptions. *True or False?*

QUESTION 2

The Old Testament teaches that a major indicator of the depth of our walk with God is the number of children we have. *True or False?*

QUESTION 3

The Bible teaches that the total responsibility for sin in the next generation lies with the parents. *True or False?*

QUESTION 4

The phrase "when he is old" probably refers to **when he is mature**, or old enough to grow a beard. *True or False?*

QUESTION 5

The type of training implied by Proverbs 22:24-25 might be described this way: some behaviors are picked up from others, and not directly taught to you. *True or False?*

QUESTION 6

What does Deuteronomy 6:7 suggest about child-rearing?

- A. Family devotions are critical for child development.
- B. Formal teaching is God's primary means of instructing our children.
- C. It is critical that children rededicate themselves to the training process by repeating the *Shema*.
- D. The main classroom for child-rearing is the classroom of life.

QUESTION 7

What is the most important characteristic of a parent to be effective in growing a child for God?

- A. How much he loves his wife
- B. His personal intimacy with Christ
- C. His practical knowledge of the Scriptures
- D. His ability to articulate biblical truths in a clear and concise manner

QUESTION 8

Based on the article on the Four Commitments, which of the following statements are valid perspectives on child training? *(Select all that apply.)*

- A. Disciplining our children is an indicator of our love for them
- B. A child left to make his own decisions will probably turn out well if he is not disciplined.
- C. Loving discipline is the best path to take in the discipline of our children.
- D. To better exercise wisdom in our training, we must be saturated with the Word of God.

QUESTION 9

Which of the following is a probable translation of the word "train" in Proverbs 22:6?

A. Initiate

B. Discipline

C. Correct

D. Teach

QUESTION 10

I have memorized Deuteronomy 6:4 and can write it out from memory. *True or False?*

Lesson 1 Answers to Questions

QUESTION 1: *Your answer*

QUESTION 2

Scripture	View of Children
Psalm 127:3	Gift of the Lord
1 Samuel 1:5	Gift not given to all
Psalm 127:4	Arrows in a quiver
Psalm 128:3	Seedlings growing into olive branches
Matthew 18:4-5	Children to be received as Christ is received

QUESTION 3: *Your answer*

QUESTION 4: *Your answer*

QUESTION 5: *Your answer*

QUESTION 6: True

QUESTION 7

    A. Disciplining our children is an indicator of our love for them.

    C. Loving discipline is the best path to take in the discipline of our children.

    D. To better exercise wisdom in our training, we must be saturated with the Word of God.

QUESTION 8: *Your answer should be similar to the following:*

The basic idea, taken from motivating a child to suck by rubbing the gums with honey or crushed dates, is that parents are to motivate a child in the direction he should go.

QUESTION 9

Scripture	Training Goal
Ephesians 3:14-19	Our children should experientially know the love of God.
Ephesians 5:16	We should take every opportunity to train our children.
1 Timothy 1:5	The goal of training is love from a pure heart and a clean conscience.
2 Timothy 3:14-17	We must thoroughly teach the Scriptures to our children.

QUESTION 10: *Your answer*

QUESTION 11

    B. The child becomes an adult, that is, a male child is old enough to grow a beard [Thus, the phrase "when he is old" probably means when he is old enough to grow a beard or when he reaches adulthood. Solomon appears to be envisioning a training responsibility that carries the child into adulthood.]

QUESTION 12: *Your answer*

QUESTION 12

    A. Proverbs 10:4

    B. Proverbs 10:22

    C. Proverbs 10:27

    D. Proverbs 28:16

    E. Proverbs 12:21

[Many biblical scholars agree that the Proverbs represent likelihoods rather than absolutes with God's personal guarantee attached. It is generally true that most children who are brought up in Christian homes under the influence of godly parents who both teach and live by God's standards follow that training. Though Proverbs 22:6 is generally true, exceptions occur because of the self-will or deliberate disobedience of a child who chooses to go his own way.]

QUESTION 13: *Your answer*

QUESTION 14: *Your answer*

QUESTION 15: *Your answer*

QUESTION 16: False [Moses recorded these verses of Deuteronomy at a time when the Israelites were preparing to enter the land of Canaan. At such a time the Lord emphasized the spiritual training of children. The spiritual dangers facing the Israelites, and especially their children, were formidable. Ahead of them lay not only physical battles but spiritual battles against powerful forces. Sadly, the Israelites of Moses' day failed to heed the warning of Deuteronomy. They neglected to teach their children, who became easy prey to the false religions of Canaan, as we see in Judges 2:10-13.]

QUESTION 17: *Your answer*

QUESTION 18: *Your answer should be similar to the following:*

We are told that Jesus grew in wisdom (mental growth), in stature (physical growth), in favor with God (spiritual growth), and in favor with man (social growth).

QUESTION 19: *Your answer*

Lesson 1 Self Check Answers

QUESTION 1: True

QUESTION 2: False

QUESTION 3: False

QUESTION 4: True

QUESTION 5: True

QUESTION 6

    D. The main classroom for child-rearing is the classroom of life.

QUESTION 7

    B. His personal intimacy with Christ

QUESTION 8

    A. Disciplining our children is an indicator of our love for them

    C. Loving discipline is the best path to take in the discipline of our children.

    D. To better exercise wisdom in our training, we must be saturated with the Word of God.

QUESTION 9

    A. Initiate

QUESTION 10: True

Lesson 2: Building the Temple of Wisdom

Lesson Introduction

Have you ever pleaded with God to give you wisdom? Sometimes it seems that we Christians are aware of our need for wisdom only when we face adversity. When our family life is going well and our children are happy and obedient, we are not so inclined to ask for God's wisdom on a daily basis. Yet when we have problems at home, we are quick to cry out, "Give me wisdom, Lord."

It is easy to confuse wisdom with quick solutions to problems. Yet in the Bible, wisdom is something very different. The entire book of Proverbs was written with the objective of imparting an intimate acquaintance with wisdom. The word used for wisdom actually refers to skill. Thus, the purpose of Proverbs is that we might become adroit at the greatest skill of all—the skill of living.

Our society today possesses more knowledge than any previous one, yet people are suffering from a lack of this skill for living. Frequently, university graduates, while trained in their profession, have no idea how to raise a family or have a successful marriage.

As parents with the responsibility of raising children to love the Lord in the midst of a perverse world, we are in special need of godly wisdom. In this lesson we will look at the book of Proverbs to see what it has to teach us about the skill of living and to consider how we might inculcate wisdom in the lives of our children.

Lesson Outline

Topic 1: The Temple of Wisdom

Topic 2: The Pillar of the Fear of the Lord

Topic 3: The Pillar of Discipline

Three Kinds of Discipline

Natural Consequences

Reproof

The Rod

Topic 4: The Pillar of Discernment

Defining Discernment

Teaching Discernment

Topic 5: The Pillar of Wise Behavior

Topic 6: The Pillar of Prudence

Topic 7: The Pillar of Knowledge

Topic 8: The Pillar of Discretion

Topic 9: Examining Our Own House of Wisdom

Topic 10: Conclusion

Lesson Objectives

By the end of this lesson, you will be able to do the following:

- Explain the purpose of the book of Proverbs
- Define the "fear of the Lord" and each of the "pillars of wisdom," determining at least one practical way to implement them in your family
- Demonstrate how to use natural consequences and logical consequences in child-rearing

Topic 1: The Temple of Wisdom

> Wisdom has built her house, she has hewn out its **seven pillars** (Prov 9:1, emphasis added).

Seven goals for child raising are presented in the book of Proverbs. They are called *"pillars of wisdom."*

In this study, each pillar will represent a principle, or concept, founded on a goal: The Fear of the Lord, Discipline, Discernment, Wise Behavior, Prudence, Knowledge, and Discretion. We recognize that the meanings of each overlap to some degree. There is not always a sharp distinction between them. On the other hand, the fact that the course writers chose to use these different words suggests some valid distinction in their meanings. We further recognize that the various Bible translations may not always reflect these distinctions. Thus, you may have some difficulty answering some of the questions that ask you to look up verses containing these Hebrew words. In those cases where it is not so clear, then look for the concept being discussed, for ultimately the issue is the concept, not the word itself.

In this lesson we will explain the meaning of each word and what it means for a parent to adopt these pillars as goals in raising their children.

Assignment

- Please read the following article:

The House of Wisdom
What Is a Proverb?

The Proverbs of Solomon comprise one of the three "wisdom" books in the Old Testament, along with Job and Ecclesiastes. According to 1 Kings 4:32, Solomon spoke three thousand proverbs and wrote the majority of the collection of proverbs in this book. There are two other authors—Agur, the author of Proverbs 30, and Lemuel, the author of Proverbs 31.

What exactly is a proverb? The Hebrew term for "proverb" means "a comparison" and came to be used for any wise or moralistic pronouncement. A proverb is a short but profound statement that expresses a commonplace truth or a useful thought. The collection of sayings we find in the book of Proverbs is essentially the instruction given by a king to his son on how to rule and to live wisely.

For people who like quick, black-and-white answers, reading Proverbs can be frustrating. Material set in proverbial form is meant to encourage the reader to slow down, to think and compare. Each couplet serves as a kind of thesis for discussion.

At the outset it should be made clear that a proverb is not a promise. A biblical promise is something to which God commits Himself, something His people can depend on as always being true. The wise sayings found in Proverbs, on the other hand, are generalizations based upon the observation of life, generalizations for which there may be, and often are, exceptions.

The Purpose of the Book of Proverbs

Read Proverbs 1:1-7, the prologue to the book.

The theme running throughout the book of Proverbs is wisdom for living. The book deals with specific instructions on a number of topics, including folly, sin, wealth, poverty, pride, humility, justice, strife, laziness, friendship, and many others. Many facets of human relationships are dealt with in Proverbs. Part of the instruction is addressed to an older boy addressed as "my son." We surmise that he is older because he is mature enough to understand some very profound instructions and symbolic language. The book of Proverbs has much to offer to older children and adults, since it provides instruction on how to acquire life's most priceless possession—wisdom. It is a key book to study in order to see what important issues parents should be communicating to their children. It is also a good book to study together with older children.

The first seven verses of Proverbs introduce four objectives for the book. These are as follows:

1. To impart an intimate acquaintance with wisdom and discipline (v. 2)

2. To impart understanding of wisdom sayings, a common mode of discourse among the sages of Solomon's day (v. 2)

3. To impart moral insight (v. 3)

4. To identify the intended recipients of wisdom (v. 4)

The fourth verse tells us that the book is particularly addressed to the naive and the young. Wisdom is not for the fool, who will only despise it. But the young and the naive can become acquainted with wisdom. Indeed, fathers were responsible to see that they conveyed wisdom to their children, so that they would not enter society without this valuable asset.

Verse 5 presents the means of becoming wise. In order for anyone to be intimately acquainted with wisdom, he or she must be willing to hear. The one who seriously desires wisdom must be receptive. This is the key to wisdom—a simple one, yet not always easy to achieve. To become wise, we must learn to be receptive. Thus, to impart wisdom to our children, we must first teach them to be receptive, to listen. Proverbs 2:1-4 presents two conditions for wisdom: a trained ear and a heart inclined toward instruction.

What exactly is wisdom, and how is it to be imparted? In the Old Testament the word *chokma* refers to the skill of craftsmen, tailors, singers, mourners, administrators, and counselors (Ex 28:3; 31:3, 6; 35:35). People who were proficient in their areas of expertise were considered skillful; they were therefore "wise." Thus, if a person has wisdom, he is able to live life skillfully, to live it as a thing of beauty. As Christian parents we have a magnificent goal to set before our children—the goal of skillful living, living wisely! God has given us the book of Proverbs to assist us in the important task of building wisdom into the lives of our children.

The Structure of the House of Wisdom

In Matthew 7:24-27 Jesus used the illustration of a man who built his house on the rock. He was a man who heard the Word of God and acted upon what he heard. When the rains came and the floods rose and the winds blew, this house stood firm. Jesus called this man wise, and indeed he illustrates many of the aspects of wisdom outlined in Proverbs, as we will see. Proverbs 24:3-4 says:

> By wisdom a house is built, and through understanding it is established; through knowledge its rooms are filled with rare and beautiful treasures. (NIV)

These verses in Proverbs are symbolic of the life of an individual or a family. A house or family is built by wisdom and established by understanding between husband and wife, parent and child. Every area of family life can feel the touch of God's blessing when family members are committed to wisdom. Wisdom, as we will see, has many aspects, including sound judgment, sensitivity to others, and the ability to discern and avoid paths that lead to what the Bible calls folly. Wisdom involves learning from our successes and failures and putting what we learn back into the building.

This kind of wisdom has only one source. Proverbs 2:6 says, "For the Lord gives wisdom; from His mouth come knowledge and understanding." Psalm 127:1 says, "Unless the Lord builds the house, they labor in vain who build it." God is at work in our lives—supervising the building of the house, making a little correction here and there in our calculations, guiding our hands in craftsmanship—if, and only if, we allow Him to do this for us. The wise builder allows Him to be the Architect and relies on the layout and design in God's Word.

Proverbs 8 depicts wisdom calling out to all who pass by, saying, "Here, come and try me. I speak what is true and just."

> Take my instruction, and not silver, and knowledge rather than choicest gold. For wisdom is better than jewels; and all desirable things cannot compare with her. ...For he who finds me finds life, and obtains favor from the Lord. But he who sins against me injures himself; all those who hate me love death (Prov 8:10-11, 35-36).

Proverbs 9:1 depicts wisdom building her house, supported with seven pillars. She prepares a feast for those who will join her and learn her ways. By now it is clear that wisdom is available to us— she calls to all the simple. She can be found, for she says, "I love those who love me; and those who diligently seek me will find me" (Prov 8:17). The only condition set forth in Proverbs is that we must seek her.

If we desire to build a home that pleases God, we need wisdom to do it right. To find wisdom, we must seek wisdom; God promises it is available to us.

But folly, too, has a house and gives parties that seem to be well-attended. For a while, at least, it seems like everyone is having a good time. But the end of folly's parties is the grave (Prov 9:13-18). We have a choice to make: to build our families on the foundation of wisdom or on another foundation. But any choice other than wisdom is folly.

Some begin building on the right foundation but later tear down what they have built (Prov 14:1). Perhaps they are dissatisfied with the master plan, or perhaps they have been building with wood, hay, and stubble.

Wisdom is needed in every step of the building process, from laying a strong foundation to putting up walls, to painting and wall papering, to occasional redecorating, to doing maintenance and upkeep. Whenever we let wisdom go, the house will begin to crumble a bit and may eventually decay and collapse.

This lesson is designed to encourage you in your house-building task—to set before you the goal of wisdom, to examine wise counsel on child-rearing, and to look at some goals suggested in Proverbs. As you study these materials, we pray that God will use them to motivate you to build your house on the rock and to remind you to seek wisdom in maintaining and refurbishing your home as God desires.

Solomon exhorts his readers, "Wisdom is supreme; therefore get wisdom" (Prov 4:7, NIV). In this lesson we will examine some of the aspects of wise living set forth in Proverbs and encourage you to develop these areas in your child. We have labeled these aspects of wise living "pillars" because each one contributes to the building of an individual life based on the solid foundation of which the Bible speaks. Let us look at the "pillars" necessary for the building of a house of wisdom and see how each can be emphasized in the child-rearing process.

QUESTION 1

Look up Proverbs 22:9, 11, 16, 29. We should interpret them as representing absolute promises. *True or False?*

Topic 2: The Pillar of The Fear of the Lord

Proverbs 1:7 gives us the guiding principle for the pursuit of wisdom: the fear of the Lord. Using our "house of wisdom" image, the fear of the Lord is at the front of the house and the other pillars are behind it, for it is the only way a person may acquire genuine wisdom.

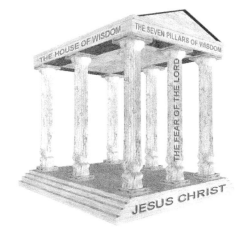

QUESTION 2

The following passages illustrate the two fundamental ideas involved in the fear of the Lord in the Bible. Look them up, and make notes in your Life Notebook. Do you think there is any connection between "A" and "B" below?

 A. Leviticus 19:3; Joshua 4:14

 B. Genesis 22:12; Deuteronomy 10:12-13

What is this "fear" that we must have before we can build a house of wisdom? When the word "fear" is used in reference to the Lord, the emphasis is upon submission to the Lord, to whom we ascribe awe and respect. Such a fear expresses itself in total commitment of one's life to Him, resulting in obedience and deliberate avoidance of evil.

But how do we help our children develop the "fear of the Lord?"

Assignment

- Read 2 Timothy 1:5; 3:14-15.

QUESTION 3

What about Lois and Eunice enabled Paul to have great confidence in Timothy's walk with God? *(Select all that apply.)*

  A. Their sincere faith

  B. Their diligence in teaching Timothy from a young age

  C. Their ability to impart conviction to Timothy

  D. Their regular involvement in Christian ministry

  E. Their ability to impart wisdom, not just knowledge

QUESTION 4

Write in your Life Notebook reflections on some ways you think you could help your children develop the fear of the Lord. It would be an excellent discussion topic with some close friends who are also Christian parents. To get you started in your thinking consider the following suggestions:

  • Pray regularly for the needs of your family.

  • When your child has a problem, take him to the Scriptures to find a solution.

  • When family needs come up, initiate taking those needs to God in prayer.

  • When your child has a problem, listen carefully, make practical and scriptural suggestions, and then lead him in prayer.

  • Build a climate in your home of music, laughter, good books, and good friends.

  • When a missionary or a godly Christian person is in town, have him to dinner and ask him to share how he came to know Christ and the difference it made in his life.

  • If a Christian summer camping program is available, send your child to it.

  • Take advantage of holidays like Christmas and Easter and even some national holidays in your country to teach and discuss Christian perspectives.

  • Introduce your child to key people in your church and ensure he is comfortable there.

  • Put pictures of missionaries on a family bulletin board and pray for them at dinner.

  • When your child is a teenager, send him on a summer mission trip of some kind sponsored by your church.

These ideas are just to get you started. Discuss them with your spouse and then add to the list.

In the early years of life we are helping our children to build upon their fear of the Lord. At the same time the structure of our own home is being established. We have selected seven major emphases from Proverbs that relate to the task of child-rearing. By focusing upon each of these "pillars," we will gain biblical insights into the fundamental elements that God wants each parent to use in child-rearing.

Topic 3: The Pillar of Discipline

The second "Pillar of Wisdom" is the pillar of discipline. A more accurate translation might be "instruction."

Assignment

- Read Proverbs 1:1-7 again and particularly focus on verse 2.

Here we are told that one of the goals of Proverbs is that the king's son might know "wisdom and instruction." The word translated "instruction" is the Hebrew word which actually means to instruct with the goal of correcting. Instruction can be imparted either by oral teaching or by discipline.

In this topic we are going to discuss some biblical principles regarding discipline of children. Our focus will be more on correction rather than the positive side of discipline that involves instruction in living life skillfully.

Solomon addresses many verses to the boy he calls "my son" on the subject of correction. The Hebrew word *musar*, sometimes translated "discipline," involves more than simply punishing a child when he misbehaves.

QUESTION 5

Look up the following verses in Proverbs, and note in your notebook what each has to say about the subject of discipline (Prov 3:11-12; 4:1, 13; 5:11-13; 6:23; 22:15; 23:13-14; 24:30-32).

In Lesson 1 we emphasized the instruction aspect of *musar*, but in this lesson we will concentrate more on the aspect of correction, or discipline. What do you do when your child misbehaves? While Scripture does mention the use of the rod in discipline, there are other biblical methods of discipline that should be considered first.

Three Kinds of Discipline

Sometimes parents think of discipline in only one way, often spanking. Actually, the Bible never tells us to spank small children. In fact, the use of the rod in the Bible is very rare and only when there is willful defiance. Small children often misbehave without being defiant and so the rod should not be used. The Bible teaches that there are three different kinds of discipline: natural consequences, reproof, and the rod. Let's take a look.

QUESTION 6

Proverbs 3:1-2; 14:23; 22:24-25; 29:1 suggest what kind of correction or discipline? *(Select all that apply.)*

    A. Natural consequences

    B. Reproof

    C. Rod

    D. None of the above

QUESTION 7

Proverbs 3:11-12; 29:15 suggest what kind of correction or discipline? *(Select all that apply.)*

    A. Natural consequences

    B. Reproof

    C. Rod

    D. None of the above

QUESTION 8

Proverbs 13:24; 22:15; 29:15 suggest which kind of correction or discipline?

    A. Natural consequences

    B. Reproof

    C. Rod

    D. None of the above

We will look briefly at each of these three methods of correction.

Natural Consequences

Assignment

- Please read the following article:

The Pillar of Discipline

Natural Consequences

The discipline of natural consequences simply means that a parent may sometimes want to let a child suffer the inevitable consequences of his own choices or actions. When should parents rely upon natural consequences? Obviously it would be cruel to let a child touch a hot stove in order to learn that he will get burned. However, there are some occasions when natural consequences may be the most helpful method to use. For example, if a child refuses to eat the meal that his parents have provided, he will not have a meal until the next time the family eats together. In general, parents should not try tp protect their children from the consequences of their actions.

At other times it may be necessary for parents to design what may be called "logical consequences." This is an extension of the idea of natural consequences that parents can use when no natural consequence is available. Parents can design a logical consequence, where the punishment is logically related to the "crime." For example, to teach a young child to put away their toys when they finish playing with them, his parent could "confiscate" the toys that are not put away. The parent could tell the child that if toys are out after he goes to bed, he will not be able to play with them for a set period of time. The parent would keep these toys in a location the child cannot access and consistently follow through with this consequence.

It is far better to use God's main method of disciplining us. Let's follow His example with our children by allowing them to experience natural consequences for their actions.

QUESTION 9

Read Luke 15:11-24. What principle of discipline is illustrated here? What do you think of the father's response? How would his response apply to situations in your home? Did natural consequences work?

Read Galatians 6:7 and Proverbs 22:8. These verses teach the law of natural consequences in God's discipline of us.

QUESTION 10

Which of the following are valid reasons we are slow to apply this same law to our children? *(Select all that apply.)*

A. It is difficult for us to trust God and allow natural consequences to work.

B. God seems to take too long to work His solutions.

C. We are afraid of what will happen if we do not quickly intervene.

D. We want to argue our case.

Little Ronnie does not want to eat. Read the following story "Ronnie doesn't want to eat," and then consider the question that follows.

Ronnie doesn't want to eat

Ronnie was a picky eater. He ate very little and then only with much help from mother. Every meal was a repeat. Mrs. Evans put a small helping of each kind of food on Ronnie's plate. Ronnie just looked at it. Mrs. Evans said, "Eat your food, Ronnie. You want to grow up and be a big boy, don't you?" Ronnie ate a bite or two and asked for some Coke. "Eat your food, and you can have some," bribed Mrs. Evans. Ronnie ate a little more and then played with his fork. "Hurry up, Ronnie, or you can't have any dessert," Mrs. Evans threatened. Finally Ronnie finished half his food and his mother let him go at that.

QUESTION 11

Which of the following solutions would be likely to secure the best result?

A. Offer Ronnie some cookies if he will eat his meal

B. Tell him that if he eats his food he will grow up to be a big boy.

C. Threaten him with a spanking

D. Let him go hungry and remove the food from him when everyone else has finished

QUESTION 12

As a parent try to determine the major discipline problems you are having with each of your children. If possible, discuss this question with your spouse. See if you can determine whether you could solve some of these problems using natural consequences or logical consequences. If you can apply one of these methods, write out your plan. Record your responses in your Life Notebook.

Reproof

The second means of discipline described in the Bible is reproof.

Assignment

- Please read the following article:

Reproof

Proverbs 29:15 says, "The rod and reproof give wisdom." Reproof is reasonable instruction. It is not nagging or screaming at a child but talking to him in a reasonable manner. Children often respond when a parent makes the effort to explain. A child needs to know what is expected of him and why certain rules have been established. For example, he can be told that his parents will not permit back talk. When the child sasses his parents, he should be disciplined, but it is not necessary to spank a child if the child responds to reason and indicates that he is sorry for what he has done.

Reproof can be very effective as a means of correction. Some children respond much better to parental reproof than to spanking. When you need to reprove a child who has disobeyed, you can ask him a series of questions to encourage him to think through his actions.

    1.   *"What did you do?"*

Listen well, be fair, and probe until you think you have the whole picture of what happened. The child will probably rationalize and excuse his behavior, and it takes some skill to lead him to see where he has erred. Be sure you are in emotional control as you start this process, lest you lose your objectivity and patience and punish in anger.

    2.   *"Was what you did the right or wrong thing to do?"*

Encourage the child to relate his action to Christian values. With a younger child you may phrase this question, "What would Jesus want you to do?" or "Would this action please Jesus?" The purpose of this question is to draw out of the child a moral judgment on his own sin. He needs to see that what he did offended God, and perhaps others as well, before he can genuinely feel sorry. If the parent's focus is on instructing and training the child in righteousness, his goal will be for the child to feel true sorrow and regret over having offended God first, and then regret over how he has offended and hurt others by his sin.

    3.   *"How might you have handled this situation in a better way, so that Jesus would have been pleased with you?"*

Together list other ways the child might have handled the situation, and choose one you both agree would most please God. Doing this helps the child to see that he has other alternatives. This is essential if he is to learn to make wise decisions.

    4.   *"The next time a similar situation arises, how will you handle it?"*

If this method has been successful, the child should select the alternative he thinks will most please God.

The purpose of using a sequence of questions similar to those given is to get the child to see that what he did was wrong and that he has other choices. It will also encourage him to know that you believe he is capable of making a better choice the next time to honor Christ and you as his parents. Some children respond well to this form of reproof without the use of other methods.

If the child expresses sorrow for his action, assure him of your forgiveness and love, and comfort him with your affection. When the incident is over, forget it. Do not keep referring to it throughout the day, reminding the child of his wrongdoing. God deals with us this way. "As far as the east is from the west, so far has He removed our transgressions from us" (Ps 103:12). We can be thankful that He does not keep bringing up the matter of our past sins over and over again. Then we need to remember this in dealing with our children.

QUESTION 13

Review the series of questions to use with reproof, and copy them in your Life Notebook. On the next occasion when it is appropriate, use this series of questions to reprove your child. Record your observations on its effectiveness and your child's response.

The Rod

The third means of discipline described in the Bible is the rod (spanking). We will cover this in more detail in Lesson 7, Topic 3.

Assignment

- Please read the following article:

The Rod

Let us now look briefly at the use of the rod, or spanking. Many of the biblical references to "the rod" occur in Proverbs. You have looked at several of these references. Some parents have mixed feelings and are hesitant to spank their children. Certainly it is good to approach the use of the rod with caution, lest you rely too heavily on it.

Many authorities on Christian child-rearing agree that the use of the rod, or spankings, should be limited to situations in which willful defiance is the issue. In the Bible it is never used with small children because they are still developing their understanding of what is right and wrong behavior. Furthermore, with children older than seven years old your spanking might have to become a beating in order to convince them, and we cannot advocate any form of spanking that could threaten a child's physical or emotional well-being. The use of the rod should be minimal with any child. Other methods are clearly more useful, especially with older children, and yield better results.

We will deal with the rod in greater detail in Lesson 7. For now, we would like to suggest a number of questions you might ask yourself before you spank:

1. Did the child know what was expected of him? Sometimes a child may not understand what he has done wrong, although we may assume he knows. Before spanking, be certain that the child did in fact know that what he did was wrong and that his limits were clearly spelled out in advance.

2. Did I reprove or rebuke previously? A child may deserve a less severe punishment for the first offense. Did I verbally rebuke him or warn him the last time he did this?

3. Is there a natural consequence I could use in this instance, which might be more effective than spanking?

4. Is there a logical consequence I could devise that would be more effective?

5. Is the child being rebellious or simply acting childish? Spanking should be reserved for willful defiance. Childish behavior should be handled in other ways.

6. Was the child's misbehavior intentional or accidental? It is wrong, for example, to spank a two-year-old for accidentally knocking over a glass of milk at the dinner table or accidentally breaking a precious art object that sits on the living room table. Accidents happen to everyone.

7. Am I in control of my emotions? Never discipline in anger. We discipline in love and do not want to communicate hateful rage or rejection to our children.

8. Does the child have a legitimate excuse for his behavior? Sometimes we demand a perfection of our children that we do not even achieve ourselves. When a child is ill or overtired, we may be demanding too much to expect perfect behavior.

As a child matures, his will strengthens and often a power struggle can develop between parent and child. Because the parent is bigger, he can often force his will upon the child but that rarely solves the problem.

QUESTION 14

Go over each of the questions in "The Rod" with your spouse. Discuss instances where you have failed to ask such questions before using the rod, and reflect together on the results. How might your actions have been different if you had asked yourself these questions? Think of several specific situations.

QUESTION 15

Reflect on several instances in which you used the rod on your child in the past. Ask yourself the following questions:

- Did I demonstrate love and reassure my child?

- Did I pray with or for my child?

Now read Hebrews 12:6-7 and Hosea 6:1, and answer the following questions in your Life Notebook.

- What do these verses say about the relationship between love and discipline?

- In what ways have you related love and discipline together when you spanked your child? Discuss this issue with your spouse, and record some of your observations.

Topic 4: The Pillar of Discernment

Proverbs also speaks of the need for our children to develop discernment. In Proverbs 1:2 Solomon tells us that we are "to discern the sayings of understanding." The Hebrew word *bina*, translated "discernment" or "understanding," comes from a word meaning "to become separated" or "to be distinct." Discernment is the ability to compare concepts and form judgments, and thus perceive a wise course of action. A man of discernment is a man of perception, one who is able to draw distinctions between God's wisdom and man's, or to separate wisdom from folly.

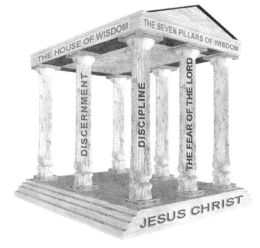

In Lesson 11 we will look more closely at the particularly relevant issue of training children to stand firm against the world's determined call for conformity.
It is particularly in the adolescent years when the child's need for discernment is greatest, as he must increasingly choose between wisdom and folly.

Defining Discernment

Let us explore Proverbs once again and read a few verses which use the term for discernment. Remember the Hebrew word *bina*, translated "discernment" is often translated "understanding."

QUESTION 16

Read each of the Scriptures and then match the passage with the aspect of discernment described.

Scripture	Aspect of Discernment
Proverbs 1:2-7	Discernment should become your child's intimate friend, as close as a family member.
Proverbs 4:4-7	Discernment is of greater value than silver, gold and riches.
Proverbs 7:4	True discernment gives on intimate knowledge of the Holy One.
Proverbs 9:6	Living in the way of discernment enables your child to escape folly, live richly and not foolishly.
Proverbs 9:10	Having the mental and spiritual ability enables your child to comprehend words of insight.
Proverbs 16:16	Understanding leads to a meaningful life.

QUESTION 17

Read Proverbs 1:2-7; 4:4-7; 7:4; 9:6, 10; 16:16 again and note how discernment is described. Record one personal situation where having biblical discernment would make a difference in a situation you have faced in the past or are facing now.

Teaching Discernment

Discernment, then, is the ability to compare concepts and to perceive a wise course of action. But how is discernment developed? First of all, we grow in discernment as we spend more time in God's Word and gain an understanding of God's point of view. We read in Scripture of godly men who made good choices and perceived a wise course of action and, conversely, of men who made mistakes and chose foolish courses of action. From childhood on we can teach those stories and discuss them with our children. Questions such as, "What would you have done if you were Abraham?" or "What would God want you to do in this situation?" can encourage children to develop discernment.

Introducing our children to the book of Proverbs can also help. Consider using Proverbs in family devotions and discussing the proverbs together so that the precepts become implanted in your child's mind. You can also discuss a proverb each night at the dinner table, for example, and encourage children to dig for meanings and applications.

QUESTION 18

With your spouse consider the following ideas, and select one of them to apply in your home this week. Write up your plan and the outcome and be able to discuss it with other parents. If none of these ideas appeal to you, then devise one of your own.

1. Read one proverb each night, at the dinner table or at bedtime, and discuss what it means and how it can be applied.

2. Select ten or fifteen proverbs that relate to specific situations you know your children are faced with. On a card put the verse reference of the proverb, and on the other side of the card write a question which relates to a life situation facing your children. The question should begin, "What would you do if...?" Mix the cards up, and ask each person to select one at the dinner table. Then each person is to answer the question, and the family should discuss the biblical perspective from the verse in Proverbs. It may be best to have some cards which are appropriate for adults and others appropriate for children.

3. Do a special topical study of Proverbs. In advance select five or six verses on a particular subject. Then go around the dinner table, having each person read one of the verses. Some good subjects to begin with are:

- **The fool** (Prov 1:7; 10:1; 15:14; 17:21, 24-25, 28; 26:7, 9, 11)
- **The sluggard** (Prov 6:6-11; 12:27; 13:4; 21:25-26; 22:13)
- **The friend** (Prov 3:29; 11:12; 14:20-21; 17:17; 18:24; 19:4, 6-7; 21:10; 25:17; 27:6-9)

We are not suggesting that topical studies in Proverbs will provide all that is necessary to teach a child discernment. One of the best ways for a child to learn discernment is to see it in the lives of his parents and to see how they apply Scripture in their daily decisions and choices.

The need for discernment in our children's lives is evident. In the schools young people are continually taught perspectives and values which are contrary to God's. Here in the West our children are confronted with a philosophy which says that man and his achievements are of greatest significance in life, that material well-being is the ultimate goal of life, and that their value as persons is dependent upon their appearance, intelligence, or abilities.

The child who lacks discernment and grounds his life on these false values is pursuing what Proverbs calls the path of folly. It is our responsibility as parents to point out the falsehood of the world's values and to encourage our children to value what is inside them rather than only what is external. We can help our children gradually learn to make good judgments and perceive a wise course of action.

Please read the following article:

Learning Discernment

The process of developing discernment in your child takes many years. As King Solomon wrote the book of Proverbs, he gave much wise counsel to this son regarding the importance of discernment. Yet, how many of us have ever considered this as a specific goal of raising children or have any idea how to practically help our children develop this critical skill?

An excellent way to teach this skill to your child would be to set up an imaginary role-play situation and play "What if." Ask your child, "What if this happened to you? What would you do?" Then go through these seven steps of the decision-making process together.

1. Determine what needs to be decided and purpose in your heart that you only want to do what would bring honor to Christ and that you want to do it in a manner which would glorify Him.

2. Determine what the options are. Consider every possible way the decision could be made. Go beyond the obvious alternatives and include even ideas that seem "way out"; this is the time for brainstorming, and sometimes a crazy idea can lead to a practical one. Write down all ideas.

3. Think about the strengths and weaknesses of each choice. Now is the time to consider pros and cons, and to determine what is feasible and what is not. Search for all the possible consequences of each choice. It may be helpful to draw a chart on a piece of paper listing the pros and cons of each possible alternative.

4. Read through the book of Proverbs and possibly the application sections of the Epistles (e.g., Rom 12–16; Eph 4–6; Gal 5–6; Jas 1–5) and look for principles that would apply to the strengths and weaknesses of each choice. Obviously this method is best for major decisions which do not have to be made immediately. Nevertheless, reflecting on what the wisdom passages have to say is critical if we are to get God's viewpoint on important decisions and learn to apply it to real life. You usually will

not find a verse which says, "Do this," or "Choose that," but you will find principles which apply to the pros and cons of the decision you need to make.

5. Choose what appears to be the best alternative. Ask yourself, "Will I be happy with this decision 10,000 years from now?"

6. Do what you've decided to do, trusting the results to God. Sometimes there may be some negative consequences and you have to settle the issue that your purpose is to please God and honor Him. He promises that He will remember and reward you for your faithfulness.

7. Evaluate the decision after you have seen the results. Decide whether or not it was a good choice, and whether you would make the same decision if you had to choose again.

QUESTION 19

As you read through the steps toward making wise decisions, identify with your child and your spouse a particular situation that is not easy, not black and white, and walk through the steps of discernment with your child. You might consider some hypothetical situations like these:

- What if the teacher is promoting unbiblical viewpoints in class and your grade depends upon a term paper he wants you to write? How should you write it and what should you say?
- What if your best friend asked you to help him or her cheat on a math test?
- What if someone asked you to marry him or her?
- What if you were graduating from secondary school and had to choose a college?

Topic 5: The Pillar of Wise Behavior

Assignment

- Please read the following article:

The Pillar of Wise Behavior

Related to discernment is the pillar called "wise behavior." The Hebrew word *sakal* means "to be prudent and possess good judgment, to behave wisely." The sentence structure of Proverbs 1:3 indicates that the three qualities that follow are intended to explain what is meant by wise behavior or skillful living: righteousness, justice, and equity. Thus, wise behavior is the result of discernment and is seen in the actions of the person who possesses it.

The Hebrew word for righteousness *tsedeq* carries the idea of "conformity to God's will and standards." The word for justice, *mishpat*, refers to the quality of dealing fairly, honestly, and righteously in our relations with one another. It is the social outworking of righteousness. Equity (Hebrew *meshar*) suggests gentleness or attractiveness.

All of these words relate to the actions of a person. What Christian parent does not desire a child who behaves wisely, fairly, honestly, and in conformity with God's standards? These actions are the result of training. It takes time to build these qualities in a child's life. Often parents cannot see the evidence of wise behavior until a child is nearly grown. Your responsibility as parents is to love, encourage, instruct, and correct. It is the Holy Spirit's responsibility to implant the character traits over a period of years. He uses our example and instruction as seeds and the circumstances of life as fertilizer to cause growth in the child's life, so that ultimately he may behave wisely.

Children must be instructed in God's standards so they will be prepared to resist the pressures of the world. The pressures in today's world are particularly great: drugs and alcohol and sensual living seem to be gaining in their appeal to young people. In view of the pressures facing young people today, how can parents help a child learn to behave wisely? Here are a few suggestions:

1. Be a living example of wise behavior to your child (Prov 4:1-5; 5:1-2; 20:7).

2. Encourage your children to walk with God's "wise men" (Prov 13:20). This can be done in several ways. Whenever possible, expose them to vital Christian leaders. You might consider a regular practice of inviting such men and women for dinner and then asking them to share their Christian experience in family discussion around the dinner table.

3. A child can complete a short topical Bible study assignment in which various standards of righteousness are emphasized. It helps to reward a child for completing assignments and to discuss with him what he has learned.

4. Expose your child as often as possible to Christian service (Mt 28:18-20). Take your children with you when you minister. Give them opportunities to minister.

5. Appeal to a child's courage to count the cost and be willing to abandon all to follow Christ (Mk 8:34-38; Lk 6:22-23).

The Hebrew word translated "wise behavior" can be summarized by the notion of living wisely with a balance of grace and truth (Jn 1:14). Obviously, wise behavior, discretion, and prudence are closely related.

QUESTION 20

Based on your reading of "Wise Behavior," match the quality with the corresponding definition.

Quality	Definition
Righteousness	Conformity to God's standards
Justice	Gentleness and attractiveness
Equity	Ability to distinguish between right and wrong or good and bad courses of action
Discernment	Dealing fairly, honestly, and righteously in our relationships with others

QUESTION 21

One way to teach all of the pillars of wisdom is to expose children constantly to God's "wise men," men or women who manifest the seven pillars in their lives. This can be done in many ways including having them read the biographies of great Christian leaders of the past and of missionaries. Take a look at the suggestions for imparting wise behavior mentioned in the article, and in conversation with your spouse, select several items you might try to implement this month. Write up your plan in your Life Notebook.

Topic 6: The Pillar of Prudence

Imagine for a moment that your son is eighteen years old and he has just been drafted into the military. Unexpectedly, a minor war develops in a distant country, and your government has decided to commit troops to the conflict. There is no time to run the new recruits through boot camp and give them basic military training. Instead, your son, along with the rest of the untrained troops, is sent abroad to fight in a war. He disembarks from the airplane, is handed a helmet and a rifle, and told to march through totally unfamiliar territory and face the enemy. The terrain is covered with land mines, and he is accordingly warned to avoid them, but of course he has received no training in how to do this.

Your son in this context is what the book of Proverbs calls "simple." He is naive, untrained, gullible, and completely incapable of dealing with the situation into which he has been thrust. Danger awaits him at every turn, and he has no expertise in dealing with the enemy. His chances of averting destruction are not very good.

For youth, according to Proverbs, life is like that enemy mine field: it is full of traps. Satan places them in a young person's path in numerous attempts to destroy his life. The naive, simple, untrained young person needs the ability to avoid traps. That ability is called "prudence" in Proverbs, based on the Hebrew verb *arom*, meaning "to be shrewd and crafty" in a good sense (see Mt 10:16). Prudence is skill in avoiding the traps of life.

QUESTION 22

Match the Scripture with the characteristics of the prudent man.

Scripture	Characteristics of Prudence
Proverbs 12:16	Is alert to danger and takes refuge from it.
Proverbs 12:23	Gives careful thought to his way or course of life
Proverbs 14:8	Responds positively to correction
Proverbs 14:15	Overlooks insults
Proverbs 15:5	Thinks before he takes a step
Proverbs 22:3	Keeps his knowledge to himself

QUESTION 23

Proverbs also mentions a number of traps which the prudent man avoids. In your Life Notebook, record some of the traps in these verses. Discuss these verses with your children, and see how they respond to them: Proverbs 1:10-14; 5:1-23; 14:16-17; 20:10; 10:19-21; 21:20.

Obviously, there are many more traps in life than those mentioned above or even in the whole book of Proverbs. Solomon seems to be saying that our children should receive some specific instruction on the various traps in life; in other words, they need to be forewarned. Presenting these items as traps rather than as a list of rules may make them more digestible to a young person and lead to some fruitful conversations.

Our children need to see the consequences of sin. Just telling them about these consequences, however, often has little effect. In some cases they need to be shown. Is your child attracted by the "trap" of alcohol? Let him see the results of alcohol in the lives of the local drunks. If possible, take him to a section of town where the drunks are sleeping in the streets!

What an important quality prudence is! The child who acquires it will be spared the anguish which comes upon those who step on Satan's land mines and have their lives blown apart.

Topic 7: The Pillar of Knowledge

One of the purposes of Proverbs, according to its author, is to give knowledge to the young (Prov 1:4). The acquisition of knowledge is, of course, intrinsic to all of the aspects of wisdom. But even though the various aspects overlap somewhat in their content, each, as we have seen, has its own distinctive emphasis.

What then is the distinctive significance of the pillar of knowledge?

The Hebrew word *da'at* is a general word for knowledge, which is acquired by both learning and experience. In Proverbs the primary emphasis, although not the exclusive use of the word, is on a life-related knowledge of truth. Proverbs emphasizes the personal and experiential aspects of knowledge. This kind of knowledge is of great value. Indeed, it is the only kind of knowledge which will keep the Scriptures and the Christian life from becoming dry and lifeless.

QUESTION 24

Summarize in your notebook what the following verses say about the value of knowledge: Proverbs 8:10; 19:2; 11:9; 20:15; 13:16; 24:4-5

These passages all teach that knowledge, a life-related experience of divine truth, is much to be desired. Such knowledge is the only kind of spiritual truth which can really be communicated to others. If our knowledge of truth is simply theoretical, or head knowledge, our ability to influence others will be severely limited. We can influence other lives only insofar as our knowledge of truth has been acquired in life and has transformed our hearts, our minds, and our actions.

As believers grow in knowledge through the experiences of life, we might say that a "life message" is being formed in us. In each life God is building a distinct life message, a statement of His reality expressed through that individual, fashioned on the anvil of his experience of God.

QUESTION 25

If you were asked to formulate the life message God has been expressing through you, what would you write down? Write out a paragraph or two in your Life Notebook.

Topic 8: The Pillar of Discretion

The final pillar in wisdom's house is discretion. What is meant by discretion? Normally when that word is used, ideas such as finesse, tactfulness, or diplomacy come to mind. But the Hebrew word *mezimma* (from the root *zamam*, meaning "to consider, purpose, devise") means "to decide wisely for himself to attain a desired end." Though usually used in a context of evil thoughts or judgment (e.g., Ps 37:12; Prov 12:2; Jer 23:20), it is used in a positive sense in Proverbs, meaning the ability to formulate and carry out wise plans. Simply put, then, **discretion is wise planning or decision making.**

QUESTION 26

Look up the following passages in Proverbs and match the Scripture with the corresponding characteristic of discretion.

Scripture	Characteristic of Discretion
Proverbs 2:11-12	Discretion is never to be let out of our sight.
Proverbs 3:21	It is a source of protection.
Proverbs 5:1-2	A major source for learning discretion is our father.
Proverbs 8:12	It is a quality to be possessed.

According to Proverbs 3:21-24, wise planning based on God's sound principles will be "life" for our children. In addition, it will keep them from stumbling in their walk along the path of life. It is even a key to a good night of sleep (Prov 3:24) We have all experienced the sense of anxiety that comes when life is completely out of order or when we make decisions that are not thought through in advance. This experience is common to our daily lives, so it is not surprising that God elevates wise planning as a key to skillful living.

It is apparently a parent's responsibility to help his children learn to plan wisely (Prov 5:1-2). Some examples of this are helping a child organize a study session in preparation for an exam or organize his homework into some coherent system, showing how to plan out the term's study with a monthly calendar and weekly schedules, teaching how to manage finances according to biblical principles (see Prov 31:16), organizing and scheduling household chores for the week, and helping a child use his time wisely by establishing priorities and a schedule.

QUESTION 27

Throughout the Bible we are reminded of the importance of time. Our days on earth are limited. Read the following passages with your child and discuss the eternal significance of time.

Psalm 39:5

Psalm 84:10

Psalm 90:12

Psalm 103:15

Psalm 139:16

Topic 9: Examining Our Own House of Wisdom

We have examined seven aspects of wisdom in the book of Proverbs. Perhaps you have noted, as you read these pages, a lack of wisdom in your own life. When it comes to these various facets of wisdom, we are all lacking in one way or another. Maybe several of the pillars in our own lives are sawed off or were never properly built. The result is an uneven house, which tends to shake or even crumble when bad weather sets in.

Dwelling excessively upon our own shortcomings can be discouraging, and we are not suggesting that you do that. But we encourage you to examine your own house of wisdom and make repairs that are needed. Are there cracks that need repair? Are the pillars firmly in place, or is there one that is crumbling? Acknowledge to God the weak areas you discover, seek His strength, and then begin again to actively pursue building the pillars of wisdom in your own life.

As Solomon declared in Proverbs 4:7, "Wisdom is supreme; therefore get wisdom" (NIV). If God calls wisdom supreme, then it is something to get, to go after, to seek to possess at all costs. To become wise, we must work at it. As parents the path of wisdom is not an option for us; it is an absolute necessity. God's desire for us is that we continually develop in wisdom, becoming mature men and women in Christ.

What is wisdom? Its basic definition is **"skill in living life gracefully in fellowship with God."**

QUESTION 28

To help you memorize the seven pillars of a well-built house of wisdom, match the pillar with its correct definition.

Pillar	Definition
The fear of the Lord	The use of natural consequences, reproof, and the rod in the training of children
Discipline	The ability to distinguish between God's wisdom and man's and to perceive a wise course of action
Discernment	The result of discernment, expressed in righteous, fair, and gentle actions toward others
Wise behavior	The ability to make and carry out wise plans
Prudence	A life-related experience of truth, not a mere theoretical "head knowledge." A "Life Message"
Knowledge	Reverential awe, respect, and a response of obedient service to God
Discretion	The ability to avoid hidden traps

Topic 10: Conclusion

If this discussion on wisdom reminds you of your own shortcomings, remember that God can use instruments which are not perfect. In spite of your shortcomings as parents, the Holy Spirit can use you to instruct and train your children in wisdom. For the daily task of living wisely we must rely on the Lord's strength. When it comes to training up our children in wisdom, we can trust the Lord to help us. We must ask Him for wisdom every day.

> **The Most Important Concept:** In this lesson you have been exposed to God's priorities in child raising—the seven pillars of wisdom. What is so striking about these pillars is that many of them are never discussed and few are ever implemented with definite intention and purpose. These pillars of wisdom show us where to place the emphasis, what battles to fight, and most of all, what is important to God.

QUESTION 29

In this lesson, seven pillars of wisdom have been discussed, and suggestions have been provided on how to help your children to develop in each of those areas. We have asked you to write your thoughts in your Life Notebook. In this final question, with your spouse, list each pillar and *one* practical suggestion with how you might implement it in your home.

Lesson 2 Self Check

QUESTION 1

Proverbs are like promises. When faithfully applied, we can be assured that they will work out in daily life. *True or False?*

QUESTION 2

What about Lois and Eunice enabled Paul to have great confidence in Timothy's walk with God? *(Select all that apply.)*

    A. Their sincere faith

    B. Their diligence in teaching Timothy from a young age

    C. Their ability to impart conviction to Timothy

    D. Their regular involvement in Christian ministry

    E. Their ability to impart wisdom, not just knowledge

QUESTION 3

Discipline with the rod is not the major means of discipline taught in the Bible. *True or False?*

QUESTION 4

God has so arranged life that, when we violate His spiritual laws, there are often certain natural consequences which follow. However, it is usually necessary and productive for parents to punish children in addition to these consequences. *True or False?*

QUESTION 5

To possess discretion means to be able to make a good decision. *True or False?*

QUESTION 6

In this lesson what is the definition of discernment?

    A. Wise planning or decision making

    B. A skillful course of action manifesting God's standards, fairness, and grace

    C. The ability to avoid traps

    D. A life related experience of truth; a life message

    E. The ability to compare concepts and devise a wise plan of action

QUESTION 7

The lesson suggested that the rod be used only in cases of willful defiance and after a number of key questions had been answered. *True or False?*

QUESTION 8

When reproving a child, which of the following questions were *not* suggested?

    A. What did you do?

    B. Why did you do it?

    C. Was what you did the right or wrong thing to do?

    D. How might you have handled this situation in a better way?

QUESTION 9

What is the definition of wise behavior?

A. Wise planning or decision making

B. A skillful course of action manifesting God's standards, fairness, and grace

C. The ability to avoid traps

D. A life related experience of truth; a life message

E. The ability to compare concepts and devise a wise plan of action

QUESTION 10

What is the definition of prudence?

A. Wise planning or decision making

B. A skillful course of action manifesting God's standards, fairness, and grace

C. The ability to avoid traps

D. A life related experience of truth; a life message

E. The ability to compare concepts and devise a wise plan of action

Lesson 2 Answers to Questions

QUESTION 1: False

QUESTION 2: *Your answer*

QUESTION 3

    A. Their sincere faith

    B. Their diligence in teaching Timothy from a young age

    C. Their ability to impart conviction to Timothy

    E. Their ability to impart wisdom, not just knowledge

QUESTION 4: *Your answer*

QUESTION 5: *Your answer*

QUESTION 6

    A. Natural consequences

    B. Reproof

[God has so arranged life that, when we violate His spiritual laws, there are certain natural consequences which follow. It is often unnecessary and unproductive for parents to punish the children in addition to these consequences.]

QUESTION 7

    B. Reproof

    C. Rod

QUESTION 8

    C. Rod [The rod should only be used where there is willful defiance. Also, in the Bible, it is never used on small children.]

QUESTION 9: *Your answer*

QUESTION 10

    A. It is difficult for us to trust God and allow natural consequences to work.

    B. God seems to take too long to work His solutions.

    C. We are afraid of what will happen if we do not quickly intervene.

    D. We want to argue our case.

[When we try to force our will upon a child, the power-hungry child fights back, making his parents miserable. A cycle of rebellion begins: the child misbehaves, the parent tries to force his will on the child, and the child resists and rebels more. In this cycle there is no peace and attempts at discipline are met with a power struggle. We have to learn to trust God with our children; He is more concerned with their behavior than we are.]

QUESTION 11

    D. Let him go hungry and remove the food from him when everyone else has finished [A parent may try bribing, nagging, and punishing when all they need to do is get out of the way and let God and nature do their work. Why do parents not do this? Parents try these other, ineffective methods mainly because they feel guilty or overly sympathetic when the child experiences the natural consequences of his actions.]

QUESTION 12: *Your answer*

QUESTION 13: *Your answer*

QUESTION 14: *Your answer*

QUESTION 15: *Your answer*

QUESTION 16

Scripture	Aspect of Discernment
Proverbs 1:2-7	Having the mental and spiritual ability enables your child to comprehend words of insight.
Proverbs 4:4-7	Understanding leads to a meaningful life.
Proverbs 7:4	Discernment should become your child's intimate friend, as close as a family member.
Proverbs 9:6	Living in the way of discernment enables your child to escape folly, live richly and not foolishly.
Proverbs 9:10	True discernment gives on intimate knowledge of the Holy One.
Proverbs 16:16	Discernment is of greater value than silver, gold and riches.

QUESTION 17: *Your answer*

QUESTION 18: *Your answer*

QUESTION 19: *Your answer*

QUESTION 20

Quality	Definition
Righteousness	Conformity to God's standards
Justice	Dealing fairly, honestly, and righteously in our relationships with others
Equity	Gentleness and attractiveness
Discernment	Ability to distinguish between right and wrong or good and bad courses of action

QUESTION 21: *Your answer*

QUESTION 22

Scripture	Characteristics of Prudence
Proverbs 12:16	Overlooks insults
Proverbs 12:23	Keeps his knowledge to himself
Proverbs 14:8	Gives careful thought to his way or course of life
Proverbs 14:15	Thinks before he takes a step
Proverbs 15:5	Responds positively to correction
Proverbs 22:3	Is alert to danger and takes refuge from it.

QUESTION 23: *Your answer*

QUESTION 24: *Your answer*

QUESTION 25: *Your answer*

QUESTION 26

Scripture	Characteristic of Discretion
Proverbs 2:11-12	It is a source of protection.
Proverbs 3:21	Discretion is never to be let out of our sight.
Proverbs 5:1-2	A major source for learning discretion is our father.
Proverbs 8:12	It is a quality to be possessed.

QUESTION 27: *Your answer*

QUESTION 28

Pillar	Definition
The fear of the Lord	Reverential awe, respect, and a response of obedient service to God
Discipline	The use of natural consequences, reproof, and the rod in the training of children
Discernment	The ability to distinguish between God's wisdom and man's and to perceive a wise course of action
Wise behavior	The result of discernment, expressed in righteous, fair, and gentle actions toward others
Prudence	The ability to avoid hidden traps
Knowledge	A life-related experience of truth, not a mere theoretical "head knowledge." A "Life Message"
Discretion	The ability to make and carry out wise plans

QUESTION 29: *Your answer*

Lesson 2 Self Check Answers

QUESTION 1: False

QUESTION 2

    A. Their sincere faith

    B. Their diligence in teaching Timothy from a young age

    C. Their ability to impart conviction to Timothy

    E. Their ability to impart wisdom, not just knowledge

QUESTION 3: True

QUESTION 4: False

QUESTION 5: True

QUESTION 6

    E. The ability to compare concepts and devise a wise plan of action

QUESTION 7: True

QUESTION 8

    B. Why did you do it?

QUESTION 9

    B. A skillful course of action manifesting God's standards, fairness, and grace

QUESTION 10

    C. The ability to avoid traps

Lesson 3: Patterns of Parenting

Lesson Introduction

Parents in all cultures are very committed to their children. They want them to grow up to be mature and healthy human beings. Christian parents are no different, but they also want their children to grow to love Christ and live for Him. Yet every culture is different in how they approach parenting methods. Parenting styles in Africa and China, for example, may differ substantially from those in the Middle East or Latin America. In this lesson, we will address different patterns parents have adopted in their efforts to raise godly children. The challenge for you will be to ask, "What is biblical about my pattern for raising my children and what is derived from my culture?" There may, of course, be considerable overlap. However, in some cases you may need to rethink what you are doing in the light of Biblical revelation, which is trans-cultural and applies everywhere.

Probably the most important influence in a child's development is that of parental behavior patterns. The way that we as parents behave at home, whether it's toward our children, our spouse or other family members, will leave a lasting impression on our children. Often when we think of training a child, we think in terms of communicating information or ideas to the child. Yet it is our daily life before our children that is the most powerful teacher.

What we teach by our example can be either positive or negative. Unfortunately, many of our patterns of parenting tend to be negative and therefore produce negative results in our children. In this lesson we will look at some of these negative patterns of parenting to which we are often prone and see where each of these patterns falls short of the standard God desires for us as parents. We will also look at how we can become more biblically balanced as parents.

Before we can begin to take steps toward changing our parenting style, we must have a picture of what God wants us to be as parents—and does **not** want us to be. So the purpose of this lesson is to set before you some common negative patterns of parenting and then to suggest some practical, biblical means of countering the negatives. There is hope for change once we recognize error. Thus, we must examine the errors in order to motivate us to greater maturity as parents.

Lesson Outline

Topic 1 Countering Negative Parenting Patterns

The Permissive Parent

The Overprotective Parent

The Nagging Parent

The Manipulative Parent

The Authoritarian Parent

The Inconsistent Parent

The Child-Centered Parent

Topic 2: Seeking Balance

Lesson Objectives

By the end of this lesson, you will be able to do the following:

- Describe seven faulty patterns of parenting, the weaknesses of each, and the commonly produced effects of each on children

- Articulate ways the wise parent can seek to counterbalance each of the negative patterns of parenting

- Recognize how a child can choose to respond positively or negatively to his parents' patterns of parenting

- Seek help from God in changing poor parenting habits and desire to call on Him for daily strength in the tasks He has given us

Topic 1: Countering Negative Parenting Patterns

The Bible presents family development as a primary responsibility of both parents, who together form the family core. Healthy families were often observed to share the characteristics of:

1. Commitment

2. Time spent together

3. An affirming environment

4. The ability to communicate

5. The ability to resolve conflict

6. A solid core of moral and spiritual beliefs

In addition to observing family strengths, some researchers have observed particular parental patterns that, in turn, tend to produce predictable negative behavior patterns in a child as he develops. Seven of these behavior patterns will be described in this lesson. If we as parents can learn to control and change these negative patterns, many hindrances to our children's spiritual development will also be removed.

One of the most difficult goals of the Christian life is finding balance. Every negative pattern of parenting takes some characteristic of biblically balanced parenting to its extreme. Whenever we emphasize one single truth to the exclusion of other truths, we become unbalanced. We will examine the way in which each of these patterns of parenting is out of balance and see how it needs to be counterbalanced to make it positive.

The Permissive Parent

Assignment

- Read Psalms 51:5-7 and Hebrews 12:5-11, and answer the following questions.

- Please read the following article:

The Permissive Parent

The Imbalance

You have seen parents who are too permissive. The result is easy to observe: a child who runs wild, doing exactly what he pleases when he pleases. The permissive parent tends to view limits and the

---

use of discipline (especially spanking) as a hindrance to the child's development and to his natural curiosity and creativity. The goal of the permissive parent is to provide his child with an environment that has as few boundaries or restraints as possible. The permissive parent does not place his primary emphasis on the goals of obedience and acceptable behavior for children.

If we look more closely at the philosophy behind this parental pattern, we might see that it could be based upon the belief that human nature is basically good, or at worst, neutral. If children are viewed as basically good rather than evil, the natural response is to let them be what they are. Self-expression, self-direction, and self-determination are central to a permissive view of the child. Thus, most restraints are viewed as a hindrance to personality development and natural expression. The assumption is that a child who has complete freedom to interact with his environment without restraint will grow up to be a self-disciplined, well-adjusted adult.

But how does this view of the child mesh with what the Bible says? Look up Psalms 51:5 and Hebrews 12:7-11, and reflect on the following questions:

- What does Psalms 51:5-7 teach about the child?

- According to Hebrews 12:7-8, what does God's discipline prove?

- Why does God discipline His children according to Hebrews 12:10?

- What are the goals of God's discipline according to Hebrews 12:11?

- How can the model of God's discipline of His children be practically applied within your family?

The Counterbalance

The philosophy behind the permissive pattern of parenting is contrary to biblical teaching. The Bible tells us that by nature every man has an irresistible bias toward evil. When the psalmist says, "Behold, I was brought forth in iniquity, and in sin my mother conceived me" (Ps 51:5), he means that from the moment of conception the child bears a sin nature.

Even in your own child whom you love dearly, you could detect this nature quite early. The young child is self-centered by nature. He or she begins very early in life to express this self-centeredness in negative actions like demanding, lying, deceiving, and using other manipulative means to gain what he wants. Proverbs 22:15 says, "Foolishness is bound up in the heart of a child; the rod of discipline will remove it far from him." One author notes that the word "foolishness" in this verse:

> "...primarily refers to moral perversion or insolence, to what is sinful rather than to mental stupidity... One must keep in mind that this discipline is to curb moral insolence that might lead in turn to rebellion against God." (Goldberg, 1:19-20)

Certainly, the Bible teaches that every human being is bent toward sin from birth. Thus, the idea that a child who has complete freedom to experience his environment without restraints will grow up to be a self-disciplined, well-adjusted adult is inherently false. If you deny your child discipline, an integral part of training him up, you will cripple your child's own development, particularly as it concerns the various facets of wisdom. How can your young child learn wise judgment if you pronounce all of his choices as good? How is he to learn self-discipline if you allow him to do whatever he pleases without restraint?

Children brought up in permissive homes often struggle with discernment; they find it difficult to draw distinctions between God's wisdom and man's, or to discern truth from folly, because they have not been corrected and properly instructed in the consequences of disobedience. Imagine a child who receives no correction from his parents: how can he understand correction from a heavenly Father? How can he understand that God's discipline and correction exist because He loves us, because we are His children and He corrects us for our good? God's discipline keeps us from the path of folly that leads to destruction. Whether through misunderstanding or otherwise, the permissive parent allows his or her child to continue to pursue the path of folly rather than reproving him or applying the rod.

Likewise, children who have not been disciplined often struggle with prudence. They remain naive and unprepared for the spiritual battles of life, finding it difficult to recognize Satan's traps and the temptations of sin. Training involving temptation and the consequences of yielding to temptation is essential for the development of prudence, as is using correction when a child willfully disobeys.

Research has shown that children raised by permissive parents generally experience several common problems: insecurity, anxiety, limited development of self-control, and lack of respect for people, property, and authority. Inwardly, a child who has been allowed to do whatever he wants often feels unloved. "If my parents really loved me," he feels, "they would set limits for me and punish me when I disobey." Often, when an undisciplined child exhibits bad behavior, it is simply an anguished cry, an unconscious way of saying, "Please stop me; please correct me."

How do you avoid making your child feel this way? When your child exceeds the limits set by you and your spouse, some form of discipline is in order. This is how your child is trained. Along with the discipline comes the opportunity for you as a parent to explain why you discipline: because you love your child and you want him to learn obedience and self-control. As your child grows, you can explain to him that God has entrusted to you the tasks of disciplining and training him to live for God. You should also explain that one day he will be directly under God's discipline and training, just as you are.

In an effort to avoid permissiveness, some parents go to the other extreme of authoritarian control of their child. They order their offspring around like little robots, which is certainly not a balanced approach to parenting. We will review this imbalanced way of parenting later in the lesson.

The balanced parent learns to allow his child some freedom, but he also knows when to pull in the reins and take control. Children need boundaries and limits, depending on their age. So as your child becomes older and gains self-control, make sure you gradually lift some of the limits or boundaries to give him increased freedom. When your child knows where the limits and boundaries are, he will be both secure and content, even though he will test these limits from time to time. As a result he will be more confident in what he attempts and less fearful of failure. Likewise, he will learn to respect the rights of others, rather than always demanding and getting his own way.

QUESTION 1

What does Psalm 51:5-7 teach about the child?

While many contemporary theories and books begin with the premise that children are innately good or at least neutral, the Bible firmly teaches that beginning at birth, we need to be trained to be selfless, honorable, and good.

According to Hebrews 12:5-11, God disciplines us for our good. This provides us with a pattern and philosophy for the discipline of our children. Remember, discipline is more than correction; it involves instruction and guidance as well.

QUESTION 2

Hebrews 12:5-11 says we should view disciplining our children as proof of which of the following? *(Select all that apply.)*

    A. That our children are basically sinful

    B. That we love our children

    C. That our children need correction

    D. That we are treating them as sons

QUESTION 3

Read Hebrews 12:5-11 again. Open your Life Notebook and answer the following questions.

- Why does God discipline His children (Heb 12:10)?

- What are the goals of God's discipline (Heb 12:11)?

- How can the model of God's discipline of His children be applied practically within your family? Reflect on one recent situation and record your thoughts.

QUESTION 4

Do you recognize a permissive pattern of parenting in the home in which you grew up? In your home now? If so, reflect on what results you have seen.

QUESTION 5

Discuss with your spouse some recent incidents in your home that required discipline. Write down your thoughts on these questions in your Life Notebook.

- Was the motivation of your discipline to show your love? Did you discipline for the ultimate good of your child?

- Was the discipline given with the ultimate goal of training for righteousness and wisdom?

The Overprotective Parent

Assignment

- Please read the following article:

The Overprotective Parent

The Imbalance

The overprotective parent is motivated by different ideas than the permissive parent. He or she either strives to control the environment or shelters the child from it to such a degree that the child may never encounter and learn from the realities of life. This type of parent desires to supervise every move the child makes. The parent is often motivated by fear, which springs from a lack of trust in a loving, sovereign God, or by his own inner need to feel competent and in control. An overprotective parent sometimes controls the child so completely that he has no opportunity to do anything wrong. A child raised in this environment is unfortunately protected from experiencing the natural consequences of wrong choices.

Overprotective parents may unconsciously believe that failure of any kind must be avoided, if not for the child, then certainly for the image of the parents. Regardless of the age of the child, he is never considered mature enough to make right decisions for himself and is thus in continual need of parental oversight. Another possible reason for overprotectiveness is the need to keep the child emotionally close to the parent or the fear of losing the child's love.

The problem with this type of parenting pattern is twofold. First, the child grows up accustomed to having his parents' continual service, guidance, and approval. Thus, he never learns to function responsibly and independently. The development of discernment, prudence, and even knowledge is seriously hindered because the child has so little experience of life.

Second, the overprotective parent also tends to restrict the child's creativity. Thus, the child becomes frustrated because he or she is not allowed to experience normal childhood activity and creative play. Such shortsighted training often results in a child who is fearful and lacks self-confidence, problems that can follow him into adulthood and hinder his spiritual dependence upon a faithful, loving God.

The counterbalance

The biblically balanced parent knows when to allow his child freedom, even freedom to fail at times and to experience the natural consequences of his choices. The overprotected child lacks the opportunities to face the realities of life, both positive and negative. Thus, his knowledge of divine truth will not be related to life. True knowledge is acquired through a balance of intellectual information (i.e., head knowledge of biblical principles) and life experience. Life experience is God's proving ground.

If a child is always protected from experiencing disappointment or even personal failure in life, he will not have the opportunity to grow in knowledge. If we think about it, we realize that some of the most important lessons in life are learned through experiencing hurt, disappointment, and personal failure. Even a very young child can learn the comfort of love, understanding, and empathy from wise parents who have not protected him from ever experiencing disappointment or failure. As he experiences comfort from his parents, a child grows in his understanding of the comforts of God's love. This experiential knowledge of God's character is very important in the child's developing concept of God.

In addition, a child who is never allowed to make his own choices never experiences the satisfaction that results from wise choices. He may be told what is wise, but he is prevented from really learning for himself. A child who has been overprotected often has little sense of personal responsibility for choices he inevitably must make in life.

If you have been following an overprotective pattern, you need to recognize this and begin to allow your child to gradually make more choices for himself. Watch for situations where your children can learn by choosing a course of action. Be prepared to let your child make some wrong choices and learn by natural consequences. Begin to instruct him on traps to avoid. Parents must balance their desire to protect their children with some freedom for children to experience life for themselves.

QUESTION 6

Look up some verses on affliction, such as Psalm 147:6, James 1:12, and Romans 5:3-5. From each of these verses, determine what might be lacking in the life of a person who is sheltered from all hardship.

QUESTION 7

Study Genesis 45:1-9. What was Joseph's perspective on the trials and disappointments that had befallen him? Should we shelter our children from every possible disappointment? Record your thoughts in your Life Notebook.

QUESTION 8

Read through the life of Joseph in Genesis 37-45. List in your Life Notebook the trials and disappointments God allowed Joseph to go through. Also note what these life experiences taught Joseph. Read Genesis 50:15-21, and note Joseph's attitude toward his brothers.

The Nagging Parent

Assignment

- Please read the following article:

The Nagging Parent

The Imbalance

Many parents exhibit a pattern of child-rearing that is characterized by the constant repetition of commands or directions to their children. These commands are often followed by repeated threats when the child fails to respond.

The problem with this pattern of behavior is that the child is being trained not to listen or obey until it is absolutely necessary. He learns to ignore the parent's instruction until it becomes absolutely necessary to obey. By using a pattern of constantly repeated commands, this parent is unconsciously reinforcing noncompliance to his own requests. In a sense, the parent is actually training the child in unrighteousness, because he is training the child that it is acceptable to ignore authority. The child never learns to obey promptly but is allowed to ignore his parent until an outburst of anger makes it necessary to obey.

When a child is frequently allowed to ignore his parents' commands and instruction, he often carries this pattern of response into every area of life. He may grow up thinking it is acceptable to ignore people if he does not feel like answering. One result of this pattern of parenting is that a child may develop an attitude of rudeness and disrespect for others, especially toward adults or authority figures. If he does not learn to respect authority, he may also fail to learn wise behavior and may fail to develop a proper reverential fear of the Lord. Unlike the boy Samuel, who responded quickly when the Lord called him, such a child may be lackadaisical and lazy in responding to the Lord.

The Counterbalance

The biblically balanced parent understands the importance of teaching a child to obey promptly. Obedience brings blessing to children. Ephesians 6:1-3 says, "Children, obey your parents in the Lord, for this is right. Honor your father and mother which is the first commandment with a promise, namely, 'that it may be well with you, and that you may live long on the earth.'"

Scripture teaches that God's judgment comes upon those who do not honor and obey their parents. Proverbs 30:17 says, "The eye that mocks a father, and scorns [literally, despises to obey] a mother, the ravens of the valley will pick it out, and the young eagles will eat it." We owe it to our children to teach them the blessings of willing obedience.

The child who has been allowed to ignore his parents' instructions may grow up lacking a true knowledge of God's righteousness, because his view of the authority of God and of God's holy standard is distorted. Our understanding of God's character greatly influences what we become. A child trained to delay obedience or to ignore instruction from divinely appointed authority will likely grow up viewing God as a passive Being.

A pattern of nagging also produces guilt and frustration in the parent, who wonders why his children do not obey and why he always has to scream at them to produce results. He feels discouraged because he always seems to be nagging or yelling, and the joy of parenthood is diminished. Yet it is hard to break the cycle of nagging once it is established.

One father said his seven-year old son reacted with shocked surprise as he sat down with him and said, "Son, from this point on, I am going to expect you to obey me the first time I ask you to do something, or there will be consequences." It took several weeks for the son to see that his father was serious, but there was new respect in his eyes for his dad, and the sense of failure and frustration for the father was replaced with a sense of fulfillment resulting from the improved relationship between father and son.

QUESTION 9

It can be very difficult to evaluate ourselves in how we deal with our children. Without realizing it, we can form habits of nagging and threatening and postponing discipline for many reasons. In the next two weeks, both you and your spouse should take note of how the other is training your children. Spend time together discussing instances when you threatened to discipline and did not carry through, and when you found yourself nagging in order to elicit obedience. Do not discuss this in the presence of your children.

Discuss the reasons why you continue to nag or threaten rather than apply needed discipline. Some of the reasons could be:

1. You are in a hurry and plan to deal with the problem later, and then you forget

2. You are too tired

3. You do not like confrontation, even with a child

4. Other people are around, or you are in a public place and plan to deal with it in private, but then you do not carry through on the discipline when in private

Discuss your reasons with your spouse, and determine if you are lacking in the area of expecting prompt and willing obedience.

Record your reflections in your Life Notebook and be prepared to share with someone.

> Are you committed to being more consistent in your own self-discipline to overcome this problem? This habit is hard to break and will very likely take much prayer together and frankness in discussing it with your spouse.

The Manipulative Parent

Assignment

- Please read the following article:

The Manipulative Parent

The Imbalance

The manipulative parent seeks to control a child's outward behavior by manipulating the child's emotions. This type of parent uses several tools to control the child's behavior. One tool is making the child feel guilty. Perhaps unconsciously, parents do this by saying things like, "How could you do such a thing to your mother?" "I gave birth to you and you do this to me!" A more subtle approach uses statements like, "All right, go ahead and do whatever you want." The parent hopes to wound the child and thus manipulate him to do what the parent desires.

A second tool of a manipulative parent is withholding love and acceptance. A parent may say something like, "Mommy won't like you if...," or "You are not Daddy's boy or girl if you do things like that."

The negative outcome of such manipulative control can be very serious. The security of the parent-child relationship based on love and acceptance can be shattered. The child lives constantly with the feeling that he will never really be loved as he is. His self-concept will probably be poor. He may develop either an extreme dependence upon his parents or an extreme desire to gain their approval or the approval of others.

Sadly, the sense of insecurity produced by manipulation tends to follow a child into adulthood. The adult who has never known unconditional love from his parents will never be freed emotionally from them. Even a great distance between the grown child and his parents does not free him from the pain of unresolved emotional conflicts. If the parent dies, the child's sense of guilt may be inordinate; he may feel responsible and find it hard to deal with his emotional confusion.

Manipulation also produces other negative results in a child, including fear of failure, fear of rejection, excessive guilt, and anxiety. The child's relationship with the Lord may be affected as well, for he may find it difficult to believe that God truly loves him unconditionally. The child tends to think that God, like his parents, only loves him when he performs according to certain standards. God's standards being perfect, the child may give up trying to please Him. The child's concept of God is not one of a loving heavenly Father who loves us and accepts us even when we grieve Him through our lack of trust and disobedience. Instead, he tends to view God as severe, ready to disown him when he fails.

The Counterbalance

If we desire for our children to grow in wisdom and the fear of the Lord, we must be aware of the dangers of manipulative control. We must be willing to train and discipline without using manipulative, emotional threats. The biblically balanced parent will warn the child of the consequences of disobedience to established rules. These consequences may be natural consequences or an imposed discipline carried out in love.

The wise parent does not manipulate a child's need for love and security by using conditional love or by instilling the child with a false sense of guilt. Rather, he gives direction and warning to his children by teaching them that there are consequences to their actions. He also provides security for the child by reassuring him that he is loved unconditionally, regardless of how he acts. Thus, the child may come to know what it truly means to fear the Lord: to love and respect Him at the same time.

QUESTION 10

Did your parents ever manipulate you emotionally as described in the article? What effect did it have on you? Have you ever told your child that you do not love him when he is disobedient? Have you ever told your child that God will not love him if he is disobedient? Based on Proverbs 3:11-12 and Hebrews 12:5-11, why is it wrong to manipulate your children into obedience with fear of rejection?

QUESTION 11

If you have used manipulation to control your children, this must be corrected in both your thinking and the child's. Begin making steps to correct this in your habits and to correct it in your child's thinking. Two steps toward correction could be:

1. Take time during family devotions to focus on Scriptures dealing with God's love and His unconditional acceptance.

2. On a regular basis, reassure your child verbally that you love him no matter what he does and that he can never do anything that will cause you to stop loving him.

What other thoughts come to mind that could help to correct a pattern of manipulation? Record your thoughts along with some steps you have determined to take toward correction of wrong patterns. If you have not been a manipulative parent, suggest some steps you think would be appropriate to help others break this pattern.

The Authoritarian Parent

Assignment

- Please read the following article:

The Authoritarian Parent

The Imbalance

The authoritarian parent believes it is essential for him to have the upper hand in his home. He sees the error of permissiveness and is determined to avoid it. The problem again is one of imbalance. He goes so far in controlling his family that he often alienates his children. He is always right, he always has the last word, and his word is final.

Even if the child has a legitimate protest or appeal to offer, he is never permitted to express it. To allow a child to appeal, in the mind of an authoritarian parent, is to allow the child to gain a measure of control. Many authoritarian parents simply cannot be appealed to, and they become unapproachable. Some parents may prefer to maintain this distance with their children because it shelters them from having to deal with the child's emotional needs, which they may be emotionally incapable of meeting.

The authoritarian parent may also communicate either nonverbally (unintentionally) or verbally that he does not want to be bothered by the child. He may be too busy doing supposedly more important things to take the time to talk or play with his child. When he does interact with his child, he is impatient with the child's inabilities and limitations, and his communication often consists of commands and directions. He orders his children around like robots and punishes even the smallest failure to respond promptly and correctly.

An authoritarian parent tends to demand perfection from his child. The child receives little encouragement when he does do well but is sure to hear a barrage of advice or criticism when he does not. The child learns that he cannot do anything well enough to please his parent.

Not surprisingly, one consequence of authoritarian parenting is that children often develop a fear of failure, which in turn may keep them from even trying to achieve. The risk of failure and of consequent belittling from the parent is simply too great. Emotionally and socially, and perhaps intellectually as well, the child will have difficulty reaching his full potential. He will likely struggle for many years with a poor self-concept.

A child growing up in a home like this may also develop an unhealthy fear of his parent, who rules the home with an inflexible hand. While the parent may or may not punish too harshly, he is lacking in the area of knowing how to give love to a child. The younger child may appear to respect an authoritarian parent, but this respect is usually based on fear rather than love. When the child is older, he may rebel under this kind of harsh authority.

The parent too will suffer disadvantages as a result of his pattern of authoritarian leadership. He will miss the blessing of emotional closeness with his child, developed on a daily basis through close and loving contact. He may desire to be closer to his children but feel unable to break down the growing barrier between them. Eventually, when his children are grown, he will feel isolated from them. Yet day by day, perhaps without realizing it, he sacrifices closeness for the sake of feeling that he is absolutely in control. He pushes the child farther and farther from him. He equates his child's fear of him with respect and believes he must never admit to being wrong. Though he may elicit obedience from his children, he usually fails to elicit genuine respect and love.

A common consequence of authoritarian parenting is that the child also tends to view God as distant, unapproachable, and demanding. He finds it hard to accept God's unconditional love or to believe that God is a loving heavenly Father who is always ready to listen to him (Ps 91:14-15; 145:18; Jer 33:3; Heb 4:14-16; 7:25; 10:22). He views God as he views his earthly father, and he feels distant from Him as he feels distant from his earthly father.

The Counterbalance

The wise parent recognizes the need to establish authority in the home but understands the difference between authority and authoritarianism. He or she works at having a close and trusting relationship with the child by being available to talk with, and especially to listen to, the child and by being patient to answer the many seemingly silly questions the child may ask.

Of course, the parent recognizes that he cannot be available every time the child wants attention, but he tries to give the child his full attention for a period of time each day. He is careful not to get so busy that he has no time for his children in his schedule. He communicates that he loves them and enjoys being with them.

While the wise parent establishes rules and expects obedience, he also lets the child know that he is approachable. For example, after disciplining a child, he may give the child a hug to affirm his love. He admits when he has made a mistake and is willing to say "I'm sorry" to those involved. He requires obedience, but he gives love and encouragement that earn him the genuine respect of the child. He leaves the door open for the child to appeal to him.

The wise parent also gives generous praise and words of encouragement to his child. When a child fails in his attempt to do something, his father and mother should be there to encourage him to get up and try again. They help the child not to view himself as a failure.

Another important part of parenting is recognizing that each child is different and should be treated accordingly. The authoritarian parent tends to think that his training should be inflexible and should apply to all his children alike. While the authoritarian parent often thinks in terms of getting the respect he deserves, the wise parent thinks in terms of earning the respect of his family by being the person God asks him to be.

QUESTION 12

If you tend to be too authoritarian with your children, take some time to ask yourself the following questions:

1. Why do I demand absolute obedience of my children?

2. What do my children really think of me? Do they love me, or are they merely afraid of me?

3. How can I take steps to change this pattern of authoritarian control as a parent?

4. How committed am I to changing?

Record your reflections in your Life Notebook.

After you have worked through those questions, read and meditate on Psalm 103:13-14. Reflect on any changes you notice in your actions as you meditate on the Fatherhood of God.

If you realize that you have had an authoritarian attitude with your children, try the following steps to break your habits and heal your family:

1. Take time during family devotions to focus on Scriptures dealing with God's availability and His desire for an intimate relationship with His children.

2. Physically turn away from your task at hand the next time your child approaches you with a question or concern. Look him in the eye and address his concern with as much respect as you would give to a friend or colleague.

3. The next time your child does something well, verbally and physically affirm him with words and a hug. The next time your child makes an innocent mistake, encourage him to try again with no criticism.

The Inconsistent Parent

Assignment

- Please read the following article:

The Inconsistent Parent

The Imbalance

The inconsistent parent vacillates from one kind of behavior to another, giving confused messages to his child. At times this parent may be permissive, allowing the child to do what he pleases; at other times he may be authoritarian, ruling with an iron hand. In other words, the child is never sure just which Mom or Dad he is dealing with today. He does not know for certain what his limits are because they are not clearly established. One day he may get away with an action but be punished for the same action the next day.

The inconsistent parent often has not thought through his philosophy of child-rearing and thus is uncertain of how to react to his child's actions and attitudes. Some inconsistent patterns are the result of moodiness. For example, Mom may punish her son today for spilling his milk because she is in a bad mood over something that has happened or she is not feeling well. Dad may swat at his son when he is irritated over his financial problems or his job.

Sometimes an inconsistent parent punishes a child harshly for breaking an unspoken rule that the parent has never bothered to explain, without warning the child of the impending consequences of his actions. Another common pattern of inconsistent parenting is for a parent to show limitless tolerance for a child's misbehavior until the parent reaches a breaking point where he or she reacts impulsively and punishes the child too harshly.

The child raised by parents who greatly vacillate in moods and in their patterns of dealing with him may develop insecurity and emotional problems. As a result of his training the child may live in constant uncertainty and even fear, wondering when something will come crushing down on him or when he will be caught and punished for crimes he has gotten away with before. Life is like a roller coaster for him, now up, now down. Even in the good times he knows insecurity because his boundaries are not clearly defined. He is never sure how his parents will react to him.

Children raised by inconsistent parents often have difficulty learning discernment or wise behavior because they have not been taught to look ahead and see the consequences of their choices. They have not been trained to recognize warning signs in life. Their parents have either failed to warn them of consequences or have been inconsistent in warning them. The child may also struggle with self-control, since he has been allowed too much freedom at times and has been harshly punished for small offenses at other times. He has not learned to control himself properly.

The Counterbalance

Did you see some of your own actions in the description of the inconsistent parent? Let us make it clear that at times all of us are inconsistent as parents and will exhibit some of the poor patterns mentioned above. Yet our goal should be to be consistent in our training as well as consistent in our example.

Many inconsistent parents are sincerely struggling to live a godly life. They are trying to be patient and to practice self-control, both fruits of the Spirit (Gal. 5:22-23). Perhaps they carry patience too far, interpreting it to mean that they should tolerate everything a child does because he is, after all, only a child. Each misbehavior on the part of the child builds tension in the parent, however. Then when he can tolerate no more, he loses control and may erupt in anger and punish harshly.

The wise parent will take the time to think through a philosophy of child-rearing, at least in broad terms, and will discuss it with his or her spouse. Together they will set up standards for the child's conduct and will attempt to be fair and consistent in dealing with the child. Each time the child exceeds the boundaries he should receive a warning before he is punished. Thus, the child will learn to recognize the rewards of obedience—praise and pleasure of his parents—and the consequences of disobedience.

Later on, as he grows up, he will be more likely to recognize God's warnings in Scripture concerning the path of folly and will be better equipped to control himself. He will also be more secure. The child who has well-defined rules to live by, such as the Israelites had, and a consistent enforcement of the rules will usually grow in self-confidence and security and will be well-adjusted. These characteristics will carry into adulthood and into his relationship with God also.

QUESTION 13

What ways can you suggest to break this pattern of permissiveness and loss of control? Look up the following verses, and summarize what they are teaching: Proverbs 16:32; 25:28, Romans 12:18, Galatians 5:22-23, Ephesians 4:26, James 1:19, 26, 2 Peter 1:3, and 1 John 5:4.

The Child-Centered Parent

Assignment

* Please read the following article:

The Child-Centered Parent

The Imbalance

Parents who center their entire world around the nurture of their children are child-centered. With such a parent every decision, large or small, is made in light of how it will affect the child. Certainly children should be considered in all decisions affecting the family but never at the expense of the family core: the husband-wife relationship.

Child-centered parenting is based upon the philosophy that good parenting can be determined by the amount of attention and sacrifice children receive from their parents. This approach is deceptive because it seems to be biblically sound. However, the major shortcoming is that it neglects the priority of the husband-wife relationship as established in Scripture. When the husband-wife relationship becomes subservient to the parent-child relationship, the divine plan for successful family development is violated and undermined.

One true story illustrates how this can happen. A four-year-old insisted that his mother sleep with him every night, and she willingly complied, although her husband was upset at being left to sleep alone. The child learned to control his mother until he was able to dictate mealtimes, menus, and many other aspects of life in this home. The husband felt increasingly alienated from his wife, who thought she was performing her motherly tasks with the greatest devotion.

Several negative behavioral patterns are commonly found in the children of child-centered parents. These children learn to get their own way by manipulating their parents, playing upon their emotions, and even playing one parent against the other. This often divides the parents against each other as one or the other feels it necessary to take up the child's cause.

A child raised in a home where he is always the center of attention will generally grow up to be selfish and ungrateful, having nurtured a false sense of his own importance. Everything has always revolved around his needs and desires; his parents have centered their lives around him. Such a child also grows up with little respect for other people or property; he continually seeks and expects self-gratification. Obviously, child-centered parenting is harmful to the character development of the child, and it can create havoc in the family as well.

The child raised in the child-centered home will have difficulty developing discernment because he or she will lack the ability to make unselfish judgments and decisions. Similarly, he will find it difficult to plan a wise course of action because he has been trained to view everything strictly in terms of how it affects him. He does not learn to view life from the perspective of the welfare and good of others, as Scripture admonishes, nor does he experience the joy of serving others. Having been trained to view himself as the most important person in every situation, he will also lack in wisdom. He will not be able to think in terms of what is fair or just in dealing with human relationships.

The Counterbalance

The parent who has been centering all of his attention on his child or children needs to recognize the mistake he is making. First, he needs to think through his priorities again and recognize the priority of cultivating the relationship with one's spouse. Second, he needs to recognize that he is harming his relationship to both the spouse and the child by placing the child at the center of all his plans and by focusing so much attention on the child. Third, he must begin to teach the child that he is merely one part of the whole that is called family.

The child needs to be reeducated to see that his needs and his desires are not the only ones. The parent who desires to balance his training will look for opportunities to teach his children that others come first: first Jesus, then others, then oneself. He encourages his child to think of how his behavior will affect other people. Teaching the principle "do unto others as you would have others do unto you" is important in Christian homes. Helping the child grow in empathy, sympathy, and sensitivity to others will help keep the parent from being too child-centered and the child from becoming too self-centered. The child who grows up in a home knowing that his mother and father are committed to God first, then to each other, and then to their children will be secure.

One of Billy Graham's daughters was asked the question, "Did you resent the time your father spent away from home to be involved in his ministry?" Her answer was, "No, because I knew first of all my parents loved God, second they loved each other unconditionally, and they also loved me unconditionally." The biblically balanced home keeps these three love commitments in proper priority and balance.

QUESTION 14

Review briefly each of the patterns of parenting discussed thus far. Make a chart listing the seven negative patterns of parenting and some of the weaknesses of each pattern and negative effects on children.

As you read through your chart, evaluate your own parenting style:

1. Which of these negative patterns do you tend toward?

2. In which areas do you need more balance?

3. How can you achieve this balance?

4. Suggest some practical things you can do to bring balance to your parenting. If possible, discuss the patterns of parenting with your spouse, and share with each other tactfully the tendencies you think you may have.

Topic 2: Seeking Balance

Assignment

- Please read the following article:

Seeking Balance

Wise and balanced parenting is an ideal, a goal toward which we aim as mothers and fathers. Not only do we aim for our children to be obedient, but we want them to be happy, fulfilled, and secure. Our training must balance love with discipline. Love without discipline produces a child who is not capable of self-discipline—a spoiled child. Discipline without love produces a discouraged child with a broken spirit. Likewise, biblical training involves both teaching and parental example. Teaching without example produces a child who is bitter and full of resentment. An example without teaching produces a child who is exasperated and insecure.

The biblically balanced parent puts the husband-wife relationship first, aiming at a strong marriage that is truly one flesh and one spirit, just as God designed it. In His plan the children are welcome members of the family, gifts of God loaned to the parents to love and enjoy and to instruct and discipline.

Before you had children, you may have had definite ideas about child-rearing that later proved unworkable. In the process of raising children we often learn to refine and develop our early philosophy of child-rearing. Hopefully we can and do learn from our mistakes and the mistakes of others, some of which we have looked at in this lesson.

We must also keep in mind here that, just as we are committed to our children and desire for them to grow to spiritual wisdom and maturity, so also God our heavenly Father is committed to us. We will fail many times as parents, but we have the promise that God's love and grace are constant. Our heavenly Father will continue to teach and train us and guide us toward spiritual maturity, helping us to set aside the sins that beset us daily in the task of raising children. He has promised to give us wisdom when we ask (Jas 1:5). He has also promised His unconditional faithfulness (2 Tim 2:13).

A story illustrates His faithfulness and His very present help to us as parents. Paderewsky, the great Polish pianist, was to perform a concert at the Opera House in London. A mother wanted to take her young son, who had just started to take piano lessons, to hear this great artist play.

On the night of the concert, the mother told her son to stay in his seat while she went to the back of the auditorium for a few minutes. As she returned to her seat, her heart almost stopped. She heard childlike music coming from the piano up on that great concert stage. Afraid to look up to see who was playing, she knew in her heart that her son had made his way up onto that stage to play that great piano. Sure enough, when she reached her seat, the boy was gone.

The huge crowd of people had begun to murmur because of her son's playing. She could scarcely think what to do, when all of a sudden she heard beautiful music coming from the stage. She looked up to see the great Paderewsky standing behind her little boy, his hands sweeping over the keys to produce lovely music, while the little boy continued playing his simple childlike tune. Paderewsky leaned over the boy and encouraged him to "keep playing, keep playing," and the beautiful music floated forth from the grand piano.

As parents we are like that little boy, inept at times, unsure of ourselves. We do not always know the right way to handle every situation that arises with our children; we are not always the parents that we should be. But God is standing behind us encouraging us and using our feeble efforts to be faithful in the task. All along He is whispering in our ear, "Keep playing, keep playing."

QUESTION 15

Patterns of parenting are passed on from generation to generation. You learned them from your parents and often will pass them on to your children. This project is designed to get you to analyze those styles and to begin to modify them to reflect what you learned in this lesson. Please open your Life Notebook and record your thoughts.

1. Analyze the parenting style that you learned from your parents by answering the following questions:

a. Describe the parenting style of your parents in one or two sentences.

b. What is the worst thing your parents taught you? What is the best thing you learned from them?

2. Analyze your own parenting style by answering the following questions:

a. Describe your own parenting style in one sentence.

b. What are you repeating in your style that you saw in your parents' style?

c. What are you doing that is different from what your parents did?

d. What areas of your style suffer from imbalance?

e. What steps can you take to balance your parenting?

f. How have you experienced God's grace to counter mistakes you may have made in parenting?

3. Conclude the project by answering the following:

a. What would you most like to teach your children?

b. List three or four positive steps you want to begin working on right away.

Check on your own progress in one month to see what you have accomplished.

We have dealt with seven patterns of parenting that are common to many homes but often prove to be negative factors in raising wise or spiritually mature children. Many children raised in homes where negative patterns predominate may have some of the problems mentioned above. But some may not.

Sometimes a boy or girl comes out of the worst circumstances imaginable and grows up to serve God in a wonderful way. We must emphasize that this is in spite of his parents, not because of them. When this happens, it is usually because a child has learned to look to God for what is lacking in his own family, whether it be love, consistency, kindness, or even standards of conduct. Such a child sees the weakness of his parents and looks beyond them to God for strength and wisdom to make it through childhood. For each of these children, however, numerous other children are bent and bruised and even broken along the way by their parents' poor patterns of parenting.

Lesson 3 Self Check

QUESTION 1

Based on Hebrews 12:5-11, we should view disciplining our children as proof of which of the following? *(Select all that apply.)*

    A. That our children are basically sinful

    B. That we love our children

    C. That our children need correction

    D. That we are treating them as sons

QUESTION 2

When God disciplines us, it is always for punishment. *True or False?*

QUESTION 3

The goal of the permissive parent is to provide his child with an environment that has as few boundaries or restraints as possible. *True or False?*

QUESTION 4

Although there are negatives, one benefit of being an overprotective parent is that the child grows up accustomed to having his parents' continual service, guidance, and approval. *True or False?*

QUESTION 5

According to the lesson, how is the nagging parent characterized?

    A. One who is characterized by the constant repetition of commands or directions to their children

    B. One who frequently gives his child good advice

    C. One who protects his child from error

    D. One who demonstrates his love by repeated exhortation

QUESTION 6

The manipulative parent often does what?

    A. Believes that he should keep the child from any difficulty

    B. Seeks to control the child's behavior by strong discipline such as spanking

    C. Gives constant commands to his child in order to secure obedience

    D. Seeks to control a child's outward behavior by manipulating the child's emotions

QUESTION 7

Children of authoritarian parents do what?

    A. Often develop a fear of failure

    B. Have a healthy respect for authority

    C. Normally grow up to be extremely obedient

    D. Often develop an emotional closeness to their parents.

QUESTION 8

The child raised by parents who greatly vacillate in their moods and in their patterns of discipline may develop insecurity and emotional problems. *True or False?*

QUESTION 9

A positive feature of the child-centered pattern of parenting is that the priority of the husband-wife relationship is frequently enhanced. *True or False?*

QUESTION 10

Discipline without love produces a discouraged child with a broken spirit. *True or False?*

Lesson 3 Answers to Questions

QUESTION 1: *Your answer should be similar to the following:*
Based on this passage and many others, it is clear that all of us are born with a disposition toward self-centeredness. Any philosophy of child raising that is based in reality must take this into consideration.

QUESTION 2

B. That we love our children

D. That we are treating them as sons

QUESTION 3: *Your answer*

QUESTION 4: *Your answer*

QUESTION 5: *Your answer*

QUESTION 6: *Your answer*

QUESTION 7: *Your answer*

QUESTION 8: *Your answer*

QUESTION 9: *Your answer*

QUESTION 10: *Your answer*

QUESTION 11: *Your answer*

QUESTION 12: *Your answer*

QUESTION 13: *Your answer*

QUESTION 14: *Your answer*

QUESTION 15: *Your answer*

Lesson 3 Self Check Answers

QUESTION 1
    B. That we love our children
    D. That we are treating them as sons

QUESTION 2: False

QUESTION 3: True

QUESTION 4: False

QUESTION 5
    A. One who is characterized by the constant repetition of commands or directions to their children

QUESTION 6
    D. Seeks to control a child's outward behavior by manipulating the child's emotions

QUESTION 7
    A. Often develop a fear of failure

QUESTION 8: True

QUESTION 9: False

QUESTION 10: True

Unit 2: Understanding Your Child

Since Adam and Eve, parents have faced the fact that their offspring can be startlingly different from one another. These differences can be the source of delight or dismay, depending on whether your child is more like Abel or Cain.

One thing is certain about each child—he is unique. On the other hand, he bears certain similarities to other children of the same age and sex. This unit will attempt to expand on these two statements, emphasizing both the individual nature of your child's personality and the way in which his actions can be characteristic of his age group. We will examine the general characteristics of children from birth through adolescence and then go on to present material showing how to train a child, demonstrating love, respect, and firmness.

Unit Outline

Lesson 4: Dealing with Children from Birth to Age Six

Lesson 5: Dealing with Children Ages Seven to Twelve

Lesson 6: Dealing with Adolescents

Unit Objectives

By the end of this unit, you will be able to do the following:

- Define appropriate goals for training at each of the three age levels based on the characteristics of each

- Articulate the importance of teaching children a proper biblical view of human sexuality and its context within marriage

- Examine the values in your own home and in your culture as a whole which either coincide with or contradict biblical values

- Explain the need for firm and loving discipline of children and identify what methods of discipline are appropriate at each age level

Lesson 4: Dealing with Children from Birth to Age Six

Lesson Introduction

Maintaining a sense of humor is often the key to survival during the years when your children are small. Being able to laugh can help you keep all those daily minor calamities in perspective. One mother of two small children described this scene in her home:

> A few months ago, I was making several phone calls in the family room where my three-year-old daughter, Adrianne, and my five-month-old son, Nathan, were playing quietly. Nathan loves Adrianne, who has been learning how to mother him gently since the time of his birth.
>
> I suddenly realized that the children were no longer in view. Panic-stricken, I quickly hung up the phone and went looking for the pieces. Down the hall and around the corner, I found the children playing cheerfully in Adrianne's bedroom.
>
> Relieved and upset, I shouted, "Adrianne, you know you are not allowed to carry Nathan! He is too little and you could hurt him if he fell!"
>
> Startled, she answered, "I didn't, Mommy."
>
> Knowing he couldn't crawl, I suspiciously demanded, "Well, then, how did he get all the way into your room?"
>
> Confident of my approval for her obedience, she said with a smile, "I rolled him!" [Dobson, *Parenting Isn't for Cowards*, 101-2]

Poor Nathan. Can't you just visualize him rolling and bobbling down the hall to the bedroom? This is the stuff of which family life is made. Your memory album has its own special shots—a picture of Samuel with ice cream everywhere but in his cone, a photo of Mariana with no front teeth (you remember well the day she knocked them out), and that precious shot of Ruth sleeping (when did she ever sleep!?)

The days of childhood, with its laughter and its tears, will be gone before you know it. Early childhood is a precious time when our little ones can be most easily influenced. As parents we can leave a lasting impression on their little hearts. In this chapter we want to look at what we need to know to effectively instruct, discipline, and care for the little ones from birth to age six.

Lesson Outline

Topic 1: Introducing Your Child

    The Variations are Endless

    Age-Related Behavior Characteristics

Topic 2: Discover the Specific Tendencies in Your Child

    The Good Tendencies

    The Good Tendencies Applied

    The Bad Tendencies

Lesson Objectives

By the end of this lesson, you will be able to do the following:

- Discuss the uniqueness of each child and the need to treat each child according to his personality and abilities

- Study your children to determine their specific bents and make a specific plan to raise each child

- Define some ways to build a positive sense of self-worth in your child and take steps to implement those ideas

- Take steps to be a godly parent in actions as well as words

Topic 1: Introducing Your Child

As we begin this lesson, we would like to introduce you to your child. Perhaps you would reply, "I already know my child better than anyone else. I feed him and clothe him and teach him and care for him." Yet it is possible to give birth to a child, to nurse, clothe, discipline, and teach your child, and yet not really know him or her. Sometimes parents are lacking in sensitivity; sometimes they just do not take the time out of a busy schedule to sit and listen to their children. Consequently, they may be missing the signals their child is sending and missing out on a wonderful opportunity to share their child's world.

God's Unique Design

Knowing your child is very important if you are to love your child and train him as God would have you to do. Your training can be so much more effective if you take the time to understand your child and the things which are important to him. Knowing your child means becoming familiar with his temperament, abilities, and interests, all of which are unique to him.

The Variations are Endless

Most mothers will tell you with great conviction what a unique temperament each baby possesses from the day he is born. From the time that little bundle is placed in your arms, you can see that he has his own personality. Some come kicking and screaming and struggling into this world; others are docile and content.

Each has his own temperament, the product of genetic material that was mysteriously woven together in secret and which Scripture says was carefully overseen by God. Your precious little child is not an accident; God put him together. He may possess your eyes, your spouse's nose, your father's ears, your grandmother's hair—the possibilities are seemingly endless.

A genetics textbook points out that there are 16 million different chromosome combinations possible for each child. Does that figure dazzle you? Such a wonderfully creative God we have! Each child is truly an original, a unique creation of God, unique in his looks, temperament, feelings, intellectual capacity, and talents. There has never been another one just like him, and there will not be one after him. (Some parents may breathe a sigh of relief here!)

Every child God places in our arms has an inborn temperament, a set of characteristics already established. Think of your children for a moment, or of your brothers and sisters. Are they all alike? Think of Cain and Abel or the twins Jacob and Esau. Although brothers, these boys displayed distinct differences in personality and in interests. As we saw in Lesson 1, the wise parent desires to tailor his training according to the personality and abilities of his child. Recognizing that God has placed a unique set of characteristics within each child, the wise parent tries to see how God has made each one; then he establishes that child's training accordingly.

Two common parental mistakes violate this principle and are to be avoided.

- The first mistake is using an identical approach with all our children. What worked with one child may unfortunately not work with another whose temperament is very different.

- A second mistake is comparing our children. At times parents may find themselves thinking or saying, "Why can't you be like your sister?" Meanwhile, the child longs for her parents to realize that she is totally different from her sibling.

This does not mean that parents should allow a child to rebel or defy her parents just to assert her identity. But comparing your child with a sibling or another child seldom has the desired effect, and children often resist efforts to make them fit into the same mold. Trouble frequently begins when parents try to do just that.

QUESTION 1

Stop for a moment and think about your own childhood. Did your parents or teachers ever compare you with a brother or sister whose temperament and abilities were different? How did the comparison with another sibling or child affect you?

Age-Related Behavior Characteristics

In this topic we are introducing a theme to which we will refer many times in the following lessons: the characteristics of children at various stages of their development. As parents, we have found this information very helpful. Why? Because it is comforting to know that the behavior our child exhibits may be perfectly normal!

It is interesting that the Hebrew Bible has eight different words for "child" and each word is applied to various ages.

Assignment

- Please read the following article:

The Stages of Child Development in the Bible

According to Alfred Edersheim in *Sketches of Jewish Social Life in the Days of Christ*, there were eight different terms in the Hebrew Bible for the word "child," each depicting a fresh stage of life.

Jeled

The newborn was called a *jeled*. It was applied to Moses (Ex 2:6-8). This word was applied to our Lord Jesus in the great prophecy of Isaiah 9:6, "For unto us a child (jeled) was born."

(See also Isa 29:23; 57:4; Jer 31:20; Eccl 4:13; 1 Kgs 12:8; 2 Kgs 2:24; Gen 42:22.)

Jonek

The next child name, in point of time, is *jonek*, which literally means "a suckling" and describes a child up to their first birthday. We are told that the Lord Jesus will grow up as a *jonek* ("tender shoot" in Isa 53:2), describing the period of time between birth and roughly three years. The word is sometimes overlaps with the next stage, the *olel*.

Olel

The third stage is life was designated by the word *olel*, which indicates age one to three. He is still nursing but it is no longer satisfied with only this nourishment, and is "asking for bread," as in Lamentations 4:4.

Gamul

The *gamul* is the "weaned one," typically age three to six. Hebrew mothers typically nursed their children until age three (see Ps 131:2; Isa 11:8; 28:9). The verb form of the word means "to complete," hence, he has completed the period of nursing. When the period of weaning was over, it was celebrated by a feast.

Taph

The *taph* refers to that period in the child's life from age seven to twelve when he clings to his mother and the mother is constantly watching him or her.

Elem

The sixth stage is called the *elem* and the feminine form is *almah*. This corresponds to the period of early adolescence, thirteen to fifteen years of age. The word means "to become firm and strong." The *almah* was the designation of the virgin Mary in the virgin birth prophecy of Isaiah 7:14.

Naar

The seventh stage of development was designed by the word *naar*, "youth." The word means "to break away." It refers to one who shakes off or shakes himself free, an appropriate term for the teenage years from fifteen to eighteen.

Bachur

The final stage, the eight stage of development was the *bachur* or "ripened one." This was used, for example, of the young warrior, as in Isaiah 31:8; Jeremiah 18:21; 15:8.

Topic 2: Discover the Specific Tendencies in Your Child

A pediatrician I know once told me that raising children was somewhat like cooking a meal and accidentally using the wrong ingredient in place of another, much different-tasting one. You don't realize you've got a disaster until it's too late!

In Lesson 1 we studied Proverbs 22:6:

> Train up a child in the way be should go, Even when he is old he will not depart from it. (NASB)

A paraphrase might read something like this: "Adapt the training of your child so that it is in keeping with his God-given characteristics and tendencies; when he comes to maturity, he will not depart from the training he has received."

In this topic we want to look at some of the Scriptures which describe two innate tendencies in our children: a tendency toward sin and a tendency toward good.

The Good Tendencies

Read Psalm 139:13-16. Keep the following points about the language in mind as you read:

- The Hebrew word translated "wove" denotes God's intricate involvement in forming us.
- "Sewed together" (Ps 139:15) in Hebrew is the same word used in Exodus for the intricate design of the curtains of the Tabernacle
- The word "saw" means "watched over."

QUESTION 2

Based on Psalm 139:13-16 it is clear that:

A. God is responsible for my formation

B. Nature is responsible for my formation

C. My characteristics are a product of random chance

D. My environment is the final determiner of who I am

QUESTION 3

What are some inferences we should draw from Psalm 139:16 in relation to raising and understanding our children?

The Good Tendencies Applied

QUESTION 4

Based on Psalm 139, what error did Isaac and Rebecca make right at the beginning in their raising of Jacob and Esau in Genesis 25:27-28?

QUESTION 5

Based on the study of Psalm 139, which of the following statements represents a wise course of action?

A. To bring about obedience parents need to exert force.

B. We can often best help our children find themselves by encouraging them to be like us.

C. When observing our child's disinterest in the Lord, we can often counterbalance this by increasing our focus on Bible reading and family devotions.

D. Encourage him to accept himself and see the benefits and value of those traits that make him **him**.

QUESTION 6

Psalm 139 is an important portion of Scripture regarding children and parental perspective. Become a "student" of your children to discover what God has designed. Learn to see God's workmanship in their motivations, and gifts; help them discern God's purpose for their lives. How does Psalm 139 apply to each of your children? Record your thoughts in your Life Notebook and discuss with your spouse.

Summary of Psalm 139

Now let's put it all together. This is what David is saying: "You, God, and none other, originated my vital organs. You knitted me together in the womb of my mother. My skeleton was not hidden from You when I was made in that concealed place of protection. When my veins and arteries and personality were skillfully embroidered in variegated colors like fine needlepoint, Your eyes watched over me when I was just an embryo. And in Your book, the days that I should experience were described—the days that would shape me into the person You want me to be."

Consider this carefully: The wise parent realizes the sovereign God of heaven has given him children He has planned and arranged and prescribed with certain attributes, abilities, personalities, and physical appearances. By study and observation, this parent gets to know the child God has given him. He spends time in prayer, asking for wisdom. He spends time watching, talking with, and listening to that precious child, not just when he is little but all through the years the child is at home. The parent actually becomes a student of the child, because the parent knows this child has certain established bents. With keen discernment the observing parent takes special note of traits that begin to emerge. He studies the child in hopes of giving him wise, intelligent direction during those crucial growing-up years. (From Swindoll, *You and Your Child*, 15-39)

The Bad Tendencies

Our children also have some bad tendencies toward self-centeredness that are derived from the fact that we all have a sin nature. Since this is reality, it is the height of foolishness to approach child-raising with the assumption that all children come to us either basically good or neutral.

Assignment

- Read Psalm 51:5; 58:3
- Read Romans 5:12

QUESTION 7

Based on your reading, what do we learn about children?

    A. Children come to us as a blank slate, neither good nor bad

    B. Children are born basically good and environment corrupts them

    C. Children are born with a tendency toward selfishness

    D. Children are completely determined by their genes.

QUESTION 8

Read Genesis 12:10-13; 20:1-5; 26:6-11; 27:1-6, 37. What pattern do you observe here?

QUESTION 9

According to Proverbs 28:13 and 1 John 1:9 the pattern observed in Question 8 is avoidable. *True or False?*

As a summary of this topic, there are five major application points:

1. Do everything in your power to lead your child to Jesus Christ. Everything!

2. Spend time in prayer, asking God for insight and wisdom to see the character of your children in depth.

3. Become a student of your children. Talk about your children with your spouse. Make that a common practice in the quietness of your bedroom or around the table when the kids are not there. Determine to know those bents and characteristics in your children.

4. Do all you can to be consistent in discipline, in love, in reaction. Attitudes in our homes are far more important than actions, but they are not as easily detected.

5. Maintain open and loving communication with the whole family.

Topic 3: The Characteristics of Early Childhood

We have seen that each child is a unique creation of God and possesses his own temperament and gifts, as well as specific tendencies he learns from other family members. As a parent it helps to know what other children of his age generally have in common.

    • Other children his age are probably doing the same things.

    • Keeping your expectations realistic and based on the child's abilities at his age.

    • Do not think you have failed when your child exhibits a particular undesirable behavior common at that age.

In this topic we will briefly outline some of the behavior characteristics commonly typical of children as they mature from infancy to age six.

Infants: Birth to Twelve Months

Assignment

- Please read the following article:

The Characteristics of Infants

As your baby grows during his first twelve months of life, several characteristics should be understood.

Range of Focus

Interestingly, studies have shown that a child's field of vision closely coincides with the distance from the mother's breast to the mother's face! When he is being held and cuddled against her, he feels the warmth and security of her body while he stares intently at her face. He does not see anything outside of that range of his focus.

Physical and Mental Stimulation

Part of caring for an infant is seeing that he is properly stimulated, both physically and mentally. In order to provide mental stimulation, pictures or hanging mobiles can be hung to correspond to the infant's range of focus. Bright, contrasting colors or black and white objects are easiest for the baby to detect. Babies usually respond quite early to pictures with simple faces as they learn the concept of what a face is.

Between the third and fifth months the infant usually begins grasping at objects within his reach. This form of stimulation is good for him. If he is left lying in a darkened room with little to stimulate his interest, he may be slower to respond to visual stimuli. He needs the sensory stimulation of those who care for him, as they caress, tickle, and gently move his arms and legs, while at the same time talking to him.

The infant gradually learns to recognize the voices of his mother and father and others who care for him. Lower tones of voice tend to calm a baby, while higher tones may arouse him, which explains why sometimes a father, with a lower voice, can calm a crying infant more easily than the mother.

Fathers who share in the care of the infant feel much more a part of their baby's life and share this sense of wonder and intimacy with their wives. Most wives feel both pleasure and pride when their husband is willing to help with the baby.

Link of Emotional and Physical Needs

For an infant to have his emotional needs met, he must have his physical needs met. When he is crying at 3 a.m. because he is hungry or wet or has colic, his emotions are quite obvious. The infant is completely dependent upon the adults who care for him or her. We show him from the very beginning whether he can or cannot trust the big people in his world.

Without being aware of it, parents are sowing the seeds of trust, courage, hope, and love as they respond to their child's needs in the early months. Each of these characteristics, or its opposite, will begin to develop during this early stage of the child's growth. These characteristics also underlie the future development of the child's faith in God, so we can see just how important it is to sow these seeds.

How do we sow trust? By being dependable. The infant learns that he can depend on you to meet his needs when he is hungry or wet or he needs to be cuddled and loved. Likewise, he feels secure when he is held and cared for. He sees love in your face and hears it in your voice when you delight in him. If his basic needs are not met, if he is frequently left to cry for long periods of time with no response from his parents, he may fail to develop trust and a sense of security, or he may become too dependent emotionally on his parents.

Becoming More Active

Around four- to six-months-old, he begins to roll over and take more interest in what is going on around him. Some babies develop a strong attachment to mother during the last half of their first year and may become fearful of strangers. At about six to eight months many babies begin to crawl if they are given sufficient opportunity to get down on all fours.

Sleeping Through the Night

Although babies are physically capable of sleeping through the night by six months, many babies enjoy being cuddled in the middle of the night and will continue to wake up once, twice, or even three times every night, a fact that leaves mother feeling very weary throughout the day. The little fellow is not so cute at 3 A.M. when he is a year old.

Frequently, parents struggle with getting a baby to sleep through the night. Since during the first twelve months the baby's main means of communication is crying, the cry could be the baby's way of telling you he is wet or uncomfortable. Or the baby may just want to be held. You need to be sensitive to this possibility, for attention and affection are very important needs in a child's first year. Baby also needs to learn that nighttime is a time to sleep, not to play or eat. If he is waking up at night merely out of habit, you might want to try to break him of this.

If this is a problem for you, try this approach. First, feed him before bedtime, see that his basic needs are met, and tuck him in. When he cries, first, check to see if he is wet or cold or is experiencing some other physical problem. If he continues to cry, try rubbing his back, perhaps singing or humming softly to him, but resist the temptation to pick him up. If he still continues to cry when you leave, give him some time to cry himself to sleep. If the crying does not stop after a reasonable amount of time, the baby may be needing the reassurance of your presence.

The main thing to remember is that a parent should not, on the one hand, automatically run and pick the child up every time he cries. On the other hand, a parent must not fail to provide a child's critical need for love, attention, and security through holding and comforting the child.

One counselor put it this way:

> I would rather have a child who has had too much attention than one who has had too little. You can take a child who has had too much and, in a matter of hours or days, break bad habits. The child who has not had enough may need years to achieve a sense of security and worth. It is better to err on the side of too much love rather than on the side of too little. (Getz, 204)

Some fathers do not seem to be as bothered by a baby's crying as mother is. If this is true in your case, perhaps mother could take a walk outside at night while father oversees this transitional period of allowing the baby to cry himself to sleep. It can be hard on parents emotionally, but your baby will survive, and you are not helping your family by letting your body become physically exhausted.

Later Months of Infancy

In the later months of infancy your child's personality becomes more evident. He is more aware of other people now. He may show more anxiety toward strangers and perhaps even cry more than he did as a newborn. He may cry when you leave him with others because his primary attachment is to his parents. But it is also healthy for him to learn a little independence from you. You and your spouse need to be alone at times without your children, if only for an hour or two, when you can talk and relate to each other as husband and wife, rather than seeing yourself only in your role as parents. If your marriage is to be a healthy one, your spouse needs your attention and affection too.

QUESTION 10

Based on the article, which of the following items are true? *(Select all that apply.)*

    A. It is better to give a child too much attention during this period than too little.

    B. A parent should run to a child and pick him up every time he cries.

    C. When a child cries at 3:00 a.m. it is important to realize that there can be emotional as well as physical needs.

    D. It is normal for a baby to develop a strong attachment to his mother during this period and be fearful of strangers.

QUESTION 11

Based on the article, how do we develop our infant's trust in us during this time in his life?

Toddlers: Twelve to Twenty-Four Months

Based on the Hebrew child development pattern, the third stage of life is the *Olel*.

Assignment

- Please read the following article:

The Characteristics of Toddlers

The toddler always seems to be excited, perhaps because he has discovered that he can walk. Unsteady though he may be, he can go places now on his own power. He wears his parents out by the end of each day, making endless discoveries in every room, examining everything from daddy's tools to mommy's pots and pans, and even the mysteries of the toilet.

Natural Curiosity

It is important to make your living space very safe by the time baby begins to crawl, putting dangerous medicines, cleaning fluids, and small items a baby could choke on out of reach. Examine your baby's toys to see that they are painted with non-toxic paint and that no small parts can come off and lodge in baby's throat. Be careful too of peeling paint chips, which can be poisonous.

His curiosity can get him into trouble at times, but it is generally a very positive quality; it is the means by which the child learns about his world. Stimulate his curiosity by means of simple word games. As the child discovers each new object, repeat its name for him. He enjoys hearing your voice and beginning to try to imitate a few sounds. Make it a point to talk to him a lot, using the real words rather than baby talk for objects and repeating the words frequently. This gives him intellectual stimulation.

Sometime between ages one and two, most children begin to talk, but their vocabulary can vary widely. It should not be a source of great concern if your eighteen-month-old is not as fluent as another child. Eventually he will talk. As the toddler moves closer to his second birthday, he will add more words and phrases to his vocabulary.

Teaching Toddlers About God

Even at this age you can lay the foundation for his Christian life, as you talk about God and show the child things which God has made. As you walk outside, you may say, "This is a tree; God made the tree." Encourage your child to pray simple prayers, saying things like, "Let us thank God for our blanket that keeps us warm."

Discipline of Toddlers

Moral training of the very small child is essentially a conditioning process. He is learning the difference between right and wrong behavior through conditioning: by being rewarded for acceptable behavior (hugs, kisses, loving approval) and being spanked for unacceptable behavior.

Many of the spankings and slaps given to toddlers could and should be avoided. Too many parents slap their little child's hand throughout the day for simply investigating his world. It is not wise to squelch his natural curiosity. Instead put valuable objects out of his reach and distract him with something else to play with. Parents can structure a child's environment so that the need for confrontation and spankings is minimized.

When should a toddler be mildly spanked? When he openly defies his parents' spoken commands. If he runs the other way when called, hits his friends, screams, and throws tantrums, a firm rap on the hand may convey the message. Reserve spankings for moments of greatest antagonism. A toddler should not be spanked for spilling a cup of milk or for other acts of childish carelessness. The child's lack of fine muscle control makes accidents inevitable at times.

When a toddler openly defies you, keep in mind as you correct the child that all correction must be administered in love. Good training consists of these two elements: love and discipline. A child needs to know his boundaries. Balancing love and discipline helps a child to feel secure. He knows he is loved, and he feels safe in the framework of regular routines and limits established for him. Security is very important to a toddler.

QUESTION 12

It is best to discipline your toddler frequently as he gets into things. *True or False?*

QUESTION 13

If you have a toddler, what helpful things did you learn in "The Characteristics of Toddlers" (refer to this Article placed earlier in the lesson)? What are some of the issues which you think you need to apply? Record your thoughts in your Life Notebook and discuss them with your spouse.

Two- and Three-Year-Olds

Assignment

- Please read the following article:

The Characteristics of Two- and Three-Year-Olds
Learning to Talk

Listening to a child talk at this age is a real delight. Two- and three-year-olds are adding more words and phrases to their vocabulary, and their mistakes and misuse of words can be very entertaining. Occasionally, a child refuses to talk until he is two years old or even a bit older. Usually it is not cause for alarm; he may even begin speaking in whole sentences when he does speak. What is important to remember is that the child understands **much** more than he can say. He does comprehend what you say to him and your instructions to him, although he may pretend not to at times!

Always Learning

If you are the parent of a two-year-old, you probably fall into bed every night exhausted. Your little one is a bundle of energy at this age. He operates on only one speed—high.

All the time he is learning, learning, learning—by observation and experimentation. His natural curiosity will wear you out at times, but it is the driving force that leads him to learn and discover. Obviously certain limits must be set on your child's curiosity, for his safety. Valued objects should be out of his reach or sight in order not to tempt him, rather than to spend your day slapping his hand for touching the vase your grandmother left you. You will wear yourself out guarding your nice things and possibly stifle his natural curiosity at the same time.

Discipline of Two- and Three-Year-Olds

The child at two and three is already developing a sense of morality. As he learns to respond to his parents' directions, mother and father are slowly but surely developing what will become his conscience. It is important to train him during this period. If you are of the opinion that he is too little to be disciplined, you will find yourself faced with a formidable task a year or two from now.

By the time he is two, your child should be learning to obey your instructions. How does he respond when you call him? Does he come quickly? Does he acknowledge you by saying, "Yes, Daddy?" or "Yes, Mommy?" or does he simply ignore your calling? Just as God desires obedience of His children, so we should train our children to obey us, and it is best if they learn early to obey willingly, without complaining.

QUESTION 14

Discuss the subject of obedience with your spouse. How do your children respond to your requests? Do they usually obey willingly, without complaining, or do they frequently argue? Do you phrase your instructions kindly, or do they come across as commands? Record your thoughts in your Life Notebook.

Two- and three-year-olds tend to babble a lot and talk nonsense. It is easy for parents to "tune out" what the child is saying, to develop the habit of not really listening. Yet listening to our little ones is very important. They need to know that we will listen to them without their having to shout or whine or do something drastic to get our attention. Many times a child is not heard until he gets louder and more insistent or until he whines and we take notice of the grating tone in his voice. Even a busy parent can take a moment to respond to a child's voice, if only to reassure him that you will listen and talk about it later.

QUESTION 15

If a child is still not talking by the age of two, the parents should be concerned and seek professional help *True or False?*

The child who has learned to whine in an effort to get attention needs to be "re-programmed." You can discourage whining by saying, "I'm sorry. Mommy doesn't hear you when you talk in that voice," or "Daddy doesn't have the kind of ears that can hear whining." Then remember to respond to the child when he speaks in a normal voice, giving him the attention he needs without resorting to whining. Reward him for speaking in a normal, quiet voice. In doing so, you will reinforce this positive way of speaking.

QUESTION 16

If you have a child who whines, experiment with the two statements given above for seven weeks. Record your results in your Life Notebook. How did the child respond to your new approach?

Four- to Six-Year-Olds

This next stage is what the Hebrews referred to as *Gamul* (three to six years old).

Assignment

- Please read the following article:

The Characteristics of Four- to Six-Year-Olds

By age four the child has developed considerably—mentally, socially, emotionally, and physically. He is no longer a baby. His physical coordination is improving, enabling him to run, climb, and jump better. He can begin to sing on pitch. He undergoes a period of rapid growth, and he is learning some things that are exciting to him as well as to adults around him. Girls typically mature faster than boys, so a five-year-old girl may be a year or more ahead of a five-year-old boy in emotional and physical development.

Begins to Use Reason

At ages four and five a typical child will develop the ability to use reason in coping with his world. Instead of merely reacting to his environment as he did as a toddler, he will begin to think about the world around him and question everything. He seeks to know the reasons and the causes behind virtually everything he sees, a fact that is illustrated by his use of the question, "Why?" While a three-year-old may use this question simply to prolong a conversation he is enjoying, the four- or five-year-old usually wants an answer that will satisfy his need to know.

He desires to learn, simply for the pure joy of it, and he enjoys putting all his thoughts into words. A child at this age often gets on his parents' nerves with incessant questioning and non-stop talking.

Develops a conscience

In addition, he is developing a conscience, a moral sense of right and wrong. The kind of training we provide for our children will influence the development of their sense of morality. Parents can have great influence in establishing the child's sense of right and wrong at this age, since the child looks to them as the final authority on every subject and is intensely interested in gaining their approval.

As his conscience develops, the four- to six-year-old also learns increasing self-control. He is more capable of controlling his temper, of sharing, of doing thoughtful things for others, and of delaying the gratification of his needs. While the toddler demands things now, the four- to six-year-old can understand that it is necessary to wait for some things and that he cannot have everything he desires.

Develops socially

The preschool child is also becoming a social person. He increasingly enjoys playing with other children and learns to give and take when placed in a social situation. Children at this age like to participate in physical activities and to feel that they are contributing in group situations. A purely "sit still and listen" context is still difficult for a child this age, who has so much energy to expend.

QUESTION 17

Reflect on your child's sense of right and wrong, considering his age. What understanding does he have at this point concerning right and wrong? In what ways does your child demonstrate self-control in some areas? What role does the Bible play in your child's thinking about morality? If you have no children, try to reflect on how your concept of right and wrong developed as a child. Record your thoughts in your Life Notebook.

Topic 4: The Basic Needs of Children

Although each child is unique, educators who have studied human behavior have found that some basic emotional needs are common to all children. Some of the most important are:

- **Love and affection.** All children need love and affection. This is a God-given need. The search for love and affection is probably the most important explanation of your child's behavior. Some children do not know how to express this need and may seem distant or independent. Yet the need is universal. Parents need to be aware that many of the child's responses to love and affection are learned from his parents. If they do not feel free to hug or kiss affectionately, their child probably will not. For example, if a father returns home from work and enters his house without showing any affection and enthusiasm for his children, they will learn to respond in the same way. Conversely, if he snatches up his children in delight, they will learn to come running with open arms and squeals of laughter. Affection is taught by example.

- **Attention.** Children need to feel that someone really listens to them and appreciates their ideas and achievements. Some children demand excessive attention, which can lead to self-centeredness and spoiled behavior.

- **Belonging.** Children have a need to belong to a significant group. This need to belong tends to increase throughout childhood until, in the teenage years, the need to belong becomes almost desperate, sometimes dominating all else.

- **A sense of security and confidence.** Children need to feel both safe and wanted. They have a need for confidence. Confidence must develop in order for a child to become emotionally healthy.

- **Achievement.** Children have a need to achieve, to feel that they are good at something or that they contribute in some way.

[The material in these five points is based on Narramore, 17-22. Some information is in a different order than in the original and italics in the original have been omitted.]

QUESTION 18

Draw a simple chart for your children with each of these basic needs indicated. To what extent do you think these needs are being met in the life of the child? In which areas do you need to concentrate your efforts to meet the child's needs? Discuss this with your spouse and record your thoughts in your Life Notebook.

Topic 5: The Seven Pillars and Early Childhood Training

In Lesson 2, we studied some overall goals for child-raising as presented in the book of Proverbs (Prov 1:1-7). We call them the Seven Pillars of Wisdom.

In this topic we will discuss the application of four of those pillars to the raising of children during the early childhood years (ages 0 – 6).

- Wise Behavior
- Discipline
- Discretion
- Discernment

Before we continue, let's review briefly the meaning of the Seven Pillars.

The Pillar of Wise Behavior

Assignment

- Please review the following article:

The Pillar of Wise Behavior

Related to discernment is the pillar called "wise behavior." The Hebrew word *sakal* means "to be prudent and possess good judgment, to behave wisely." The sentence structure of Proverbs 1:3 indicates that the three qualities that follow are intended to explain what is meant by wise behavior or skillful living: righteousness, justice, and equity. Thus, wise behavior is the result of discernment and is seen in the actions of the person who possesses it.

The Hebrew word for righteousness *tsedeq* carries the idea of "conformity to God's will and standards." The word for justice, *mishpat*, refers to the quality of dealing fairly, honestly, and righteously in our relations with one another. It is the social outworking of righteousness. Equity (Hebrew *meshar*) suggests gentleness or attractiveness.

All of these words relate to the actions of a person. What Christian parent does not desire a child who behaves wisely, fairly, honestly, and in conformity with God's standards? These actions are the result of training. It takes time to build these qualities in a child's life. Often parents cannot see the evidence of wise behavior until a child is nearly grown. Your responsibility as parents is to love, encourage, instruct, and correct. It is the Holy Spirit's responsibility to implant the character traits over a period of years. He uses our example and instruction as seeds and the circumstances of life as fertilizer to cause growth in the child's life, so that ultimately he may behave wisely.

Children must be instructed in God's standards so they will be prepared to resist the pressures of the world. The pressures in today's world are particularly great: drugs and alcohol and sensual living seem to be gaining in their appeal to young people. In view of the pressures facing young people today, how can parents help a child learn to behave wisely? Here are a few suggestions:

1. Be a living example of wise behavior to your child (Prov 4:1-5; 5:1-2; 20:7).

2. Encourage your children to walk with God's "wise men" (Prov 13:20). This can be done in several ways. Whenever possible, expose them to vital Christian leaders. You

might consider a regular practice of inviting such men and women for dinner and then asking them to share their Christian experience in family discussion around the dinner table.

3. A child can complete a short topical Bible study assignment in which various standards of righteousness are emphasized. It helps to reward a child for completing assignments and to discuss with him what he has learned.

4. Expose your child as often as possible to Christian service (Mt 28:18-20). Take your children with you when you minister. Give them opportunities to minister.

5. Appeal to a child's courage to count the cost and be willing to abandon all to follow Christ (Mk 8:34-38; Lk 6:22-23).

The Hebrew word "wise behavior" can be summarized by the notion of living wisely with a balance of grace and truth (Jn 1:14).

An attitude of respect also extends to other areas of life, as a child learns to respect the rights and possessions of others. In simple ways a small child can begin to learn about the rights of others. For example, when his parents encourage him to wait his turn to speak, rather than interrupting others whenever he feels like talking, he learns that others are important too. Parental example is probably the greatest teacher of respect. We need to ask ourselves as parents, "Do I interrupt, or do I wait my turn?" Unfortunately, many of us are still trying to learn this lesson.

Proverbs 18:13 reminds us, "He who answers before listening—that is his folly and his shame" (NIV). This may seem like a very small and insignificant lesson to teach our children, but it communicates a basic respect for other people. Similarly, a child learns that he is not allowed to deliberately break or abuse the possessions of others and that he is expected to show respect for others by respecting their belongings.

QUESTION 19

What example have you set for your children regarding respecting the rights of others? How are your children responding to your training? With your spouse reflect on these issues and record your observations and possible solutions to help your child learn wise behavior in your Life Notebook.

The Pillar of Discipline

As we looked at the characteristics of children, we noted that early childhood is characterized by self-centeredness. A baby knows only his own needs, and he can be very demanding if these are not met. Only gradually does a child begin to gain a measure of self-control; he can wait a few minutes for his food when it is being prepared. He learns gradually to control his outbursts of anger.

Self-control is an important goal of training at every stage of growth. While emotions are God-given and an important part of the human personality, they can cause many problems in life if we do not learn how to control them. There is a balance between stifling or repressing our emotions and letting them totally control us. Positive expressions of emotion, such as laughter, hugs, kisses, and crying when one is hurt, are normal. Emotions that lead to destructive or aggressive behavior must be brought under control.

Thus, a child should be properly disciplined when he throws his toys at others or bites or hits his friends or family. He must be trained to recognize that he cannot always do what his emotions tell him to do at the moment. On the other hand, the child should be encouraged to give his feelings an appropriate outlet. Little boys should not be told that it is unacceptable to express emotion by crying. This only teaches them to repress their feelings, encouraging them to become inarticulate and unable to communicate genuine emotion. Helping the child to express emotion properly is an important task that will produce fruit throughout his life.

The child should gradually learn to control his temper and to ask for things politely rather than grabbing what he wants. He should learn that throwing tantrums will not accomplish his purposes. How should a tantrum be handled? The best method is to ignore the tantrum, if possible, or to remove the child to a room where he can be alone to scream until he is over it. If the child sees that having a tantrum eventually gets him what he wants, he will soon learn to scream even louder and longer next time. For some children, even a parent's negative response to a tantrum, such as spankings or screaming, rewards him with something he desperately wants—attention.

The best way to squelch a child's tantrums is to pay no attention whatsoever to them. This can be hard for parents, particularly when a child has a tantrum in public. Some parents will do anything to appease the child rather than suffer this embarrassment in front of others. So the child learns to perform in public to get what he wants. A better method is to take the child aside somewhere, if possible. He will soon stop these ridiculous scenes when he sees that he gains nothing from them.

QUESTION 21

Reflect on a child you have seen having a tantrum. What was it that the child wanted? How did his parents react? Did the child get what he desired? Who won the conflict—parent or child? How should the parents have handled it?

The Pillar of Discretion

Assignment

- Please review the following article:

The Pillar of Discretion

To the youth knowledge and **discretion**. (Prov 1:4, emphasis added)

The final pillar in wisdom's house is **discretion**. What is meant by discretion? Normally when that word is used, ideas such as finesse, tactfulness, or diplomacy come to mind. But the Hebrew word *mezimma* means "to decide wisely for himself to attain a desired end." Though usually used in a context of evil thoughts or judgment (e.g., Ps 37:12; Prov 12:2; Jer 23:20), it is used in a positive sense in Proverbs, meaning the ability to formulate and carry out wise plans.

Simply put, then, discretion is wise planning or decision making.

In Lesson 2 we learned that the Hebrew word *mezimma* means "*to decide wisely for himself to attain a desired end.*" Though usually used in a context of evil thoughts or judgment (e.g., Ps 37:12; Prov 12:2; Jer 23:20), it is used in a positive sense in Proverbs, meaning the ability to formulate and carry out wise plans. Simply put, then, discretion is wise planning or decision making.

The child at about age three or four should begin to have a few little jobs to do at home to teach him responsibility, such as hanging up his coat when he comes in, putting his shoes away, and helping to put his toys away before bedtime. Having little jobs to do makes him feel that he is contributing to the family. He gains the satisfaction of doing his tasks regularly. At the same time he learns what it means to be faithful.

This is another area where a child often learns by your example. If he sees his parents avoiding responsibility, being lazy or trying to get away with a half-hearted job, he will likely pick up some of those same attitudes. Conversely, he may learn from a parent's faithfulness to a dull or tedious activity that God desires us to be faithful in the smallest tasks.

QUESTION 22

Review with your spouse each child's responsibilities at home. Discuss whether the responsibility is appropriate for the age and abilities of the child. Then make a simple checklist of the child's jobs at home. If your child does not currently have any responsibilities, discuss ways you can apply this practice.

The Pillar of Discernment

Assignment

- Please read the following articles:

Learning Discernment

The process of developing discernment in your child takes many years. As King Solomon wrote the book of Proverbs, he gave much wise counsel to this son regarding the importance of discernment. Yet, how many of us have ever considered this as a specific goal of raising children or have any idea how to practically help our children develop this critical skill?

An excellent way to teach this skill to your child would be to set up an imaginary role-play situation and play "What if." Ask your child, "What if this happened to you? What would you do?" Then go through these seven steps of the decision-making process together.

1. Determine what needs to be decided and purpose in your heart that you only want to do what would bring honor to Christ and that you want to do it in a manner which would glorify Him.

2. Determine what the options are. Consider every possible way the decision could be made. Go beyond the obvious alternatives and include even ideas that seem "way out"; this is the time for brainstorming, and sometimes a crazy idea can lead to a practical one. Write down all ideas.

3. Think about the strengths and weaknesses of each choice. Now is the time to consider pros and cons, and to determine what is feasible and what is not. Search for all the possible consequences of each choice. It may be helpful to draw a chart on a piece of paper listing the pros and cons of each possible alternative.

4. Read through the book of Proverbs and possibly the application sections of the Epistles (e.g., Rom 12–16; Eph 4–6; Gal 5–6, Jas 1–5) and look for principles that would apply to the strengths and weaknesses of each choice. Obviously this method is best for major decisions which do not have to be made immediately. Nevertheless, reflecting on what the wisdom passages have to say is critical if we are to get God's viewpoint on important decisions and learn to apply it to real life. You usually will not find a verse which says, "Do this," or "Choose that," but you will find principles which apply to the pros and cons of the decision you need to make.

5. Choose what appears to be the best alternative. Ask yourself, "Will I be happy with this decision 10,000 years from now?"

6. Do what you've decided to do, trusting the results to God. Sometimes there may be some negative consequences and you have to settle the issue that your purpose is to please God and honor Him. He promises that He will remember and reward you for your faithfulness.

7. Evaluate the decision after you have seen the results. Decide whether or not it was a good choice, and whether you would make the same decision if you had to choose again.

The Pillar of Discernment in Early Childhood

As explained in Lesson 2, discernment is the ability to compare concepts and to perceive a wise course of action. But how is discernment developed? First of all, we grow in discernment as we spend more time in God's Word and gain an understanding of God's point of view. We read in Scripture of godly men who made good choices and perceived a wise course of action and, conversely, of men who made mistakes and chose foolish courses of action. From childhood on we can teach those stories and discuss them with our children. "What would you have done if you were Abraham?" or "What would God want you to do in this situation?" are questions that can provoke children to develop discernment.

Developing discernment is a lifelong process. There are two aspects of the pillar of discernment, however, we would like to address related to the early childhood: the development of conscience and of a healthy view toward sexuality.

In Regard to Conscience

If a child is going to development discernment in life, he must not only know the Scriptures, but his conscience must be trained by those principles so that his conscience speaks truth to him when he must make discerning decisions.

A child generally develops a sense of right and wrong during the first five years of life. A child's parents are the primary influences on his developing conscience. What standard are we writing on our child's heart? Are we teaching him early to have reverence and respect for God and His Word and to desire to do what pleases God?

When parents are good models of the qualities they desire to see in their children and when they place a positive emphasis on encouraging the child to do right, rather than simply discouraging him from doing wrong, the child usually develops a healthy sense of right and wrong.

He learns to feel a sense of guilt when he breaks the standard that has been set for him and to feel pleasure and a sense of contentment when he makes a right choice. In order for a child's conscience to develop, he should be attracted to obedience, instead of concluding that obeying is simply a way to avoid punishment.

In Regard to Sexuality

In a warm and loving family, parents are laying the foundation for children to have a healthy view of human sexuality, to be comfortable with their own sexual nature. Parents generally think of sexual training as something that should be undertaken much later on. Yet there are certain attitudes and simple explanations that can be communicated to the small child to lay a firm and godly basis for sexual understanding later.

The Formation of Sexual Identity

Studies show that a young child's sexual identity is formed during the first five or six years of life. During these years the child will learn a particular role, whether male or female. Recent research suggests that the father has a significant influence on his child's development, particularly in the area of sex direction or orientation. A father's loving presence is very significant to the young child in developing the right mental images of his or her sexuality and, in particular, sex direction. Problems can arise if the father is absent too much from the home, is too passive or rejecting, or for other reasons fails to reinforce his son's maleness or daughter's femaleness.

One study found that young boys whose fathers were absent from the home were more likely to exhibit more feminine ways of thinking, low masculinity, dependence, and either less aggression or exaggeratedly masculine behaviors than were boys whose fathers were present.

While the absence of a father can have a detrimental effect on the normal development of the masculine role in boys, overly dominating mothers can also have a negative effect on the development of healthy sex roles. A child who grows up in such circumstances may feel insecure or uncomfortable with his sexuality. Thus, in order to lay a good foundation for a child to have discernment about his true sexual identity, both parents need to be aware of the signals they are sending. A little girl needs to be satisfied that God has created her to become a woman, and a little boy needs to have positive feelings about becoming a man. These concepts come primarily from parental example. Part of our responsibility as parents is to help our child to have positive feelings about his own sexuality.

Teaching about Reproduction

When a young child asks questions about sex, parents should treat these questions as casually as they do his questions on any other subject. He is curious about everything, and he thinks in literal, concrete terms. Give him a clear, matter-of-fact answer, but do not tell him more than he really wants to know. One parent launched into a detailed explanation of reproduction when her child asked, "Where do I come from, Mommy?" only to find out that the child simply wanted to know where she was born!

To explain sexual reproduction plainly to small children, we can introduce them to the world of plants, animals, and insects. Explain the story of creation—how God created everything as male and female, plants and animals and insects, and how everything He made was good. God fashioned every living creature with seeds inside it to reproduce itself: apples from apple seeds, chickens from eggs, kittens from the mother cat.

Small children will inevitably ask, "Where do babies come from?" It is best to answer simply and truthfully, saying something like, "A baby grows in a special place inside the mother." You can explain that a baby grows from a tiny seed that was in the mother all the time. Explain that babies grow inside mothers, where they are nurtured and protected until it is time for them to be born. If you have the opportunity, let your children be present when a family pet or farm animal gives birth. Explain the miracle of birth as "God-designed." *Always bring God's plan into your teaching.*

At about age two-and-a-half or three, children begin to ask more questions related to sexuality, corresponding with the "why" stages of development. The presence of a new baby often causes a toddler to be curious about the obvious physical differences between the baby and its older siblings. Boys in particular may be concerned to discover that their baby sister is "missing" something. Parents can explain in a cheerful tone that girls and women are made differently from boys and men; God created them to be different.

It is normal for young children to display an awareness of and interest in the physical differences between boys and girls. They may sometimes play "doctor" or "nurse" in order to express their natural curiosity about the opposite sex. It is best if parents do not make a bigger issue of this interest in physical differences than is necessary. This could convey to the child that the human body is in some way nasty or dirty, laying the foundation for sexual inhibitions and problems in marriage. You should, however, explain clearly to your children that only doctors or parents are allowed to see them in the nude and that no one should touch them in their private parts, the parts of their bodies covered by their bathing suits.

Around ages four to six children often begin to make jokes about bodily parts. Parents can explain to a child that discussions about the private parts of our bodies are to take place in our own home with mother or father, not in public. Avoid giving the child the impression that these body parts are nasty or dirty in some way. In Song of Solomon, the bride's body parts are described a beautiful (Song 4:12-15; 7:1-9), and we should be sure that we do not imply to our children that this is "nasty." Answer the child's questions naturally and simply.

To summarize: our most important asset in teaching our children about sex, love, and marriage is having a healthy attitude toward these subjects ourselves. This begins by viewing our sexual nature as a God-given gift, which, when expressed within the bonds of marriage, is good. It is meant to foster intimacy and bring great pleasure to both husband and wife.

Some Christians are uncomfortable when it comes to sexual training or believe it is not appropriate to talk about sex to children. The facts are, however, that your children will hear about sex from someone. Besides, God devoted a whole book to the subject, the Song of Solomon. Is it not far better to hear it from you under controlled conditions and from a biblical perspective, with the important emphasis on moral principles included, than to hear it from some other source? Human sexuality is a part of life, an aspect of moral training which should be undertaken by parents.

Discernment, as we discussed in Lesson 2, is the ability to compare concepts and to perceive a wise course of action. But how is discernment developed? First of all, we grow in discernment as we spend more time in God's Word and gain an understanding of God's point of view. We read in Scripture of godly men who made good choices and perceived a wise course of action and, conversely, of men who made mistakes and chose foolish courses of action. From childhood on we can teach those stories and discuss them with our children. Questions such as, "What would you have done if you were Abraham?" or "What would God want you to do in this situation?" can encourage children to develop discernment.

QUESTION 23

Based on the article above, what is an important factor in helping a child develop clear and **positive** discernment of his or her own sexual identity?

A. An overbearing mother

B. A distant father

C. A loving and involved father

D. Playing "doctor" with the opposite sex.

QUESTION 24

Reflect on your own home life as a child. Did your parents convey a sense of closeness? How do you think your own attitudes toward sexuality were influenced by your home training? What attitudes are you communicating to your children? How have you handled the subject of sexuality?

QUESTION 25

Based on the suggestions in the article ("The Pillar of Discernment in Early Childhood"), when a child asks, "Where do babies come from?" what is the best response?

A. Say, "A baby grows in a special place inside the mother."

B. Avoid the subject until he or she is older.

C. Give a detailed and truthful explanation.

D. Use this question as an opportunity to teach him about sexuality from the Bible.

Topic 6: Goals for Parents for the Early Childhood Years

Assignment

- Please read the following article:

The Goals for Parents

Having goals for your children is good and necessary. But having goals for yourself as a parent is also important. We have emphasized just a few important goals to keep in mind as parents.

Realistic Expectations

One mother complained, "My son acts like a two-year-old." "How old is he?" asked the counselor. "Two," she replied, blushing. When our children do something particularly exasperating, it is easy to lose all objectivity about our parenting, as well as about our children. Often we react emotionally to some of the things our children do because we are embarrassed by how their behavior reflects on us. When things seem to be out of control, it sometimes helps to go off alone somewhere, if only for half an hour, and try to put things back in perspective.

Sometimes our expectations of a child are simply too great. As a parent I need to ask myself, "Is his behavior typical for his age? Am I expecting too much? Have I been pushing him too hard or comparing him with other children?" Asking ourselves these kinds of questions can help us to determine if our expectations of our child are realistic and encourage us to be more realistic in what we expect of our children and of ourselves.

Reliance on God

When we face problems in child-rearing, we need to know where to turn. The Word of God can give us clear answers to some problems. God speaks to us most clearly in the pages of His Word, and it is there that we know we have His will revealed. The answers are not always spelled out as clearly as we might like. We need to spend time with the Lord and seek wisdom from above when Scripture does not clearly point the way.

We can ask God to help us to make the right decision and to hold us in the palm of His hand when we are unsure of ourselves as parents. We can ask, too, for forgiveness for our failures and inconsistencies as parents. Then, we should ask for strength, courage, and wisdom to get up tomorrow and to face the task afresh with His grace.

A Consistent Example

When parents read a book on child-rearing, it is normal for them to feel somewhat guilty. Every conscientious parent immediately sees his own shortcomings and knows that he fails to measure up to the ideal standards set forth in books on this subject. It is easy to feel awed at all we are expected to know as a parent. We have covered many subjects already, and you may already be feeling a bit discouraged at all that has been presented.

We must emphasize again that these are goals. These are ideals. We will fall short of achieving these ideals, but it is better to aim at a high ideal than none at all. Someone has said, "Aim at nothing and you will surely hit it." We have set forth some high standards in this course, with the awareness that no one will achieve all of them but with the hope that every student will aim a little higher than he did before.

Probably the most important target to concentrate on is our example. What matters most to our children is not our educational methods or our understanding of childhood development. What speaks loudest to our children is what we are as parents. We may know all the right answers from Scripture and still be a poor parent if our life in our own home before our family does not measure up to what we believe. To a certain extent this is true of all believers; we know much more than we ever put into practice. Yet if our lives are full of glaring inconsistencies, our children will quickly discern that we are phonies. Children are very quick to detect phoniness. If we must repeatedly tell our child, "Do as I say, not as I do," he will hear this double message and either lose all respect for us as his parents or become just like us—another phony.

In other words, our behavior before our children needs to be consistent and real. They should see that in daily life we seek to model the fruit of the Spirit: love, joy, peace, patience, kindness, goodness, faithfulness, gentleness, self-control. These should be our goals as Christian parents. We need to set this biblical standard daily before us and ask the Holy Spirit to enable us to grow in each of these areas. When we fail to exemplify this godly character before our children, they should see our repentance. They should see us asking forgiveness, rather than proudly refusing to admit when we are wrong. Someone has said that children are much more interested in honesty than perfection. They know parents are imperfect; they just need to see parents accept it too. They want to see parents striving to fulfill their goals and responsibilities as much as the parents are expecting the children to fulfill theirs.

Far more important than the specific methods you might choose to raise your children is the example you set for them. Paul was able to say to the Corinthians, "Be imitators of me, just as I also am of Christ" (1 Cor 11:1). This is God's design for us as parents also, that we imitate Christ in our daily lives so that our children can imitate us.

What a privilege God gives us to influence these little lives to become imitators of Christ. What a high calling it is to be a parent! When our resources run dry, as they will at times, we can be thankful that His well is a never-ending stream to replenish us over and over again, supplying all that we need to bring our children to maturity in Christ.

QUESTION 26

In your Life Notebook rate yourself from 1-5 on the following parental activities (1 is very good, 5 is poor):

- Praying for your child

- Studying your child

- Consistency in dealing with your child

- Listening to your child

- Spending time with your child

- Maintaining realistic expectations

- Being an example of godly character

Take one area in which you rated yourself poorly, and write down some ways you can improve in this area in the next month. Discuss this with your spouse.

Lesson 4 Self Check

QUESTION 1

Read Psalm 139:13-16. What is clear based on this passage?

- A. God is responsible for my formation.
- B. Nature is responsible for my formation.
- C. My characteristics are a product of random chance.
- D. My environment is the final determiner of who I am.

QUESTION 2

What mistake do you think Isaac and Rebecca made in raising their children?

- A. They disciplined Jacob and Esau too severely.
- B. They compared them with one another.
- C. They failed to give them adequate discipline.
- D. They were too child centered.

QUESTION 3

Based on the study of Psalm 139, which of the following statements represents a wise course of action?

- A. To bring about obedience parents need to exert force.
- B. We can often best help our children find themselves by encouraging them to be like us.
- C. When observing our child's disinterest in the Lord, we can often counterbalance this by increasing our focus on Bible reading and family devotions.
- D. Encourage him to accept himself and see the benefits and value of those traits that make him who he is.

QUESTION 4

For an infant to have his emotional needs met, he must have his physical needs met. *True or False?*

QUESTION 5

Too many parents slap their little child's hand throughout the day for simply investigating his world. *True or False?*

QUESTION 6

If a child is still not talking by the age of two, the parents should be concerned and seek professional help. *True or False?*

QUESTION 7

What is the best way to squelch a child's tantrums?

- A. To discipline him immediately
- B. To offer him something he likes if he will stop
- C. To pay no attention whatsoever to them
- D. To attempt to reason with him in a gentle voice

QUESTION 8

Recent research suggests that the father has a significant influence on his child's development, particularly in the area of sex direction or orientation. *True or False?*

QUESTION 9

Based on the suggestions in "The Pillar of Discernment in Early Childhood," when a child asks where babies come from, what is the best response?

    A. Say, "A baby grows in a special place inside the mother."

    B. Avoid the subject until he or she is older.

    C. Give a detailed and truthful explanation.

    D. Use this question as an opportunity to teach him about sexuality from the Bible.

QUESTION 10

The principles covered in this lesson are goals to strive for. We will fall short of achieving these ideals, but it is better to aim at a high ideal than none at all. *True or False?*

Lesson 4 Answers to Questions

QUESTION 1: *Your answer*

QUESTION 2

    A. God is responsible for my formation

QUESTION 3: *Your answer should be similar to the following:*

When you read Psalm 139:16, you understand that God has, in our terms, a "book" for every child. If you have three children, He had three books in mind. And He put into living form the plan of three books as He set them in your home. As each child was born, another book was opened. Different as night and day, but each one was planned and established, prescribed by God.

QUESTION 4: *Your answer should be similar to the following:*

You notice problems already, such as the problem of comparison. You'll notice the children were loved on the basis of how they pleased their parents or how they possessed the same likes as their parents, still a common problem today. Rebekah fell in love with Jacob because he was like her. Isaac fell in love with Esau because he was like him.

QUESTION 5

    D. Encourage him to accept himself and see the benefits and value of those traits that make him him. [One of the best investments you can make is to deposit into your child's mind an understanding of himself—how he has been "bent." Help your child come to a realization of his God-given abilities and interests.]

QUESTION 6: *Your answer*

QUESTION 7

    C. Children are born with a tendency toward selfishness

QUESTION 8: *Your answer should be similar to the following:*

The sinful tendency which Abraham had in regard to lying was being passed on to his son, Isaac, and to his grandson, Jacob, and finally to Jacob's sons.

QUESTION 9: True [The descendants of Abraham did not deal with their lying bents. That is when our God of love gets tough! God forgives sin, and He wants us to forsake sin. He will keep loving-kindness, He will forgive iniquity, transgression, and sin when it's dealt with.]

QUESTION 10

    A. It is better to give a child too much attention during this period than too little.

    C. When a child cries at 3:00 a.m. it is important to realize that there can be emotional as well as physical needs.

    D. It is normal for a baby to develop a strong attachment to his mother during this period and be fearful of strangers.

QUESTION 11: *Your answer should be similar to the following:*

How do we sow trust? By being dependable. The infant learns that he can depend on you to meet his needs when he is hungry or wet or he needs to be cuddled and loved. Likewise, he feels secure when he is held and cared for. He sees love in your face and hears it in your voice when you delight in him. If his basic needs are not met, if he is frequently left to cry for long periods of time with no response from his parents, he may fail to develop trust and a sense of security, or he may become too dependent emotionally on his parents.

QUESTION 12: False [His curiosity can get him into trouble at times, but it is generally a very positive quality; it is the means by which the child learns about his world. It is not wise to squelch his natural curiosity.]

QUESTION 13: *Your answer*

QUESTION 14: *Your answer*

QUESTION 15: False [Occasionally, a child refuses to talk until he is two years old or even a bit older. Usually it is not cause for alarm; he may even begin speaking in whole sentences when he does speak. What is important to remember is that the child understands much more than he can say. He does comprehend what you say to him and your instructions to him, although he may pretend not to at times!]

QUESTION 16: *Your answer*

QUESTION 17: *Your answer*

QUESTION 18: *Your answer*

QUESTION 19: *Your answer*

QUESTION 21: *Your answer*

QUESTION 22: *Your answer*

QUESTION 23

    C. A loving and involved father

QUESTION 24: *Your answer*

QUESTION 25

    A. Say, "A baby grows in a special place inside the mother."

QUESTION 26: *Your answer*

Lesson 4 Self Check Answers

QUESTION 1
    A. God is responsible for my formation.

QUESTION 2
    B. They compared them with one another.

QUESTION 3
    D. Encourage him to accept himself and see the benefits and value of those traits that make him who he is.

QUESTION 4: True

QUESTION 5: True

QUESTION 6: False

QUESTION 7
    C. To pay no attention whatsoever to them

QUESTION 8: True

QUESTION 9
    A. Say, "A baby grows in a special place inside the mother."

QUESTION 10: True

Lesson 5: Dealing with Children Ages Seven to Twelve

Lesson Introduction

Today is an important day in Paul's life. It is his first day of school. He is excited and nervous at the same time, and he can hardly sit still to eat his breakfast. His mother seems to be even more nervous. She checks him over several times to see that his shirt is tucked in, his hair combed just right, and that he remembered to wash behind his ears. He wonders why mothers are so worried about people looking behind his ears. He himself has never looked behind anyone's ears!

On the way to school Paul's mother reminds him to be friendly to the other children, polite to the teacher, and to do his best to learn. Paul feels a little uneasy. "Will it be too hard for me?" he wonders. "What will the teacher do if I cannot learn it all?" His mother encourages him that he will do just fine. "Your father and I are so proud of you," she tells Paul.

For both Paul and his parents, school will bring some changes. Paul will spend more time with other children and learn to value the opinions of his peers. He will learn some things he has not learned at home, some of them good, some not so good. He will gain confidence if he succeeds in school. If he fails, his self-esteem will also suffer. Many new experiences and feelings await him. His parents will no longer be the sole influences on his value system; teachers and classmates will affect his thinking as well.

In this chapter we want to look at the child from seven to twelve years old. We will look at the ways in which he is changing and developing, and also discuss the important role of the parent in the continuing process of training the child toward the goal of Christian maturity.

Paul is entering the fifth stage of "The Stages of Child Development in the Bible," the *Taph*. The word refers to one who clings to his mother and she is constantly watching him.

Lesson Outline

Topic 1: Characteristics of Children Ages Seven to Twelve

    Physical Development

    Emotional Development

    Intellectual Development

    Social Development

Topic 2: Teaching the Pillar of the Fear of the Lord

    Make the Bible Come Alive for Your Child

    Motivate Your Child to Express His Faith in Action

Topic 3: Teaching the Pillar of Prudence

    Teaching Your Child About Sexuality

    Preparing Your Child for Adolescence

Topic 4: Teaching the Pillar of Discernment: Self-Esteem

    What the World Says about Self-Esteem

Lesson Objectives

By the end of this lesson, you will be able to do the following:

- Describe some specific ways to deal with children, considering their emotional, intellectual, social, and moral development

- Take appropriate steps to train your children with a moral view of sexuality, as you recognize their increasing curiosity regarding sexuality

- Explain how to deal with behavior problems at this age level

Topic 1: Characteristics of Children Ages Seven to Twelve

By the time a child is ready to enter school, he is beginning the job of emancipating himself from the family, a task that takes a number of years to complete before he will be ready to stand on his own as an adult.

During the years from seven to twelve, a child becomes more of a social individual, learning to cooperate and interrelate with others. Correspondingly, children become increasingly independent of their parents. They demonstrate this feeling of independence in different ways: a child may insist on choosing his own clothes or may refuse to eat what he is served or may question his parents' opinions on different subjects.

Parents are no longer the sole important factor in determining what the child thinks. The child is increasingly concerned with what his peers say and do and is eager to please others. This gradual increase in independence from his parents is the hallmark of the years from seven to twelve.

Let us look briefly at five areas of the child's development, making some suggestions for parents on ways to apply this information.

In this topic you will answer more Life Notebook questions than usual in order to help you understand and interact with your spouse in identifying these same characteristics in your child.

Physical Development

Assignment

- Please read the following article:

Physical Development

Growth and development are not always measurable by birthdays. Not all children develop at the same rate physically. A child's physical development may be considerably ahead of his years, while emotionally or mentally he remains babyish. On the other hand, a child may be considerably slower to develop physically than his peers, while mentally and emotionally he is just as mature or even more mature. No charts can accurately predict a child's growth at this stage.

All that can be said with reasonable assurance is that eventually the child who is slow to develop will catch up with his peers, while the child who towers over his classmates at age nine may experience a period of slower growth later on. This news is probably not very reassuring to the child who feels awkward and different right now.

In general, children at this stage are in the process of what we might call "fine tuning." While the general muscular structure is developed by age seven, children become increasingly coordinated during these years, particularly as they undertake exercise or athletics. Fine muscles can be increasingly coordinated, so that children in this age group are more capable of strenuous exercise and competition than they were when they were younger. They take pride in these new skills, valuing speed, strength, and agility. They also enjoy competition and games that have rules and require skill. Girls are often somewhat ahead of boys in physical development and can compete well with the opposite sex.

While competition can be exhilarating and fun for the child, parents need to be aware of the possible detrimental effects of too much competition, particularly on those children who are not gifted with speed or agility. It is hard to be the one who is always the last to be chosen for team sports or competitions. Help such a child to find an area where he can do well. Parents need to adjust their expectations as they recognize that all children will not be equally endowed with physical strength and skill.

QUESTION 1

What are the characteristics of physical development in this age group which you can identify in your children?

QUESTION 2

Based on the article on physical development, which of the following are true of children in the age seven to twelve stage of child development? *(Select all that apply.)*

A. We can count on all children developing as the same rate during this stage.

B. The parents continue to be the sole focus of authority for a child of this age.

C. Children in this stage are capable of strenuous exercise.

D. Often a child who develops rapidly in this stage will slow down later.

Emotional Development

Assignment

- Please read the following article:

Emotional Development

Emotionally, children mature gradually at this age, each at a different rate. From ages seven to twelve the child is developing the capacity to control his emotions. He is better able to postpone the gratification of his desires (i.e., to wait until he gets something he wants) and to check outbursts of anger when he cannot get his way. He is gaining a sense of dignity as an individual, is less self-centered, and likes to be treated with respect.

School-age children are under more pressure than they were before: pressure to perform and to perform well, as well as to relate well with their peers. Perhaps for these reasons some children develop nervous habits, such as nail-biting, stuttering, eye-blinking, sniffing, or facial grimacing. There is no point scolding a child for such a nervous habit. Concentrate your efforts on making his home life as relaxed as possible and his school and social life satisfying.

As children mature, they may become less vocal and demonstrative about their affections. Children who were affectionate between three and five years of age now may squirm when a parent tries to kiss them. They groan or roll their eyes when they see adults expressing affection. While they may avoid outward displays of their feelings, they still look to adults for approval, and they still need regular reassurance of their parents' love.

In addition, they need to gain self-respect and confidence in their own abilities. Parents need to let a child know when he is successful, and keep criticism to a minimum. This encourages him to continue making efforts in his work. Children are very sensitive to failure, but positive reinforcement—affirming our children's pleasing behavior—enables them to overcome the inevitable failures every person experiences.

To a certain extent, emotional stability can be learned, as parents provide an example of stability and self-control for their child. Parents need to be aware of their own emotional shortcomings. For example, are you subject to mood changes or uncontrolled temper outbursts? Do you have a tendency to mask all your emotions, or to repress them? These may be areas that you need to work on in order to provide a better example of emotional stability for your children.

Conflict between siblings or with other children is common at this age. Older children can become adept at teasing and tormenting their younger siblings, who respond with their own weapons. At times home may seem like a battlefield if there is more than one child present.

A wise parent can learn to use biblical teaching to help children resolve some of these daily conflicts. This does not mean long lectures using the Bible as a club to either bore or punish a child. Using the Bible in such a way can make a child resent and even hate the Scriptures.

Instead, parents can encourage children to begin a regular program of memorizing Scripture verses that are carefully selected to teach certain values, such as kindness and forgiveness (Eph 4:32), confessing our sins to God (1 Jn 1:9), taking our problems to the Lord (1 Pet 5:7), and relying on the Bible to guide us (Ps 119:105), among others.

When problems arise, encourage your child to think about a related verse he has memorized. Ask him what course of action would please God in this situation. Make use of "what if" questions to encourage children to think through the probable results of a course of action or to review what has occurred and consider how a situation might have been handled better.

If children are not fighting, they are frequently laughing, sometimes over nothing in particular. Laughing at things is another way for children to deal with their emotions. A child often giggles

---

with glee at this age over things in which parents may see little humor. Some of the silliness is just an emotional outlet for a child's energies. Try to appreciate the humor that your children use. Develop a sense of humor that is in tune with Christ-like qualities. When a child makes fun of something serious or sacred or when his humor is inappropriate, he should be gently corrected.

A child's emotions are increasingly involved in his growing awareness of economic differences. Earlier he was more easily content with his own toys and clothes. As he becomes more aware of what others have, his discontent may seem to grow.

Obviously, a child does not need to be rich to be secure. Nevertheless, children in this stage of life become increasingly sensitive to competition among their peers for the material ingredients of life. It is very difficult for a child who is forced to dress extremely different from his peers or who is aware that his friends have toys and clothes which his family cannot afford. Of course, this must be the case at times, but it helps if we as parents realize how important such things can be to a child.

QUESTION 3

Discuss your child's emotional well-being with your spouse. In which areas does he seem to be experiencing stress or difficulty? What steps do you think you could take to help the situation? Are there expectations you have which may not be correct regarding the emotional maturity in this stage? If so, discuss with your spouse and write them out in your Life Notebook.

QUESTION 4

This is a good time to begin active use of the book of Proverbs. As a project, ask your child to read a chapter of Proverbs each day for a month. Each day, ask him to select a verse which seemed significant to him and tell him that you would really like to discuss the verse he selected at the dinner table. Record some of the insights from this discussion in your Life Notebook.

Intellectual Development

Assignment

- Please read the following article:

Intellectual Development

Mentally, development varies considerably in the period from seven to twelve years old. For example, in a typical first-grade class there will be a few children who have great difficulties concentrating and learning to read, a number who are ready for reading, and one or two children who learn very rapidly and may be bored with the lessons. Sometimes parents are too eager for their children to excel and may put too much pressure on them. A general rule is to try to discover what your child's abilities are and to maintain realistic expectations for his progress.

Be careful about scolding or punishing a child who is having difficulties at school. Instead, try to find out where the trouble lies. Does the child have a special difficulty in recognizing words? Is the school using harsh or rigid teaching methods? Are the classes too large to allow the child any individual attention? When you have determined the source of the child's problem, do whatever is possible to alleviate or to assist in resolving it.

If a child is struggling and becoming very nervous about school, it is sometimes helpful to keep him back a year until he is more mature, rather than take the risk of shattering his self-confidence and having him labeled a "dummy." A child's learning problems can be discouraging, not only for him but for the parent whose expectations are too high. Sometimes a child is afraid to try in school for fear of failing. This may be because the family has been too critical of his accomplishments or has set standards too high. Some children balk at school work because they have been pushed too much. They will pursue hobbies with great enthusiasm and diligence but appear suddenly lazy when it comes to school work.

Keep in mind that not all children are ready for formal learning at the same time. Some children may need special help in school or could benefit from simply waiting a year before beginning school, if this is an option, until they are more developed emotionally and mentally. Try to assess your child's abilities objectively and maintain realistic expectations for his behavior and learning.

About ten percent of children are estimated to have more than average learning difficulties. They may have problems recognizing and remembering the appearance of words and continue to reverse many letters and words for several years. If they are labeled as stupid, they may come to hate school because they cannot keep up with their peers. They need reassurance from parents and teachers that this is a special memory problem, that they are not stupid or lazy, and that they will learn to read and write in time. Individual tutoring may help many of these children.

A child's natural curiosity about the world around him can be squelched or encouraged. Particularly at this age parents can capitalize on a child's natural curiosity by encouraging him to find answers for himself. The ones he finds for himself are usually the ones he will retain the longest. Send a child to an encyclopedia, nature book, or other appropriate source to learn what he wants to know. Take him to the library, to museums, or on nature walks—when it is possible—to stimulate his curiosity and help make learning fun.

When our children are very young, we have a great deal of control over the information and intellectual stimulation they receive. As they grow and spend more time away from us, we have less and less control over what they will be exposed to. They are certain to receive information that conflicts with the moral training and biblical standards we have taught at home.

One of the best ways to handle this is to prepare them before they are exposed to these teachings. Let the child know that he will hear many things that conflict with the moral values he has been taught at home. Children should be prepared to face false teaching so that they will not be shocked and shaken from their faith but will be able to recognize these teachings as false because they are contrary to what the Bible teaches.

It is important to train our children to recognize these secular values when they hear them and to reject them based on what the Bible teaches. Most of the spiritual battles of life are won or lost at the threshold of the mind. Early training of a child should emphasize that the Bible is our standard and that every idea we come into contact with must be tested to see how it measures up to what the Bible says.

We must conscientiously guard our children's minds. In this regard television must be mentioned, for its effect on children can be considerable. Television viewing should be limited, and programs should be carefully selected for children's viewing to be sure that they have a moral tone of which we approve. Some parents refuse to allow children to watch any television. Another approach is to teach a child to be selective in his choice of programs. Be careful to avoid programs that portray extreme violence or that are not appropriate for children's viewing. Television should not be used as a substitute for more stimulating intellectual activity, nor should it be used as a baby-sitter. Encourage your child to read good books, to study nature, or to find a creative hobby to pursue.

QUESTION 5

The article on intellectual development from ages seven to twelve, describes many characteristics of children in this state. With your spouse, open your Life Notebook and record your observations of your own children in comparison to what is said in the article. Do you see areas where your expectations may have been unrealistic?

QUESTION 6

You should be aware that many children (about one in ten) have some kind of learning disability in this stage. *True or False?*

Social Development

Assignment

- Please read the following article:

Social Development (ages 7-12)

In the age group from seven to twelve it is increasingly important to a child to have friends. Parents can encourage friendships by being friendly and hospitable when their child brings others home to play. Make your child's home an inviting place for children. See to it that he or she has plenty of opportunities to play with other children so that he can begin to build real friendships of his own. Encourage—but do not force—your child to develop relationships with children who share your moral and spiritual values.

As his peer group becomes more important, the child tends to pick up some of the language and habits of his friends. He wants the same style of clothes or hairstyle that his friends have. He may pick up bad manners and habits that upset his parents, who imagine that their child is forgetting all they taught so carefully. Without realizing it, the child is shifting to his own age group for models of behavior. Some of his annoying habits, such as a tendency toward sloppiness, may be a declaration of independence.

If parents recognize this, they can overlook some of the minor irritating habits. At the same time parents should be firm in enforcing the rules of the house in a matter-of-fact way. When you ask a child to hang up his coat, do it in a firm, but not bossy way. Nagging and bossiness irritate children in this age group and often have the effect of spurring them to further resistance.

Correlating with their need to be less dependent on their parents, children may turn increasingly to trusted adults outside the family for ideas and inspiration. Hero worship is common at this age. Parents may not always approve of the child's choice of heroes but can encourage children to emulate those who exhibit good character qualities.

By age eight or nine, children are generally interested in group activities. Clubs and gangs may become popular at this age. Membership may be limited to their own sex, since boys and girls tend to develop an aversion toward each other at this age and do not play as well together as younger children.

Capitalize on the child's love of clubs and competition by providing a Christian children's club, if such a possibility exists. Children can motivate one another to learn Bible verses, earn small prizes or stickers for attendance, memorization, and other projects, and enjoy some team games in a Christian setting. It may be best to segregate boys and girls by age ten if enough teachers are available.

Children from seven to twelve enjoy games that have rules and require skill. They like competition and speed and are learning the meaning of fairness.

This is also the age for starting collections. The child enjoys the sense of orderliness and achievement involved in collecting something which he enjoys, such as stamps or butterflies. Children do not keep their things neat for long at this age, but they may demonstrate a desire for order at times. When they arrange their comic books or toys in a certain way, they may be saying, "These are my possessions," and they may be quite upset when a younger child touches their precious objects. The need for privacy, for an area to call his own, increases at this stage. A child may not be able to have his own room, but even a special shelf or desk to call his own can satisfy this need.

Children at this age gradually learn to carry more responsibility at home and at school. They do not always work willingly, but most respond to the positive motivation of praise or rewards. At this age you should establish individual responsibilities in the home for each child, based on his abilities and his age.

Provide some motivation for the child to carry out his chores. A child can be given an allowance, an amount of money which he is free to use as he wishes. Another suggestion is to use the child's enjoyment of rewards to help him develop a sense of responsibility in performing household chores or school work. Draw up a chart, and reward the child with stars when he performs an expected task. Occasionally you may offer a special reward for completed work over a period of several weeks or months, or for extra tasks that he or she performs. Make the goal attainable; children are usually not capable of maintaining good performance for a reward that is too distant in the future.

QUESTION 7

According to the article, what characteristics typically describe children ages seven to twelve? *(Select all that apply.)*

    A. Children at this age have an increasing need for privacy

    B. Children may pick up bad language and habits from their friends.

    C. In this stage children may turn to adults outside the family for inspiration.

    D. They are typically not ready for games which require skill

    E. Children can learn about responsibility at this age

    F. Clubs and gangs are not yet of interest to children in this stage.

QUESTION 8

Based on what you learned in "Social Development," discuss and record several ways you and your spouse can strengthen positive social development in your children.

Topic 2: Teaching the Pillar of the Fear of the Lord
Make the Bible Come Alive for Your Child

Children from ages seven to twelve are very receptive to spiritual truth. The child at this age believes what you tell him about God, Jesus, the Bible, sin, and salvation. It is so important to build a solid foundation of faith in his childhood, beginning long before the child even enters school, where many of your values will be contradicted, attacked, or ignored. But children do not appreciate long sermons or lectures or lengthy Bible readings from a version which is difficult to understand. The Bible must come alive for a child.

When teaching a child from the Bible, select stories with lots of action. Tell the story with enthusiasm. Try to involve the child as much as possible. One way is to use thought-provoking questions, for example, "What would you do if you were in Daniel's place?" Because children are prone to miss the application of Bible stories, adults need to help the child at this age to apply Bible stories to his own life. As the child's reasoning develops, the parent can encourage him to do this for himself, asking questions that encourage the child to think. Some examples are: "What can we learn from this story? What does God want us to do? What pleased God in this man's life?"

QUESTION 9

Prepare some thought-provoking questions for children ages seven to twelve based on the story of Peter in Acts 12:1-18. Write these out. Try using the story this week, and see how your child responds to the questions. Record the results in your Life Notebook.

Motivate Your Child to Express His Faith in Action

Children have a natural compassion for the hurt, the sick, and the poor. This can be developed and encouraged as you motivate them to express it. Children can be taught to exercise acts of kindness at a very early age.

QUESTION 10

What are some acts of kindness which your child can undertake to give practical expression to his faith? List several that you can think of, and choose one for your child to do this week. Be prepared to tell how he responded to this opportunity and how others responded to his help.

Topic 3: Teaching the Pillar of Prudence

In Lesson 4 we mentioned the importance of teaching children a proper biblical view of human sexuality and its context within marriage. Between the ages of seven and twelve a child's interest in matters pertaining to sexuality and the opposite sex generally increases.

Remember what "prudence" is.

Teaching a child prudence involves alerting him to things which could cause him harm and teaching him how to avoid the traps which could damage his life. In this topic we want to discuss the important topic of sexuality and how to prepare your child for the traps involved by preparing him for adolescence.

Teaching Your Child About Sexuality

From ages seven to ten it is not uncommon for children to make crude or silly jokes about sex and elimination and to use some vulgar language. These are indicators of a child's increasing awareness of sexuality. Children may begin to talk about sex with their friends at this age, picking up false information as well as some facts.

By age ten most girls and some boys have gleaned some information from their friends about intercourse and menstruation, if their parents have not already informed them. It is wise to sit down and share this information with the child by the ninth or tenth year to ensure that your child has accurate information.

> It is certainly preferable that the facts about sexual reproduction come from parents who can teach it in a proper moral context, rather than from misinformed friends.

Children ages seven to ten are normally curious about conception and the process by which a baby grows inside the mother's body, as well as the father's role in conception. A general explanation of conception can be taught to a child by age nine or ten. Explain to your child that sexuality is a gift from God to be enjoyed within the framework of marriage. As parents, remember that the keys to communicating a godly view of sex are your own healthy view of your God-given sexuality and the affectionate bond between you and your spouse that your children can observe. Sexual education should be viewed as a responsibility in the moral development of your child that God has placed on you as parents.

If we deal with these matters with a relaxed attitude, our children will accept the information we give them without being upset or thinking that sex is something dirty to be whispered about. By emphasizing God's role in designing this creative process, we will communicate to our children that sex is a wholesome and positive aspect of their lives, to be enjoyed within the framework of Christian marriage.

QUESTION 11

The Scriptures have much to say about the sexual relationship. A child should learn from an early age what God says about it rather than pick up misinformation, wrong morals, and incorrect attitudes from his friends. As an introduction to this topic let's explore a few passages from Scripture. Match the Scripture on the left with the biblical instruction about sex on the right.

Scripture	Biblical Principle
Genesis 2:24-25	Rich and satisfying sex in marriage is healthy and even commanded.
Proverbs 5:1-8	Sexual love in marriage is to be free and creative.
Proverbs 5:15-19	We are to flee from sexual immorality.
1 Corinthians 6:18	Sex is to be experienced only in marriage.
Song of Solomon 7:1-9	Sex is without shame and ordained by God.

Preparing Your Child for Adolescence

Puberty

The child who is nearing puberty (age eleven or twelve) needs to be prepared for the changes which will take place in his body and in his emotional make-up. The stage of puberty is characterized by the maturing of the sexual organs in preparation for reproduction. Puberty can be especially disturbing for boys and girls who have not been properly prepared for it by their parents. We should not put off telling our children about sexual matters if they are near puberty. Going through puberty is difficult even when a young person knows what to expect. A little knowledge will go a long way in protecting children from unnecessary trauma. Lesson 6 suggests some material to use in preparing your child for adolescence.

Physical affection

Remember to continue to demonstrate physical affection to your children during the period of pre-adolescence. Some fathers feel a bit embarrassed about hugging or kissing their daughter, now that she is becoming a young lady, but both sons and daughters need the security of a father's affection as well as a mother's. The emotional storms of adolescence make it even more essential to reaffirm your love to them.

Changing Emotions

In most children the passage into adolescence is characterized by tremendous highs and lows of emotion. It is good to remember that a preadolescent girl or boy can be a child at one moment, an adult the next. Preadolescents vacillate between childlike thinking and adult reasoning. Conflicts may be more frequent between parent and child during this stage of life, and we must be ready for them.

Peer Pressure

Peer pressure also has an increasing influence on the preadolescent, who has an increasing desire to be accepted. The child who feels rejected or unpopular is especially in need of allies at home.

Physical Changes

Children in the preadolescent stage are very aware of the early bloomers and the late bloomers and often compare themselves unfavorably with those who are taller or more attractive. As parents we need to understand that our child is struggling with confusion, insecurity, peer pressure, emotional ups and downs, and self-esteem problems. Many children do poorly in school at this time because they are beginning to be distracted by all this. They need extra amounts of loving patience and support from us during these years. At times they may severely test our love or even appear to withdraw or shut us out. If we understand what tremendous pressures they face, we will be in a better position to offer support and love.

Communication

Communicating with our children in an open, responsive way is one of the keys to getting through this phase. Set the stage for a smoother adolescent experience by letting your preadolescent know that he can come to you at any time and discuss any subject on his mind. He needs to know that you are going to love him, pray for him, and help and comfort him on the journey from childhood to adulthood.

QUESTION 12

Review the training regarding sexuality which you and your spouse have provided for your children. Has it been adequate, or have you avoided speaking about sexual matters? Discuss with your spouse how you might share this with your child. By the age of nine or ten most children are ready to receive these facts. Open your Life Notebook and record your plan.

Topic 4: Teaching the Pillar of Discernment: Self-Esteem

At this age a child is acquiring many perspectives about himself, his values, and the world around him. He will receive many false impressions and ideas. It is critical that he learn discernment.

Solomon tells us that a child is to be able "to discern the sayings of understanding." The Hebrew word *bina*—translated "discernment"—comes from a word meaning "to become separated" or "to be distinct". Discernment is the ability to compare concepts and form judgments, and thus perceive a wise course of action. A man of discernment is a man of perception, one who is able to draw distinctions between God's wisdom and man's, or to separate wisdom from folly.

He is to discern "sayings of understanding." The word understanding is more than information but words of perception and insight. The child enters a world where all kinds of sayings and teachings will surround him. He needs the ability to discern which sayings are truly sayings of perception and spiritual understanding. He needs to be able to discern the world's sayings from Scripture, to discern God's wisdom from the world's wisdom.

One of the most critical areas of discernment is to discern a correct view of self. The messages from the world will continually conflict with the Scriptures. A child picks up his view of himself from those messages but more importantly, from how his parents and friends respond to him.

It is critical for his spiritual growth that he discerns God's view of himself.

What the World Says About Self-Esteem

False values about human worth exist in every society, past and present. In every generation people have tended to value physical appearance and beauty. The ideal of beauty varies from one culture to the next and changes somewhat with each new generation. Yet beauty has long been worshiped by man.

In our cultures today the world seems to value three things on which one can base one's self-esteem.

- **Beauty**— the message of physical beauty is loudly proclaimed in the media and among our children's peers. This has a profound impact on their value system.

- **Intellect**— As our children go to school, everyone knows who the smart ones are. Those who do not do as well as others assume their self-worth is less because they cannot achieve as well in school.

- **Athleticism**— Our world emphasizes the boys and girls who have athletic ability. Those who do not are often demoralized.

We must teach our children not only that these values are wrong and unbiblical, but that we possess a superior way to live.

Assignment

- Please read the following article:

What the World Says about Self-esteem

When a baby is born, his parents examine that little red, wrinkled body for signs of physical attractiveness. Adults respond very differently to an unusually beautiful child than to a particularly unattractive one. That difference in response has a profound impact on a developing personality. The pretty child is much more likely to see the world as warm and accepting; the ugly child is far better acquainted with the cold, steel eyes of rejection.

An example indicates how devastating the effects of this false value system can be. One little boy born with a harelip wrote that he was affected for life when another older boy called him a turtle. Because of this he concluded, irrationally, that God did not like him because of his harelip. At age seven, this little boy was acquainted with loneliness and despair so severe that he felt hated by the universe. Yet he is merely one victim of a false system of evaluating human worth—a system that stresses attributes not obtained by the majority of our children. Not everyone is seen as worthy; not everyone is accepted. Instead, we reserve our praise and admiration for a select few who have been blessed from birth with the characteristics we value most highly.

These characteristics vary from one society to another. Some common ones are beauty, intelligence, youth, the possession of money, and athletic ability.

Dr. Dobson recalls how people always showed attention to his little girl, who was cute and dimpled at fifteen months. One day she fell against a table and drove her tooth into her gums. Since the cut was on the inner part of her lip, she appeared to have been born that way. All of the babyish appeal was now gone. For awhile she looked terrible, and people averted their eyes to avoid looking at her. The warmth, love, and tenderness previously offered to her were replaced with rejection and coolness. People were not trying to be mean; they just did not find her attractive any longer. Their reaction illustrated the injustice in our value system, a system that rewards a child for something he has not earned and destroys him for circumstances beyond his control.

QUESTION 13

Think of some values that your culture places on things that impact self-esteem. List five to ten values. How does each value compare with what values are lasting and meaningful, according to the Bible? Does Scripture indicate that God values this characteristic? Write down any verses you can find that pertain to this value. Do you respect or admire those who possess this quality more than those who do not?

QUESTION 14

Read 1 Samuel 16:1-7. With your spouse, think about how these verses relate to what you observe in your children. Note particularly how this contradicts the world's view described in the article "What the World Says About Self-Esteem." (refer to this Article placed earlier in the lesson) Be specific for each of your children. This is the first step in developing a plan to counter the impact of the world.

Examine the Values in Your Home

Now that we have considered the negative impact of the world system on our child's view of himself, let us consider some ways in which parents can counteract this influence. This is an important aspect of teaching your child discernment. He must learn to view himself from God's point of view. He must learn to value the superior way of life which he has been exposed to in a loving Christian home.

In the following sections we will suggest six keys to helping your child develop a healthy sense of personal worth.

In a very real sense parents are products of their society. While we may condemn many of society's values, we have sometimes accepted them without realizing it. We have unconsciously learned to worship beauty, intelligence, athletic prowess, or money just like everyone else. One writer said, "We have met the enemy and it is us." The first step must be to examine the values in our home to see whether we truly have adopted God's perspective on human worth or if our own value system needs to be redesigned.

Assignment

- Please read the following article:

Examine the Values in Your Home

A child's feelings about himself come primarily from the significant people in his life—parents, teachers, friends, and relatives. All contribute to the child's self-image in either a positive or negative way, but the influence of how parents seem to view their child tends to be the strongest influence on a child's self-image.

Parents often make negative remarks in the presence of their child as if he were not listening. On the contrary, he listens to what you say about him with the greatest interest. Comments such as "My son is not very bright" or "He's a lazy child" are quickly picked up by a child. His ears are attuned to any statement you make regarding his worth. Parents need to be aware of what they say in front of their children.

Another common mistake that parents make is being too critical of their child. If all a child ever hears from us is criticism and negative evaluations, he will soon come to believe what he hears. He will eventually think of himself as a bad child. Parents can be completely unaware of the harm they are doing to their child, whose self-concept will probably always reflect what his mother or father said about him.

An exhaustive study of self-esteem concluded that parents have a tremendous influence on their child's view of himself. The child accepts the judgments of the significant adults in his life, and many of those judgments will remain with him throughout his life. Is it any wonder Scriptures note that how a person "thinks within himself, so he is" (Prov 23:7, NASB)?

Negative evaluations are not the only cause of a poor self-esteem. Many factors in a home situation can affect a child's self-esteem. For example, a younger child may find it difficult to compete with an older sibling who can run faster or climb higher. He may feel stupid or inept, particularly if his older sibling is allowed to tease him. Embarrassing family characteristics, such as having an alcoholic father, can produce undeserved feelings of inferiority in a child. Even disease and financial hardship can affect the way a child looks at himself, particularly when he compares himself with others.

Unfortunately, incest and sexual abuse is on the rise, even in Christian homes. Fathers, grandfathers, brothers, and uncles have no idea how much lifelong damage they do to their sons and daughters when they sexually abuse them. God makes it clear that those who do such things will not inherit the kingdom of God (1 Cor 6:9-10)!

Sensitivity is the key word to remember when it comes to building self-esteem. We need to be attuned to the thoughts and feelings of our children so that we are aware of their emotional needs. Then we need to make a conscious effort to build their self-esteem rather than tearing it down.

QUESTION 15

One way to evaluate your values is to examine your feelings about each of your children. For example:

- Are you secretly disappointed because one of your children is so ordinary?
- Have you rejected one of your children at times because of his lack of appeal?
- Do you think he is dumb or clumsy?
- Did you want this child when he was born?
- Did you wish for a boy instead of a girl, or vice versa?
- Does your child embarrass you by his behavior?
- Do you find it difficult to accept gross imperfections in your child?

As you examine your feelings toward your child, you can determine whether you are really accepting him and loving him as he is, or whether you are evaluating him according to a false standard of human worth. With your spouse, sit down and honestly answer these questions in your Life Notebook.

QUESTION 16

Reflect on some of the factors in your own life and upbringing which probably harmed your self-esteem and confidence. Write down some of your responses. Do any of these factors apply now to your own children? What specific factors do you think are most affecting your child's self-esteem in a negative way? Or in a positive way? Be prepared to share some thoughts on this at the next seminar

Convey Unconditional Love and Respect to Your Child

Assignment

- Please read the following article:

Convey Unconditional Love and Respect to Your Child

If it is true that we can make a child think he is worthless, it is conversely true that we can make a child feel his immense worth by showing him our unconditional love. This means we accept our children fully, no matter how they act. Love and acceptance must not depend on perfect behavior or physical appearance. Children must be loved for who they are, not just for what they can do.

Unconditional love does not mean approving the negative things a child does. When children disobey, we discipline, but we shouldn't attack their character. We may say, "That is wrong;" "You are not to do that," or "That's a bad thing to do." But we should avoid saying, "You are bad," or, "You are no good." We should focus on the misdeed, on the wrong action, not on our children's sense of personal worth. In this way we teach them right and wrong while maintaining their self-esteem.

When a child is convinced that he is greatly loved and respected by his parents, he is inclined to accept his own worth as a person. A child, like an adult, needs respect. Many children know intuitively that they are loved by their parents, but they do not believe they are held in high esteem by them. A child can conclude in his own mind, "Sure, they love me because I'm their child—I can see that I'm important to them—but they are not proud of me as a person. I'm a disappointment to them. I've let them down. I didn't turn out like they had hoped."

It is very easy to convey love and disrespect at the same time. A child can know that you truly love him, yet your doubts about his acceptability show through. For example, you may reveal your frustration when you are trying to comb his hair or make him "look nice" for an important event. He knows you think it is an impossible assignment. Certain subtle behaviors are signals to the child that he must be supervised closely to avoid embarrassing the whole family. He reads disrespect in your manner, though it is framed in genuine love. The love is a private thing between you—whereas confidence and admiration are "other" oriented, having social implications to those outside the family. Love and respect for your child both contribute to the development of his self-esteem. Respecting your children is one way to fight against the negative influences he receives from society.

If it is true that we can make a child think he is worthless, it is conversely true that we can make a child feel his immense worth by showing him our unconditional love. This means we accept our children fully, no matter how they act. Love and acceptance must not depend on perfect behavior or physical appearance. Children must be loved for who they are, not just for what they can do.

QUESTION 17

Based on what you read of unconditional love in the article, which of the following statements is true?

A. To love unconditionally means we may need to approve negative things a child does.

B. It is OK to say, "That is a bad thing to do."

C. We should focus more on the character deficiency behind that misdeed rather than on the deed itself.

D. When they misbehave, we should explain that they have been a bad boy or girl.

QUESTION 18

It is possible for a child to think you love him but that you do not respect him. *True or False?*

QUESTION 19

This is a good time to reflect on whether you and your spouse truly love your child in a biblical manner. Read 1 Corinthians 13:4-8. Open your Life Notebook and list the seventeen qualities of love that Paul presents. Rewrite the statements so that instead of writing "love is patient," write "Noah and Linda are patient with David." In other words put your names and the name of your child in the sentence. Then discuss whether that statement is true. Record your thoughts in your Life Notebook.

Build Your Child's Confidence Through Praise

Many problems with low self-esteem arise in families where praise is lacking. One lady struggling with self-esteem as an adult told her counselor of an incident in her childhood that scarred her. Her father had been very hard to please. She said:

> I couldn't seem to do anything right. One day he was out working and my mother was gone. I knew daddy loved chocolate cake. I took all morning and made him the nicest cake I could. I was so excited! I knew he would be so happy! Finally he came home. When he saw the cake, he said, "Who made that?" "I did!" I said proudly. With that, he took the cake and threw it in the sink. He said in anger, "I never want to eat anything you make!"

That young girl would remember this event her whole life long. Years later, she cried as she related the story. It was obvious that many of her present feelings about herself originated during her childhood experiences. Her father, whether consciously or unconsciously, had succeeded in smashing her self-image through continued ridicule and criticism.

Few parents may be as severe as this father was. But we can subtly tear at the foundation of our children's self-esteem without being aware of what we are doing.

Assignment

- Please read the following article:

Build Your Child's Confidence Through Praise

Every criticism is a blow to a child's self-image. Each compliment helps to build an inner sense of confidence.

We often unwittingly tear down our children's self-image by what we think is "constructive criticism." We are sincerely interested in our child's performance. We want him to do well. So we point out his errors. We say, "That was good, Hassan, but you could have done a little better." We mean to help. But what runs through Hassan's little mind? He thinks, "I can't do very well. Daddy said I did it well, but he really didn't like it."

Most of us have seen parents who are overly critical with their children; some of us have lived with such parents. Why do some parents criticize everything their child does? Unfortunately, this often arises from the parent's feelings of poor self-esteem. Parents with low self-esteem often want to be proud of themselves and their children.

Criticizing a child may cause him to work harder to please us. At the same time, the child's ego takes a beating. He thinks his parents do not love him unless his achievements result in their satisfaction. "We sacrifice the long-range goal of a good self-image for the present satisfaction of a high-quality performance" (Narramore, 137). This is a poor exchange, and we need to recognize that fact. It is more important for a child to develop wholesome attitudes than ideal performance. Good behavior is much more likely to flow from good feelings about oneself.

As Christian parents, we need to limit criticism as much as possible and build our child's confidence through praise and encouragement. Praise should characterize our words as parents. Praise should reinforce positive, constructive behavior and be specific in nature, rather than general. "I liked the way you straightened your room today" is better than "You've been a good boy," which is vague and does not reward specific behavior. Parents should always watch for opportunities to offer genuine, well-deserved praise to their children, but avoid empty flattery. Your child will quickly learn that your words have no meaning if your praise is insincere and unearned.

Studies have demonstrated that it takes seven compliments to your child to counteract the emotional impact of one negative criticism or remark.

QUESTION 20

The Scriptures speak often of the need for us to build up and encourage one another. As an exercise in applying this thought to your children, match the Scripture with the characteristic of praise.

Scripture	Aspect of Praise
Romans 15:7	Build up one another
Ephesians 4:32	Confidence and boasting in our children
1 Thessalonians 5:11	Kindness
Philippians 2:3	Accept one another
2 Corinthians 7:4	Regard the other person as more important

QUESTION 21

Reflect on your upbringing. Was your parents' home a place of praise or criticism? Think of an incident or two involving praise or criticism that affected you. Summarize these in your notebook. Then, in conversation with your spouse, identify two incidents where you have either praised or criticized your children. In view of what you have read, what would you do differently?

Teach Your Child Not to Criticize

Assignment

- Please read the following article:

Teach Your Child Not to Criticize

Parents can set a positive tone in the family that can be contagious. Establish a rule in your home that ridiculing others is not allowed. Encourage your child not to criticize himself or others. Healthy families should be able to laugh together, but not at the expense of hurt feelings. Even innocent humor can be painful when one child is always the object of the jokes. It is wise not to tease a child about anything he is being criticized about outside the home.

Children ages seven to twelve become increasingly adept at all forms of teasing, ridicule, name-calling, and even outright ostracism of certain children who for one reason or another are not acceptable to them. As adults we know that this stage will pass, but we must not forget how much it can hurt to be called "Fatty" or "Frog" or "Elephant Ears." We need to help our own children to avoid labeling and ridiculing others. Praise, rather than criticism, should characterize our words as parents and be reflected in how our children treat each other as well.

QUESTION 22

Discuss with your spouse the tone you set in your home. Does your child hear you criticizing others, criticizing the pastor's sermon, criticizing his friends? In your Life Notebook record your discussion and identify areas you can improve.

Teach Responsibility

A very important key to building your child's self-esteem is to give him responsible tasks to perform.

Assignment

- Please read the following article:

Teach Confidence by Giving Responsibility

Everyone needs to feel important. We want to feel that we contribute and that we belong. By giving children responsibilities, we build their self-esteem. When Martin takes out the trash each day, he feels important. It is good for his self-concept to do something useful to help the family.

This does not mean he will enjoy taking out the trash. He may even try to get out of doing it, but when his parents calmly explain, "We each have important tasks to do, Martin" and set a logical consequence for failure to do it, he will usually respond. We are not doing a child a favor by relieving him of all responsibilities in the home and allowing him to play continuously. Work is one of the ways in which we gain an inner sense of fulfillment as we carry our share of the load.

Even young children need opportunities to achieve simple tasks on their own. A child who grows up feeling inadequate to perform certain tasks may carry this sense of inadequacy throughout his life. When a child completes a task, satisfaction and confidence result. Achievement builds feelings of success, providing concrete evidence that the child is capable.

QUESTION 23

Recalling again your upbringing. What responsibilities were given to you at home? What effect, if any, do you think this had on your sense of self-worth? What are some responsibilities you could assign to your children now which are appropriate to this age?

Compensation

Assignment

- Please read the following article:

Help Your Child Compensate

Parents often long to shield a child who is ridiculed, rejected, or ignored at school. The human personality grows through mild adversity, provided it is not crushed in the process. Contrary to what you might believe, the ideal environment for your child is not one devoid of problems and trials. The child learns to cope with problems and frustration and disappointment as he confronts them.

The well-rooted tree becomes strong and steady against all assailants. This illustration applies to our children, as well: those who have learned to conquer their problems are more secure than those who have never faced them. Our task as parents, then, is not to eliminate every challenge for our children; it is to serve as a confident ally on their behalf, encouraging when they are distressed, intervening when the threats are overwhelming, and above all, giving them the tools with which to overcome the obstacles.

One tool which can help a child is compensation; to compensate means to counterbalance. A child can learn to counterbalance his weakness by capitalizing on his strengths. Bobby Fischer, the former world champion chess player, was once asked where he got the ambition and motivation to excel in chess. He replied, "It was some people thinking maybe I wasn't as good as they were when I was a kid." Many great men in many walks of life have been propelled by the need to prove something about their adequacy. While compensation has a negative side, in that the person involved may be struggling to prove something to his parents or to himself, it has a positive side as well.

Essentially, compensation is a tool that provides a child with some concrete proof of his own value. A child finds it difficult to think of his value in abstract terms. Developing skills or natural abilities in a particular area can bolster a child's confidence and self-esteem.

Compensation is one of the best weapons against inferiority. In order to help a child to compensate for his perceived weak areas, parents should make a careful assessment of their child's strengths and select a skill that has the greatest possibilities for success. It may be music, art, gymnastics, athletics, or any other area. See that the child gets through the early stage of learning this skill. Later, if you discover that the child has no aptitude for that particular skill, start over on something else, but help him to learn something in which he can excel.

QUESTION 24

Make a list of your child's greatest strengths and areas of weakness. Write down one or two ideas on how you might help him to compensate for weak areas. If you have no children, think of a child you know (a friend's child, or a child at church, etc.) and identify possible areas of weakness in his life. Write ideas on how you could help him grow stronger in those weak areas.

Topic 5: Teaching the Pillar of Discipline

A friend of mind describes the following incident:

> Joanna and I had friends over for the evening. At one point, the visiting mom needed to feed her one-year old child. It is important to realize that this mother enjoys conversation and relished the opportunity to visit with "adults." She continued talking while opening a jar of baby food for her youngster. As she opened the jar and introduced the spoon to her baby, the child began to scream. This went on for a while. Every spoonful was separated by a scream. Finally, the mother turned to me and said, "I just don't understand, she screams the whole time I'm feeding her." (Lybrand, 57)

Understanding the dynamic of what was happening in this situation is the key to modifying the behavior of your child. In this topic we will consider principles keys which, if applied, are absolutely guaranteed to modify undesirable behavior.

The Law of the Harvest

The first principle for modifying undesirable behavior is called "the Law of the Harvest."

Take a look at Galatians 6:7.

QUESTION 25

The idea in Galatians 6:7 is sometimes called the "Law of the Harvest." How does this passage apply to the problem the visiting mother faced with her one-year-old as described at the beginning of this lesson?

After entering your own answer, check The Law of the Harvest note below.

Law of the Harvest

The law of the harvest says that we reap what we sow. If you sow corn, you get corn. If you sow wheat, you get wheat. If you sow evil, you get evil. When applied to changing behavior the law can be restated this way, "whatever behavior you encourage, you will see." Or to state it in reverse, what you see, has probably been encouraged.

QUESTION 26

Let's explore the Law of the Harvest more deeply. You will find it all over Scripture. Match what a man sows with what he reaps.

Sowing	*Reaping*
Proverbs 2:1-5 - Receive your father's words	You will reap bountifully.
Proverbs 29:12 - If a ruler listens to lies	You will not stumble.
Proverbs 4:10-12 - Accept the father's sayings	The churning of anger produces strife.
Proverbs 19:19 - If you rescue an angry man	Then you will discern the fear of the Lord.
Proverbs 30:32-33 - If you do foolishly or plan evil	His servants become wicked.
2 Corinthians 9:6 - If you sow bountifully	He will only do it again.

It is evident that the reason the visiting mom had a child screaming while she was feeding her is that the child was being rewarded with food every time she screamed!

> Here is the principle: whatever behavior you encourage (what you sow) in your children, that is the behavior you will reap.

Let's now apply this to the Four Key Questions: a key to modifying your child's misbehavior.

The First Key Question

The value of these questions is that they will help you understand what is happening with your child and what you can do to encourage change. If you are not seeing the things in your child that you would like to see, read on! These questions give you a practical way to apply the Law of the Harvest. (The following discussion of key questions in Topic 5 is taken from Lybrand, 65-95)

1. "What do I see?"

This question is often the most difficult for many of us. It helps us to be objective instead of interpreting what is happening through our emotions or assumptions. For example, what do you see when you see a small child on the ground crying? Some of you see a hurt child, while others see a child crying for attention or for Mommy to pick him up. The only objective answer is that you see a child lying on the ground crying.

At first, instead of trying to figure out why something is happening, we need to simply focus on what is happening.

The important point here is that we must distinguish between what we actually see and what is our opinion about what we see.

QUESTION 27

As an exercise to help you understand the difference between what you see and your assumption about what you see, match the observation with an assumption regarding that observation.

Observation: What do I See?	Opinion: What do I assume?
"My child is answering my every request with a question"	"My child is arguing with me and showing me disrespect"
"My child is hanging around friends I do not think are a good influence on him"	"My child is undisciplined"
"My child is not turning in completed homework according to his teacher"	"My child is shy"
"My child hides behind me when meeting someone new"	"My child is growing away from the family"

We see a behavior and rush to make an interpretation. The first key question is to get the facts and not make an interpretation.

The Second Key Question

2. "What do I want to see?"

The power behind this question is that it gets us to develop a vision for our child's actions and life. It keeps us from just reacting and causes us to slow down and develop a plan. Too often we respond without thinking through what is really happening and what we could do about it. Instead we just say, "Tommy, stop that right now," or "If you don't behave I am going to spank you!"

QUESTION 28

As an exercise in not reacting but thinking carefully about the behavior you would like to see, match the current behavior with behavior you would desire to see instead.

Current behavior	Desired behavior
"My child is answering my every request with a question"	"I want to see my child stand at my side and say, 'Hello, I'm Samuel; it's nice to meet you.'"
"My child is hanging around friends I do not think are a good influence on him"	"I want to see my child obey me or commit to obey me before asking any questions"
"My child is not turning in completed homework according to his teacher"	"I want to see my child turn his completed homework in on time, and have his teacher surprise me with a note about the change."
"My child hides behind me when meeting someone new"	"I want to see my child keeping company with friends who are a good influence on him"

This kind of thinking forces you to think about solutions, instead of simply reacting.

The Third Key Question

3. "How is what I see being encouraged?"

We are now ready to apply the Law of the Harvest. It can be stated this way:

- You reap what you sow
- What is encouraged will be revealed in a child's behavior

There are, of course, numerous exceptions to this "Law." It is only a general principle when applied in this context. Nevertheless, very often when you apply it by asking the third key question, you will often be on the way to modifying bad behavior.

Let's apply this kind of thinking to the situations we have been illustrating above. The third key question takes us back to Question 1, but it takes it a step further. This question helps us understand the behavior or actions we observe. Often it is difficult to see what might be encouraging a particular behavior. However, if you persist you are likely to unravel the mystery.

QUESTION 29

Match the observation you see with how that observed behavior might be encouraged.

What I see	How is what I see being encouraged?
"My child is answering my every request with a question"	"The teacher did not inform us of the problem for six weeks; therefore my child was getting away with it. Also, we have not been checking his homework each night before bed."
"My child is hanging around friends I do not think are a good influence on him"	"When my husband pointed out that I always apologize by saying, 'She's our shy one,' I realized I have probably encouraged her to live up to that label."
"My child is not turning in completed homework according to his teacher"	"My child is getting more encouragement and support from his friends than from his family. Maybe they listen more while I lecture more? Maybe they hang out and I'm just in a hurry."
"My child hides behind me when meeting someone new"	"My child is curious OR I am answering the question before he obeys, so I am encouraging him to delay obedience by engaging in conversations with him."

These are just examples and there could be other reasons why these behaviors have been encouraged. The point is for you to begin to look for the cause behind the action.

The Fourth Key Question

4. How can I encourage what I want to see and discourage everything else?

This is the most important question of all. This question begins to set in motion the innate gift of God within parents. It moves us to become the experts for our own child.

Question 4 requires something you may not be very skilled at yet: brainstorming. The key is to simply get as many ideas as possible without criticizing or throwing away any of them. If the idea is related to the action, then all the better.

Let's apply this to the Law of the Harvest again.

QUESTION 30

Match the behavior on the left with a possible way you might encourage that behavior on the right.

What do I want to see?	How can I encourage or discourage my child?
"I want to see my child obey me or commit to obey me before asking any questions."	"I need to work on my friendship with him. I think I'll begin to let him pick one activity each month just for us. I could also begin to provide activities, or other encouragements whenever he spends time with some of his 'good influence' friends."
"I want to see my child keeping company with friends who are a good influence on him."	"I simply will not answer a question until after he obeys or tells me 'I'm going to do it, but may I ask a question?'"
"I want to see my child turn his completed homework in on time, and have his teacher surprise me with a call or note about the change in my child."	"The new rule will be Earn Fun with Homework. It will be homework first and fun second. Outside activities, friends, TV, etc., will be allowed after homework is completed. I'll also throw in a special treat when the teacher gives me that call or note!"
"I want to see my child stand at my side and politely say, 'Hello, I'm Samuel. It's nice to meet you.'"	"We'll just practice until we get right—first, in private, then as we meet people. I'll explain that 'this is my polite child' (not my shy one) and praise him as he follows the plan. I'm also going to have to have a serious consequence until he obeys."

Again, these are just a few examples. Please remember, you are to become the expert for your child. You are better able to figure out what will encourage and discourage behaviors in your child than any experts, books, or magazines. Do not be afraid to gather ideas from others, but usually the best ideas for Question 4 come from your own mind and heart; no one knows your child like you do, nor can they.

QUESTION 31

Applying these questions is very important. Work with your spouse and take time to apply the four questions by answering each one for each of your children. Answer all of these questions at the same time and use as much detail as possible for each child. More children may mean more sessions, but it will be worth it. If this is overwhelming, pick a single behavior for each child and focus the questions on it.

Topic 6: Teaching the Pillar of Discipline: The Absolute Quickest Way to Help your Child Change

In this topic you will learn the absolute quickest way to help your children change. We can guarantee you that if you will follow this advice you will see dramatic changes in your children's behavior.

Here is the central key to the pillar of discipline in the home. It is more important than the Four Key Questions and is guaranteed to get results.

Dr. Lybrand says:

> This key will dramatically affect your child's life and behavior. But let me warn you: this principle is not for the faint of heart. This shortcut is powerful, but potentially difficult.
>
> What could it be that is so powerful over the lives of our children? Many parents who turn to the next page of this lesson may find feelings of anger, hopelessness, and frustration well

up from within. If that happens to you do not stop reading. Instead, ask yourself, "What is in me that is so resistant to what I'm learning here?"

If you can keep your objectivity, you will find great hope.

Dr Lybrand continues:

> Consider an example. She was three when her parents decided to stop her from sucking her thumb. It seemed easy enough to discipline her for sucking her thumb, but suddenly she began to pull her hair out in little tufts. I was invited to help solve this dilemma, and we saw some improvement. We simply applied the questions and answers to the Four Key Questions and we saw some immediate improvement.
>
> After a short time, however, this little girl began to pull her hair out and carefully hide it under her pillow! We tried everything, but it just wasn't working. I personally thought we were taking a wise approach, but this little girl was not responding.
>
> When sound, common sense practices don't work on a three-year-old, then you can be confident that something in the family more powerful than your direct actions is encouraging the behavior.

What is that something?

The relationship between husband and wife.

> A healthy relationship between Mom and Dad is the absolute quickest way to help your child change.

> **Husbands, love your wives just as Christ loved the church and gave himself for her** to sanctify her by cleansing her with the washing of the water by the word, so that he may present the church to himself as glorious – not having a stain or wrinkle, or any such blemish, but holy and blameless. In the same way husbands ought to love their wives as their own bodies. He who loves his wife loves himself. For no one has ever hated his own body but he feeds it and takes care of it, just as Christ also does the church, for we are members of his body. **For this reason a man will leave his father and mother and will be joined to his wife, and the two will become one flesh.** This mystery is great – but I am actually speaking with reference to Christ and the church. **Nevertheless, each one of you must also love his own wife as he loves himself, and the wife must respect her husband.** (Eph 5:25-33, emphasis added)

Topic 7: Conclusion

We have covered a lot of material in this lesson. Some of it may seem a bit overwhelming. You might ask, "How can I do all this?" In some cases you might be thinking, "I have done so many things wrong?"

Implementing these suggestions will take months, even years. Take your successes and failures before the Lord and ask Him for encouragement and wisdom. He has promised that He has compassion on us and accepts us as we are. He is so pleased that you are taking this course and that you desire to give to Him a godly offspring.

Lesson 5 Self Check

QUESTION 1

Competition can be exhilarating and fun for the child, and should almost always be encouraged in during the ages of seven to twelve. *True or False?*

QUESTION 2

Age seven to twelve is:

    A. A good time to begin the active use of the book of Proverbs

    B. A good time to introduce the child into serious competition

    C. A good time to dismiss emotional issues because he is not able to talk about them intelligently

    D. A good time to stress the need for strenuous exercise

QUESTION 3

A parent does not need to be concerned that children in this age group may have a learning disability. *True or False?*

QUESTION 4

During the ages seven to twelve, children are typically not ready for games that require skill. *True or False?*

QUESTION 5

Children in the seven-to-twelve age group should be encouraged to initiate acts of kindness and compassion toward others. *True or False?*

QUESTION 6

It is certainly preferable that the facts about sexual reproduction come from parents who can teach it in a proper moral context, rather than from misinformed friends. *True or False?*

QUESTION 7

The world's view of what makes a person significant vary from one society to another. Some common ones are beauty, intelligence, youth, the possession of money, and athletic ability. *True or False?*

QUESTION 8

Studies have demonstrated that it takes seven criticisms of your child to counteract the emotional impact of one positive remark. *True or False?*

QUESTION 9

Unfortunately, incest and sexual abuse is on the rise, even in Christian homes. *True or False?*

QUESTION 10

Which one of the following statements is true of showing unconditional love?

    A. To love unconditionally means we may need to approve negative things a child does.

    B. It is OK to say, "That is a bad thing to do."

    C. We should focus more on the character deficiency behind that misdeed rather than on the deed itself.

    D. When they misbehave, we should explain that they have been a "bad boy/girl."

Lesson 5 Answers to Questions

QUESTION 1: *Your answer*

QUESTION 2

    C. Children in this stage are capable of strenuous exercise.

    D. Often a child who develops rapidly in this stage will slow down later.

QUESTION 3: *Your answer*

QUESTION 4: *Your answer*

QUESTION 5: *Your answer*

QUESTION 6: True [They may have problems recognizing and remembering the appearance of words and continue to reverse many letters and words for several years. They need reassurance from parents and teachers that this is a special memory problem, that they are not stupid or lazy, and that they will learn to read and write in time. Individual tutoring may help many of these children.]

QUESTION 7

    A. Children at this age have an increasing need for privacy

    B. Children may pick up bad language and habits from their friends.

    C. In this stage children may turn to adults outside the family for inspiration.

    E. Children can learn about responsibility at this age

QUESTION 8: *Your answer*

QUESTION 9: *Your answer*

QUESTION 10: *Your answer*

QUESTION 11

Scripture	*Biblical Principle*
Genesis 2:24-25	Sex is without shame and ordained by God.
Proverbs 5:1-8	Sex is to be experienced only in marriage.
Proverbs 5:15-19	Rich and satisfying sex in marriage is healthy and even commanded.
1 Corinthians 6:18	We are to flee from sexual immorality.
Song of Solomon 7:1-9	Sexual love in marriage is to be free and creative.

QUESTION 12: *Your answer*

QUESTION 13: *Your answer*

QUESTION 14: *Your answer*

QUESTION 15: *Your answer*

QUESTION 16: *Your answer*

QUESTION 17

    B. It is OK to say, "That is a bad thing to do."

QUESTION 18: True [When a child is convinced that he is greatly loved and respected by his parents, he is inclined to accept his own worth as a person.]

QUESTION 19: *Your answer*

QUESTION 20

Scripture	*Aspect of Praise*
Romans 15:7	Accept one another
Ephesians 4:32	Kindness
1 Thessalonians 5:11	Build up one another
Philippians 2:3	Regard the other person as more important
2 Corinthians 7:4	Confidence and boasting in our children

QUESTION 21: *Your answer*

QUESTION 22: *Your answer*

QUESTION 23: *Your answer*

QUESTION 24: *Your answer*

QUESTION 25: *Your answer*

QUESTION 26

Sowing	Reaping
Proverbs 2:1-5 - Receive your father's words	Then you will discern the fear of the Lord.
Proverbs 29:12 - If a ruler listens to lies	His servants become wicked.
Proverbs 4:10-12 - Accept the father's sayings	You will not stumble.
Proverbs 19:19 - If you rescue an angry man	He will only do it again.
Proverbs 30:32-33 - If you do foolishly or plan evil	The churning of anger produces strife.
2 Corinthians 9:6 - If you sow bountifully	You will reap bountifully.

QUESTION 27

Observation: What do I See?	Opinion: What do I assume?
"My child is answering my every request with a question"	"My child is arguing with me and showing me disrespect"
"My child is hanging around friends I do not think are a good influence on him"	"My child is growing away from the family"
"My child is not turning in completed homework according to his teacher"	"My child is undisciplined"
"My child hides behind me when meeting someone new"	"My child is shy"

QUESTION 28

Current behavior	Desired behavior
"My child is answering my every request with a question"	"I want to see my child obey me or commit to obey me before asking any questions"
"My child is hanging around friends I do not think are a good influence on him"	"I want to see my child keeping company with friends who are a good influence on him"
"My child is not turning in completed homework according to his teacher"	"I want to see my child turn his completed homework in on time, and have his teacher surprise me with a note about the change."
"My child hides behind me when meeting someone new"	"I want to see my child stand at my side and say, 'Hello, I'm Samuel; it's nice to meet you.'"

QUESTION 29

What I see	How is what I see being encouraged?
"My child is answering my every request with a question"	"My child is curious OR I am answering the question before he obeys, so I am encouraging him to delay obedience by engaging in conversations with him."
"My child is hanging around friends I do not think are a good influence on him"	"My child is getting more encouragement and support from his friends than from his family. Maybe they listen more while I lecture more? Maybe they hang out and I'm just in a hurry."
"My child is not turning in completed homework according to his teacher"	"The teacher did not inform us of the problem for six weeks; therefore my child was getting away with it. Also, we have not been checking his homework each night before bed."
"My child hides behind me when meeting someone new"	"When my husband pointed out that I always apologize by saying, 'She's our shy one,' I realized I have probably encouraged her to live up to that label."

QUESTION 30

What do I want to see?	How can I encourage or discourage my child?
"I want to see my child obey me or commit to obey me before asking any questions."	"I simply will not answer a question until after he obeys or tells me 'I'm going to do it, but may I ask a question?'"
"I want to see my child keeping company with friends who are a good influence on him."	"I need to work on my friendship with him. I think I'll begin to let him pick one activity each month just for us. I could also begin to provide activities, or other encouragements whenever he spends time with some of his 'good influence' friends."
"I want to see my child turn his completed homework in on time, and have his teacher surprise me with a call or note about the change in my child."	"The new rule will be Earn Fun with Homework. It will be homework first and fun second. Outside activities, friends, TV, etc., will be allowed after homework is completed. I'll also throw in a special treat when the teacher gives me that call or note!"
"I want to see my child stand at my side and politely say, 'Hello, I'm Samuel. It's nice to meet you.'"	"We'll just practice until we get right—first, in private, then as we meet people. I'll explain that 'this is my polite child' (not my shy one) and praise him as he follows the plan. I'm also going to have to have a serious consequence until he obeys."

QUESTION 31: *Your answer*

Lesson 5 Self Check Answers

QUESTION 1: False

QUESTION 2

    A. A good time to begin the active use of the book of Proverbs

QUESTION 3: False

QUESTION 4: False

QUESTION 5: True

QUESTION 6: True

QUESTION 7: True

QUESTION 8: False

QUESTION 9: True

QUESTION 10

    B. It is OK to say, "That is a bad thing to do."

Lesson 6: Dealing with Adolescents

Lesson Introduction

During a lively parental discussion of some of the problems encountered in the teenage years, a frustrated mother exclaimed, "I guess I look at adolescence the same way I did the childhood diseases, like measles, mumps, and chicken pox. I knew that our children would eventually catch them, and I just prayed that they would have a light case and recover quickly. But now I'm getting worried. We hear stories from other parents about their teenagers and really wonder what we'll be facing as the parents of teenagers."

Like this mother, many parents of adolescents feel at least a twinge of anxiety over their teenager's adjustment during the next few years. The teenage years present some special challenges to parents. We all know parents who have struggled with an adolescent over problems such as disrespect for authority, styles of clothing, choice of music, or even alcohol or drug use. Perhaps we have memories of our own adolescent struggles, and we assume that our children will have a turbulent adolescence. We may fear that with the advent of adolescence happy family times will disappear forever, or at least until our children pass through this dreadful stage and regain their sanity.

In reality, adolescence is not always a turbulent experience. Expecting the worst can deprive us of the positive attitude toward parenting that is so essential. Adolescence is not a disease or a natural disaster. Many parents of adolescents never encounter serious conflicts or major crises during these years, and others weather the storms without too much family disharmony. In fact, adolescence can bring some of the most rewarding moments that parents ever experience. As the teenager is reaching out for independence, we can stand at his side as an ally or enemy. If we become his ally in the maturation process, we can find the family strengthened in renewed understanding and love.

The adolescent years give us an excellent opportunity to strengthen the bonds between us. Now that our children are older, we can work together to seek solutions to problems, to mend wounds that occur, and to remove barriers to communication and understanding. To strengthen family bonds during adolescence, parents need to exercise or develop some basic attitudes or parenting skills. These parenting skills will form the outline for our lesson on adolescence.

Lesson Outline

Topic 1: Understanding the Teenager's World

 Physical Development

 Emotional Development

 Social Development

 Mental Development

 Spiritual Development

Topic 2: Communicating Love and Respect to the Adolescent

 Loving Your Teenager Unconditionally

 Giving "Focused Attention"

 Concentrating on the Positive

Topic 3: The Pillar of Discipline

Lesson Objectives

By the end of this lesson, you will be able to do the following:

- Describe your teenager's world—the thoughts, feelings, conflicts, and experiences common to adolescence

- Discuss the impact of peer pressure in the life of the teenager

- Communicate respect and love to your teenager in ways that he can understand and receive

- Develop a plan to gradually release your teenager so that he can graduate into adulthood

Topic 1: Understanding the Teenager's World

Mariana came to the breakfast table. Her short hair seemed to stand on end. Last year she had worn it longer; it had fallen softly around her face. Her dress, too, had changed. Her figure was hidden by the huge, sloppy sweater she wore; her legs emerged beneath it, looking like toothpicks.

"Mariana," said her mother, "You aren't going out dressed like that."

"Why not?" countered her dark-haired daughter, eyes flashing. "What's wrong with how I'm dressed?"

"Mariana, we've discussed this many times. Your father and I want you to dress modestly and becomingly."

"Oh, Mother," Mariana sighed, rolling her eyes up. "You are so old-fashioned. You couldn't possibly understand how I feel."

Many adolescents feel the way Mariana did when she expressed this. With the advent of teenage years many young people begin to view their parents as ancient artifacts from some archaeological dig. The same parents who have been around all these years suddenly learn that they do not speak the same language as their teenager. They express shock at his taste in clothes, haircuts, and music. They just do not seem to understand him at all.

In the Bible the teenager is called a "youth." The Hebrew word is *naar*. This word is used of children from infant to young adult but the primary use is of those in the teenage years. Scholars are not sure of the original meaning. Some say it comes from an Arabic word which means "agitated" and others from the Hebrew word for "to shake off." We cannot be sure but most would agree this is a period of time in a child's life in which there is a high degree of agitation and it is also a time in which they are "shaking off" parental authority and becoming independent.

Please look again at the following article:

The Stages of Child Development in the Bible

According to Alfred Edersheim in *Sketches of Jewish Social Life in the Days of Christ*, there were eight different terms in the Hebrew Bible for the word "child," each depicting a fresh stage of life.

Jeled

The newborn was called a *jeled*. It was applied to Moses (Ex 2:6-8). This word was applied to our Lord Jesus in the great prophecy of Isaiah 9:6, "*For unto us a child (jeled) was born.*"

(See also Isa 29:23; 57:4; Jer 31:20; Eccl 4:13; 1 Kgs 12:8; 2 Kgs 2:24; Gen 42:22.)

Jonek

The next child name, in point of time, is *jonek*, which literally means "a suckling" and describes a child up to their first birthday. We are told that the Lord Jesus will grow up as a *jonek* ("tender shoot" in Isa 53:2), describing the period of time between birth and roughly three years. The word is sometimes overlaps with the next stage, the *Olel*.

Olel

The third stage is life was designated by the word *olel*, which indicates age one to three. He is still nursing but it is no longer satisfied with only this nourishment, and is "asking for bread," as in Lamentations 4:4.

Gamul

The *gamul* is the "weaned one," typically age three to six. Hebrew mothers typically nursed their children until age three (see Ps 131:2; Isa 11:8; 28:9). The verb form of the word means "to complete," hence, he has completed the period of nursing. When the period of weaning was over, it was celebrated by a feast.

Taph

The *taph* refers to that period in the child's life from age seven to twelve when he clings to his mother and the mother is constantly watching him or her.

Elem

The sixth stage is called the *elem* and the feminine form is *almah*. This corresponds to the period of early adolescence, thirteen to fifteen years of age. The word means "to become firm and strong." The *almah* was the designation of the virgin Mary in the virgin birth prophecy of Isaiah 7:14.

Naar

The seventh stage of development was designed by the word *naar*, "youth." The word means "to break away." It refers to one who shakes off or shakes himself free, an appropriate term for the teenage years from fifteen to eighteen.

Bachur

The final stage, the eight stage of development was the *bachur* or "ripened one." This was used, for example, of the young warrior, as in Isaiah 31:8; Jeremiah 18:21; 15:8.

Understanding the adolescent experience is critical to survival of the next few years ahead for you as a parent. Perhaps you will never understand everything your child is thinking and feeling, but you can refresh yourself on how it feels to be a teenager. Remind yourself that certain natural changes, inner turmoil, and even conflicts are common at this stage of life. Understanding your teenager's world is the first and most important step to living peacefully with him and being able to help him through these most difficult few years.

Can you remember your early adolescent years? One parent recalls how he felt when he was on the threshold of adolescence.

> What horror fills my mind when I recall the beginning of my adolescent years. Skinny legs. Pimples. Perpetually imagining what others thought of me: Did they notice my crooked nose? …Why did I have to be a runt—small and skinny?

Feelings of inferiority tend to be characteristic of the adolescent years. Surveys show that up to eighty percent of young people do not like themselves. During a United States Senate hearing Dr. Yuri Bronfenbrenner, eminent authority on child development from Cornell University, was asked, "What are the most critical years of a child's development?" The senators expected him to emphasize the importance of the preschool experience, since studies show that much significant learning takes place during the first six years of life.

Instead, Bronfenbrenner replied, "Yes, the preschool years are vital, but so is every other phase of childhood." He went on to tell the Senate committee that the early adolescent years are probably the most critical to the development of a child's mental health. During this period of self-doubt the personality is often assaulted and damaged beyond repair. (This and the preceding paragraph adapted from Kesler and Beers, 157.)

As parents and Christian leaders we need to understand the nature of this time of self-doubt that our children undergo during adolescence. This period is characterized by change—physical, emotional, and social change.

Physical Development

Dramatic physical changes take place during the teenage years, when a complete transformation from the body of a child to the body of an adult takes place. Puberty generally begins for girls somewhere between the ages of eleven and thirteen. Breast development, the first menstrual period, the growth of pubic hair, and the widening of hips are all a part of the growth process for a teenage girl. For boys, puberty generally begins about two years later, at age thirteen to fifteen, and includes rapid and uneven growth spurts, changing voice, the growth of pubic hair, and nocturnal emissions. Increased sexual awareness is true of both boys and girls in the stage of puberty.

Another physical change which is not outwardly observable, but which has tremendous influence on the adolescent, is the production of male and female hormones. During the period of adolescence the onset of hormonal changes can cause extreme fluctuations in emotions for the teenager. Even an easy-going child can experience mood swings.

The tendency toward moodiness is complicated by the adolescent's anxiety about his changing appearance. Every young person is anxious to some degree about beginning puberty and has an idea in mind about how he or she should look when physical development is completed. Most adolescents are inwardly somewhat disappointed when they fall short of attaining their ideal of femininity or masculinity. They are convinced that they are too tall or too short, too fat or too thin. They imagine when they enter a room that every other person is looking at their big nose or their receding chin or the single pimple on their nose.

One of our responsibilities as parents is to help our teenager feel comfortable with his or her developing body, so that he or she can eventually thank God for the final result, whatever it is. We need to accept as normal any defects perceived by our adolescent, to encourage the adolescent about his physical appearance, and to refrain from making any remarks about him that could easily be misinterpreted. We should be careful not to laugh at teenage clumsiness, which is often the result of growth spurts. We also need to help our teenagers learn to refrain from ridiculing one another.

Teenagers have high amounts of energy that need to be used or channeled. If you work with young people, you need to provide an outlet for their energy. Plan lots of recreational activities for young people and plenty of group games, but do not place too much emphasis on competitive activities, which can contribute to a sense of failure and low self-esteem in those young people lacking in athletic ability. Instead, emphasize the fun aspect of activities and the group sense of togetherness.

Assignment

- Please read the following article:

The Awkward Years

Try to remember how you felt about your body when you were thirteen or fourteen years old. Can you honestly say that you liked everything about it? What upset or worried you most about your physical appearance? How did you handle your feelings in this area? You may want to record your thoughts in your Life Notebook.

Most of us, if we are honest, probably did not like everything about ourselves as adolescents. We were convinced that we were too tall or too short, too heavy or too skinny, too clumsy or too pimply, or too something else. The way we felt about our bodies affected other areas of our lives. With the advantage of hindsight, parents tend to view the rapid physical changes of adolescence as perfectly natural, and we can overlook their emotional importance. Yet these physical changes are the basis for most of the personality changes our adolescents undergo and for many of the problems they encounter.

We need to step into our teenager's shoes and remember how we felt when we were undergoing the physical changes of adolescence. Any aspect of physical development that sets a teenager conspicuously apart from his peers can become a serious problem.

Chang, for example, was a tall, gangling fifteen-year-old who grew twenty centimeters taller in a short time. When he tried out for the school basketball team, the coach had high expectations of him. Chang had the height to be a strong forward. Unfortunately, he had grown so quickly that his coordination had not caught up with his size. Though tall, he was awkward and had trouble getting both feet going in the same direction at the same time.

Though he skipped rope, jogged, and tried all kinds of calisthenics, nothing cured his lack of coordination. Soon his friends began to tease him about his height and his clumsiness. Although their comments were good-natured and Chang tried to laugh them off, they hurt inside. His self-image suffered because Chang saw himself as unacceptable to the other kids.

Faced with what they perceive to be their inadequacies, many adolescents will try to compensate for their shortcomings. Compensation can be a helpful means of bolstering a sagging self-concept, as we discussed in Lesson 5. Sometimes, however, a teenager tries to compensate in an inappropriate way, by learning to make people laugh or by acting like a tough guy to shield his ego. Some go to the extreme of withdrawing physically or emotionally to isolate themselves from hurt.

Physical characteristics create similar dilemmas for both boys and girls. For a girl, being exceptionally tall or overweight or having a flat chest can be a severe burden to bear. Sometimes the problem of a negative self-image is compounded by the reaction of the adolescent's peer group. Recently the mother of a fourteen-year-old girl said, "Our daughter is likeable, attractive, and bright, but some of her classmates tease her unmercifully because she is very tall. Nearly every day she comes home in tears and retreats to her room to be alone." Teenagers are deeply hurt by the negative remarks of their peers and are quick to misinterpret remarks in the worst possible way.

The awakening of sexuality is alternately one of the most exciting and confusing experiences for the teenager. The process of dealing with one's developing sexuality is a major task of adolescence. It is important to note that a teenager's feelings about his or her sexuality are not simply a reflection of actual physical attributes. In fact, the most important determinants of teenagers' feelings about their sexuality have been forged long before they reach physical sexual maturity.

The relationship of a child with his parents during the preceding years and the parents' relationship with each other have helped to shape the fundamental features of the child's attitudes toward himself, his sexual identity, and the opposite sex. Boys, for example, need a good relationship with their father as a living model of what it is like to be a man. They also need a secure relationship with a loving and reasonably relaxed, happy mother in order to anticipate rewarding relationships with females.

In much the same way girls need mothers they can trust and admire to make womanhood appealing. They also require sensitive and caring fathers if marriage is to look attractive and the opposite sex appealing, rather than intimidating. If parents have provided good examples of male and female roles and if the parent-child relationship has been a close one, your teenager will most likely adjust positively to his or her developing sexuality.

As mentioned in Lesson 5, it is important for parents to adequately prepare their teenagers for puberty. Teenagers should be told of the physical and emotional changes which they will undergo. Girls should also be prepared for the onset of menstruation. Unfortunately, many parents have not felt sufficiently comfortable with their own sexuality to talk freely about their body functions and prepare their children emotionally for puberty.

Large numbers of children receive no explanation of even basic sexual functions. Imagine the effect of the onset of menstruation for a girl who is totally unprepared for these physical changes. The reaction is one of distress and confusion. Some parents attempt to explain basic physical changes but do it in such a negative way that fear is created. As one girl expressed it, "My mother talked about my period as if it were the plague."

When parents have talked openly with preadolescents about sexuality and have demonstrated wholesome attitudes toward their own bodies, children's adaptation to sexual development usually proceeds smoothly. No undue curiosity about sex will dominate their minds, and a deep respect for their bodies will protect them from abusing the gift of sexuality.

QUESTION 1

With your spouse, discuss how the points raised in this article may apply to your teenagers. Record your thoughts in your Life Notebook.

QUESTION 2

"The Awkward Years" mentioned a number of issues that can negatively affect an adolescent's sense of self-esteem. Which of the following are issues raised in the article? *(Select all that apply.)*

　　A. For a girl, being exceptionally tall

　　B. Clumsiness in physical activities

　　C. A good relationship with one's father.

　　D. A healthy understanding of sexuality.

Emotional Development

Have you noticed your teenager shifting unexpectedly from one mood to another? Is your son emotionally "up" one minute and "down" the next? Is your daughter outgoing and vivacious one day and morose and introverted the next? One day your daughter may come running into the house, exclaiming, "Mom, I met the most wonderful friend today!" A few days later she may angrily exclaim, "Don't ever mention that name around me again!" You shake your head and wonder what has happened. Be reassured: your teenager is normal.

Beyond understanding the physical changes of adolescence, we also need to understand more about our teenager's emotional world. Many teenagers have significant mood shifts. Some vacillate from elation to depression. One day they are effervescent, happy, and enjoying life; the next day they act like the world has come to an end. They shuffle into the house after school and want to be left alone. In response to queries, they may have nothing to say except "Leave me alone," or they may insist, "Nothing's wrong." They may mope around the house, doing nothing except making everybody else share their misery. They may shift rapidly from surprising politeness to ornery negativity.

One mother of two teenage daughters said, "Sometimes I can hardly cope with our youngest daughter. She is like a doll with two faces sewn on. At times she is as sweet, warm, and loving as you could hope for. Then she shows her other face, acting defiant, hateful, and uncooperative."

Of course, this unpredictability is hard for parents to cope with. If a teenager is consistently cheerful and outgoing or even consistently withdrawn and reticent, we can at least learn to adjust to a dependable pattern. But when we do not know what to expect from one moment to the next, it is difficult to get our bearings. We do not know which personality or mood he or she will be wearing when we next interact.

Roller-coaster mood changes frustrate us as rational adults, but an understanding of this phenomenon can help quiet our reactions. There is a physical basis for the mood swings common to adolescents. The hormonal changes associated with puberty can upset one's entire emotional balance, causing some teenagers to go through rather lengthy periods of emotional upset. Time, increasing maturity, and parental understanding usually help smooth out these peaks and valleys.

Moodiness is sometimes compounded in girls by hormonal changes experienced as a regular part of the monthly menstrual cycle. The week before menstruation, and possibly for several days around the time of ovulation, some girls experience extreme emotional tension, which can produce outbursts of anger or tears. These symptoms have been discovered in many women and are now referred to as "premenstrual tension." Parents of a teenage girl should check the calendar on a monthly basis, for explosions can sometimes be predicted and defused.

QUESTION 3

Discuss the subject of premenstrual tension with your spouse. Does strife tend to occur in your family most frequently during the week preceding menstruation? If you have never done so, take note of how your moods or your spouse's moods are affected by premenstrual tension. How can this information be helpful to you?

In addition to these physically-caused emotional upsets, a second cause of emotional swings is learning to cope with new roles and responsibilities. Physically speaking, teenagers are able to take care of themselves and to carry a greater measure of responsibility. No longer must parents cater to their needs. Adult habits must be learned. Increased responsibility, however, also means that greater emotional pressure is placed on the adolescent. He is expected to act more like an adult, yet at times his thinking is still immature. He may lack discernment, for example, in choosing friends or in matters of dress.

Until your child reaches adolescence, you have probably taken charge of meeting most of his needs. You have seen that your young child was fed and clothed, made sure your child completed his homework and household chores, and had some influence in your child's choice of friends and activities. However, a teenager is increasingly free to make his own choices and demonstrate his ability to handle more responsibility.

This time of changing roles and expanding responsibilities can be exciting but perilous at the same time. The teenager views every endeavor in terms of success or failure. If a teenage boy reaches out to a potential girlfriend and is rebuffed, he may withdraw, afraid to be so vulnerable. If a girl is not invited to a prominent school event, she may be devastated. Self-esteem plunges to its lowest depths with greater frequency during the adolescent experience.

Teenagers are striving to please others, forging new self-reliance, and trying to cope with conflicts and wounded feelings all at the same time. It is no wonder that teenagers are understandably vulnerable to extreme fluctuation in attitude and mood. Everyone benefits when we parents learn to accept these temporary emotional swings and patiently and understandingly give our teenagers time to adjust and learn to cope. It is important that we develop the ability to understand our teenager's fluctuating moods, if we are to help him through this complicated time of life and stand as his ally beside him.

QUESTION 4

From the discussion above summarize two major causes of the tremendous mood swings characteristic of adolescents.

Our heavenly Father paid the ultimate sacrifice for us. He gave us His Son, so that we might be acceptable in God's sight as we are purified by Christ's blood (Rom 5:1, 8-9). It cost God a tremendous sacrifice in order to demonstrate His love in this concrete way. It will cost us too as parents to make a sacrificial effort to hear, understand, and accept our children.

It is all too common for a teen to feel as if no one understands—not his parents, not his teachers, and maybe not even God. Often the greatest gift to a child who is feeling that way is simply to listen. Take the time to be available, and just let your child talk. Sometimes when he has heard himself say what he is thinking, he will straighten himself out, without any advice on your part. If he is prone to keep his feelings to himself and is quiet and withdrawn, the parent must try to win his confidence, gently encouraging him, but not forcing him, to share his feelings. Above all, continue to accept him at his level of maturity and help him grow from there.

QUESTION 5

Study Hebrews 4:14-16. According to these verses, what particular qualities characterize Christ? What does He offer to us in time of need? What should we offer to our children in their time of need?

Social Development

At the top of every list of adolescent problems is the problem of peer pressure. Ahn, a sixteen-year-old Christian, described his feelings about peer pressure:

> This is the area that's hardest for me. My friends want to do things that I know are wrong, and it's hard not to go along. I guess this means my friends aren't good for me, but knowing this doesn't make it easier. No one likes to be an oddball.

Assignment
- Please read the following article:

Social Development

Few things strike more fear in the hearts of parents than the threat of the negative influence of peer pressure. We look around at adolescents in our neighborhood or the local school and quake inwardly just at the sight of some of them. We wonder about their moral standards, their spiritual commitment, their attitudes toward authority, and their sense of responsibility or lack of it. We wonder about their music, their dress, and other current fads. In the face of many disagreeable aspects of today's adolescent experience, we may be tempted to brace ourselves for the worst.

To complicate matters, our child's urge to conform usually sharpens during the pre-teen and teenage years. Susceptibility to peer pressure generally peaks around middle adolescence and thereafter begins a gradual decline. This relatively predictable cycle tells us a great deal about the dynamics of peer pressure.

It begins its most rapid growth in early adolescence when our children are, for the first time, moving out on their own and establishing their own identities. At this time they are starting to loosen the ties at home but do not yet have the inner resources necessary to stand on their own. For several years they will seek their identity in peer groups that offer emotional reinforcement for their struggle; to go against the group puts insecure teens in an emotional void.

As they move into the later stages of adolescence, they gain more confidence in their own abilities and decision-making powers. This growing sense of self-assurance enables them to learn to stand against the group and begin to assert their individuality once again. To go through this entire process, however, takes several years.

It may help us to realize that this cycle is somewhat predictable and natural—from extreme dependence on peers to a gradual assertion of individuality. Teenagers are susceptible to their friends' influence precisely because they are in the process of weaning themselves away from us and learning to think for themselves. For years they have grounded their identities in parental relationships. What we said and did was, for the most part, what they accepted as right or true.

Physical and intellectual growth incites both independent action and thought. Part of the process of maturing is learning to think for oneself and being open to opinions other than those of one's parents. Thus, one's friends gain in influence during this period. In a sense our teenagers pass from one form of dependency (parental) to another (peer) on their way to constructive self-reliance and dependence upon God.

Now as adults we realize that the carbon-copy speech, dress, and music of teenagers do not seem to be a great indication of individuality and thinking for oneself. In fact, the opposite seems true to us, but from the teenager's perspective his temporary "cookie-cutter conformity" is an exercise in individuality, as he frees himself from conformity to some of the standards his parents have chosen for him.

As our teenagers turn outward and try to find their own autonomy, they may also feel a sense of distance or even loneliness. Their reaching out for independence gradually separates them from parental control and can make them feel more isolated, although it is a chosen isolation. At the same time they need acceptance more than ever. Consequently, peers often provide the needed approval, and our teenagers may be willing to trade some of their values, ideals, and individuality to receive it.

A teenager's search for acceptance by his peers also stems partly from trying to find his place in a big and potentially frightening world. After a dozen years of being a child, teenagers are suddenly thrust into a world where they must learn to make their own choices and live with the consequences. They must learn to adapt to new people and accept responsibility. They feel vulnerable and insecure.

In the middle of all of these conflicting possibilities, where can they turn for help? Parents are one potential source, and many teenagers do turn to their parents for guidance, particularly if communication has been open and support has been freely given in the past. However, there are limitations to this source of guidance. Since the teenager is trying to put dependence behind him, turning back to his parents may be difficult or disagreeable for him. It can be far more agreeable to turn to his friends for advice.

The influence of peers is not always negative. We need to recognize that a teenager can learn a great deal by identifying with others his own age who are in similar circumstances. Although understanding parents still have the opportunity and capacity to aid their teen's development, we must face the fact that he needs broader influences in his life if he is ever to reach maturity. Our prayer should be that with our continued guidance our teenagers will choose to associate with Christian young people who will be a positive influence in their lives. Having a Christian peer group can be a strong encouragement to their faith.

QUESTION 6

Open your Life Notebook and in discussion with your spouse, summarize the major reasons teenagers are susceptible to peer pressure.

QUESTION 7

Evaluate your child's present peer group. Does he have some Christian friends? What values does he seem to share with his friends? What influence do you think he has on them? What influence do you think they have on him?

Some other aspects of social needs should be mentioned in addition to peer pressure. Young people at this age are looking for love from friends and family. If it is not found, they may turn to illicit sexual involvement. With awakening sexuality comes an increased desire for tenderness that makes it only too easy to mistake sex for love. One girl confided to a Christian counselor, "I started going to my boyfriend's home every day because my parents never really cared to listen to my problems. He really seemed to care. But eventually we got involved physically in a way that I had never intended to happen. I wish someone had cared at home."

Teenagers are looking for a place to belong and for a place to be accepted. We need to be sure that we communicate this important message to them: you are loved and accepted here at home. Some parents assume that the adolescent does not need them much anymore, except to provide meals and basic care. That is not the case. The adolescent may need his parents more than ever during these years, although he may not be able to articulate his needs.

What are some of the needs of adolescents which parents should be aware of? Teenagers want to be a grown-up. They want us to trust them and respect their choices, even their choice of friends. We should avoid referring to adolescents as children, yet also help them see that they must earn the right to be treated like adults. Since they want independence, they must accept the responsibility that accompanies it. Gradually give them more freedom and responsibility, a little at a time. When they abuse the privileges, take away a little of the freedom and explain the reason. Remember, they are still in the process of becoming adults, so they will act grown up one day and very childlike the next.

Teenagers want to be noticed, and some will do just about anything to gain recognition. Have you ever wondered why a perfectly normal young person would suddenly desire to look so different? The latest and wildest clothes and hair attract attention. Loud music attracts attention. The latest clichés of speech also attract the desired attention, as will crude or abusive language.

Young people are also looking for fulfillment. They may try to fill the void in their lives with the latest music, alcohol, or relationships with the opposite sex. However, the love, acceptance, attention, and fulfillment they seek are only to be found through Jesus Christ.

As young people seek to fulfill these needs, they will inevitably face a variety of enticing temptations. The Scripture offers both examples and promises for the godly person who is willing to stand firm in his faith. In Lesson 11 we will take a closer look at the issue of standing firm against the world.

QUESTION 8

In what ways should parents be involved in the life of their teenager? *(Select all that apply.)*

    A. Do as little as possible for the teenager.

    B. Treat the teenager with respect.

    C. Let the teenager decide how late to stay out at night.

    D. Love and accept the teenager during this stage.

QUESTION 9

What teenage behaviors have you noticed in your culture? What are ways that you can communicate love, acceptance, attention, and fulfillment to a teenager?

Mental Development

In Lesson 2 we learned about the sixth pillar of wisdom: knowledge of the Scriptures applied to life. In order for a teenager to gain wisdom, he must go through a process of applying what he knows to life. In the process of doing this, he will probably question his parents' ideas and values.

Since teens are developing their independence and learning to think for themselves, they may even challenge what you say, asking "Why?" with almost as much frequency as a three-year-old. At times they may do this just to irritate you, but often young people are sincerely looking for answers. They want to know why you believe what you do, or why they are not allowed to do something they are sure "everyone else" is doing. Adolescents need reasonable answers; they will not be content if you simply reply, "Because I said so." Try to be patient and explain your rationale. Keep an open mind to the young person's point of view, and consider legitimate counter-arguments.

The teenager has much to occupy his mind. In addition to the daily interaction with his peers at school, the future also begins to concern teens. They face a lot of decisions regarding schooling, career, and the choice of a mate. Parents need to be available to listen to their teenager whenever he brings up these subjects. Ask probing questions to get him thinking about what he would like to do with his life and where his strengths lie. Encourage him gently to consider what the Lord wants for his life, but do not preach or lecture when you do this.

As teenagers begin to ask many questions, it is important that you do not respond too quickly. Ask him questions; you need to find out what is behind the question, what he thinks. We must demonstrate appreciation that he is thinking and even doubting even though we might be nervous. If he feels he is going to receive a strong response or that his questions are not appreciated or are summarily rejected, that may be the end of his ever asking questions again.

QUESTION 10

Does your child feel free to approach you with his doubts about his faith? With your spouse, think though some situations where your teen did ask a question. How did you respond? Is there anything you could have done differently? Do you need to ask forgiveness for an improper response?

Spiritual Development
QUESTION 11

Take a few moments to recall how you felt physically, emotionally, and spiritually as a teenager. What spiritual struggles did you face? In what ways did your feelings about yourself physically and emotionally impact you?

The spiritual development of an adolescent is closely tied to his physical, social, and mental development. Adolescents are often deeply interested in spiritual issues but tend to have many questions and doubts. During the teenage years a young person may reevaluate the faith of his parents and come to his own conclusions about God and faith in Jesus Christ. He is in the process of internalizing faith, or making it his own. In this process he may have to deal with many doubts and questions.

Doubting God is not necessarily denying God; rather, it often indicates a faith that needs strengthening. It is common for a teenager to question the truth of the indoctrination he has received. He will conduct an intensive self-examination during these years. Encourage your adolescent to articulate his doubts and questions. If he is in the habit of having a daily quiet time, a time of personal Bible reading and prayer, encourage him to read some passages that address his questions. Rather than telling him some pat answers, help him discover for himself what the Bible teaches. Do not expect him to spend an hour in personal quiet time; a short but consistent program of reading God's Word is better than an hour once a month.

Adolescents tend to be hero worshipers. Unfortunately their choice of heroes may not coincide with ours. They may idolize a movie star, a television personality, or a rock singer. Again, we must remind ourselves of the importance of providing good models for teenagers. Studying the life of Christ can encourage young people to compare true values with the false ones offered by the world.

Young people are hungry for a practical faith. They want to see faith in action. Help them to apply biblical principles to their daily experiences at school, work, and home. Encourage them to act out their own faith by helping others who are in need, and take the leadership by providing an example in this area yourself.

What a challenge lies before us as parents and Christian leaders to develop the ability to understand a teenager's world—the thoughts, feelings, conflicts, and experiences common to adolescence. We need to understand the sweeping physical and hormonal changes, the fluctuating moods, and the impact of peer pressure in our teenagers' lives. If we recognize the normality of the adolescent's sometimes abnormal behavior, it will help us to relax and encourage us to commit each roller-coaster day to the Lord.

QUESTION 12

Discuss with your spouse how you can encourage your teenager to develop Christian friends who are a positive influence. Summarize your conclusions in your Life Notebook, and use this as you pray for your teenager.

QUESTION 13

What can your church do to offer support and encouragement to teenagers? How can the church help adolescents deal with feelings of inferiority, emotional struggles, and spiritual questions? Write out your answers and suggestions in your Life Notebook.

Topic 2: Communicating Love and Respect to the Adolescent

We have discussed the need for us as parents to understand our teenager's world. We have talked about the physical and emotional changes in our teenager and about peer pressure. Our focus has been primarily on our teenager, but now we want to shift the focus to the parent. We want to talk about developing the ability to communicate respect and love to our teenager in ways that he can understand and accept.

Loving Your Teenager Unconditionally

A short study on the unconditional love of God may help us understand how to put His love into practice.

Assignment

- Please read the following verses about God's love: Psalm 106:1; 145:15-16; Matthew 5:45; Romans 8:35-39; and 1 Corinthians 13:4-7.
- Please read the following article:

Unconditional Love

As we begin to look at this all-important topic, consider the following thoughts: What would it be like to be loved by someone whose love for you is not influenced by anything you ever did, are now doing, or will do; whose love could never weaken or fluctuate? You can know what it would be like! For God's love for you is not influenced by anything you ever did or will do (Deut 7:6-8; 2 Tim 1:9). His love is unconditional. God chose to love you, and the moment He did, His personal love and happiness became identified or "tied up" with you (Ps 104:31). You became the object of His affection, "the apple of [His] eye" (Ps 17:8). Love does not exist in a vacuum. It must express itself, so God desired to express Himself to you through a personal relationship made possible by the death and resurrection of Jesus Christ.

The love God has for you will never change. He loves you as much today as when He gave His Son for you (Gal 2:20; Tit 2:13-14), and He will keep on giving in love to you (Rom 8:32). God's love will never weaken or fluctuate, for in Him "there is no variation or shadow due to change" (Jas 1:17). His personal love for you is eternal; thus, He loved you before you had any being, with a love that is everlasting (Jer 31:3).

This everlasting love of God has been poured into our hearts through the Holy Spirit who has been given to us (Rom 5:5). You have God's love inside of you to empower you to love one another (1 Jn 4:11). "One another" includes your teenager. If we are to love our teenager as God loves us, then we are to accept him or her unconditionally.

If our love for our teenager depends on certain conditions, if it depends upon his acting in a certain way, we can be sure that he will suffer and we will suffer. He will feel unaccepted and insecure, and we will experience the pain of his withdrawal and isolation from us. Unconditional love, love with no conditions attached, is basic and essential to parenting. It is from within this framework that we can guide our teenager and meet his needs on a daily basis.

Dr. Ross Campbell, a Christian counselor, defines unconditional love for a teenager:

Unconditional love means loving a teenager, no matter what.

- No matter what the teenager looks like

- No matter what his assets, liabilities, and handicaps are

- No matter how he acts

This does not mean that you always like his behavior. Unconditional love means you love your teenager, even when you detest his behavior.

Unconditional love is an ideal that parents must strive for, for our human love, apart from God's strength, falls far short of the standard of 1 Corinthians 13. We are incapable of the type of unconditional love described in this chapter. In our own strength we cannot accept our child or our spouse or anyone else one hundred percent of the time. But we can continue to grow in love, and as we do, our child will be more secure in our love.

Campbell suggests that, while you may not feel love for your teenager every minute of the day, you can work at the goal of loving him unconditionally by constantly reminding yourself of the following:

1. Teenagers are children.

2. Teenagers will tend to act like teenagers.

3. Much of teenage behavior is unpleasant.

---

4. If I do my part as a parent and love them despite their unpleasant behavior, they will be able to mature and give up their immature ways.

5. If I love them only when they please me (conditional love), they will not feel genuinely loved. This in turn will make them feel insecure, damage their self-esteem, and actually prevent them from developing more mature behavior. Therefore, their behavior development is as much my responsibility as theirs.

6. If I love them unconditionally, they will feel good about themselves and be comfortable with themselves. They will be able to control their anxiety and, in turn, their behavior, as they grow into adulthood.

7. If I love them only when they meet my requirements or expectations, they will feel incompetent. They will believe it is fruitless to do their best because it is never enough. Insecurity, anxiety, and low self-esteem will plague them. There will be constant hindrances in their emotional and behavioral growth.

8. For my sake, as a struggling parent, and for the sake of my children, I pray my love for them will be as unconditional as I can make it. The future of my teenagers depends on this foundation.

(Adapted from Campbell, *How to Really Love Your Teen*, 23-26)

Without realizing it, your adolescent is constantly asking, "Do you love me?" He asks it primarily through his behavior, rather than in words. "Do you accept me?" he asks, as he tests the limits of your love. Your answer is absolutely critical. If you answer yes sometimes and no at other times, your teenager's sense of worth may suffer, and he may do things to prove that he is indeed unworthy of acceptance. Your answer to that single critical question, "Do you accept me?" can greatly influence your teenager's basic attitude toward life.

Many parents do not answer yes to this question. Some do love and accept their teenagers, but they do not know how to convey this love and acceptance in a way that a teenager can understand. Teenagers are primarily behavior oriented, while adults are primarily verbally oriented. Let us use an illustration to explain this. If you called your wife on the phone and said to her, "Honey, I just wanted to tell you how much I love you," she would be elated. But if you called your nine-year-old son and said, "Hi, this is your daddy. I just wanted to tell you I love you," his reaction would probably be quite different. He might say in a puzzled voice, "Yes, Daddy, but why did you call?"

Verbal expressions of love and acceptance are deeply meaningful to your wife; she has learned to value them. Your son is still more behaviorally oriented. While your verbal expression of love to him is important, it is simply insufficient to make him really feel accepted emotionally. A thirteen-year-old's reaction would still be similar to a nine-year-old's. The teenager needs to hear you say "I love you," but it is not enough. For your teenager to know and feel that you love him, you must also show him by your actions that you accept him (preceding three paragraphs based on Campbell, 26-27).

Five teenagers were asked how they knew that their parents loved them. These were their answers:

1. I know my parents love me because they help me with my studies.

2. My mother got up at six o'clock in the morning to study with me for my history test.

3. My dad gave me the money to buy a new sweater, and he went without a new sweater because he knew I wanted one so much.

4. My mother always invites my friends to the house and cooks for them and cooks for me and makes me feel good.

5. My parents always take time to listen to me and to talk to me, and to encourage me to be my best.

Notice the common element in each of these answers. The teenagers were convinced of their parents' love by specific actions. Is that not what convinces us that God loves us, His specific act of sending His Son to die in our place? God loves us unconditionally, and He showed it. He wants us to learn to love and accept our teenagers unconditionally and to show it.

QUESTION 14

Based on how God's love is described in the verses you read, reflect on ways God expresses His love to you personally.

QUESTION 15

How do you show love in physical ways to your family?

According to Romans 5:6-8, Ephesians 2:8-9, and 2 Timothy 1:9, in no way did we earn or deserve this life-giving demonstration of God's love.

QUESTION 16

Jesus Christ gave the parable of the prodigal son (Lk 15:11-32) to illustrate God's love. What do you learn about God's love through this parable? *(Select all that apply.)*

A. It is quick to forgive.

B. It is limited to one person at a time.

C. It brings restoration.

D. It is extravagant.

E. It is removed when we squander His gifts.

QUESTION 17

Can any situation, action or anything others do to you keep God from loving you (Rom 8:35-39)? Should anything your teenager does or any situation your teenager finds himself in keep you from loving your teenager? Why? Record your responses in your Life Notebook.

When we begin to comprehend the depth and the breadth of the love of God for us, we can begin to feel secure emotionally. Our deepest emotional needs can only be filled by the Lord. We as parents help meet our children's emotional needs by striving to love them unconditionally. Dr. Campbell visualizes this as a process of filling a child's "emotional tank."

> Your teenager has an emotional tank. This tank is figurative, of course, but the concept is very real. Your teenager has certain emotional needs, and whether these emotional needs are met (through love, understanding, discipline, etc.) helps determine how he feels— whether he is content, angry, depressed, or joyful. Also, it strongly affects his behavior— whether he is obedient, disobedient, whiny, perky, playful, or withdrawn. Naturally, the fuller the tank, the more positive the feelings and the better the behavior. . . *Only if the emotional tank is full, can a teenager be expected to be his best and do his best.* It is your responsibility as a parent to do all you can to keep the emotional tank full. (Campbell, 27)

Earlier we pointed out that teenagers are still children emotionally. In some ways we might compare a teenager with a two-year-old. Both a teenager and a two-year-old have a drive for independence, and figuratively speaking, both have an emotional tank. Each will strive for independence, drawing on energy from the emotional tank. When the emotional tank is empty, both the teenager and the two-year-old will return to the parent for a refill so they can again strive for independence.

For example, suppose a mother brings her two-year-old to a strange place, such as a school meeting. At first, the child may cling to his mother for emotional support. When he receives this, his emotional tank fills up. Gradually the child may begin exerting his independence by exploring a bit. At first, he may simply stand next to his mother and look around, then he may venture out farther and farther from mother. Eventually, as his emotional tank becomes empty again, the child will seek his mother once more for a refill—seeking eye contact, physical contact, and her focused attention. Now the child is again ready to try his independence.

A teenager uses different means for exerting his drive for independence, but he still needs the energy from his emotional tank to do this. Where should he go to get his emotional tank refilled? To his parents.

> A teenager will strive for independence in typical adolescent ways—doing things by himself, going places without family, testing parental rules. But he will eventually run out of emotional gasoline and come back to the parent for emotional maintenance—for a refill. This is what we want, as parents of teenagers. We want our adolescent to feel free to come to us for emotional maintenance when he needs it. (Campbell, 29)

This refilling is important for teenagers to be able to function at their best and grow to be their best. With full emotional tanks they feel the security and self-confidence needed to cope with peer pressure and to uphold moral values. While the emotional refilling is taking place, it is possible to keep open lines of communication between parents and teenagers. When a teenager comes to refill his tank and to seek parental love, vital communication is so much easier.

QUESTION 18

Summarize in your own words what Dr. Campbell means by an "emotional tank." Discuss with your spouse how full you think your child's emotional tank is and some ways you could constructively fill it to the brim. How can you apply what you learned about God's unconditional love to your relationship with your teenager?

Giving "Focused Attention"

We have said that teenagers are behavior-oriented and need to be shown that they are loved unconditionally. One way to show our teenagers that we love them is to communicate that we want to be with them and to give them our full attention. Campbell refers to this as giving "focused attention" to your teenager. This does not mean simply sitting in the same room watching television with him but giving him concentrated attention, really listening to him.

Focused attention means giving your teenager full, undivided attention in such a way that he feels truly loved, that he knows he is so valuable in his own right that he warrants your watchfulness, appreciation, and uncompromising regard. Focused attention makes your teenager feel that he is the most important person in the world to you, his parents.

Doing this can be demanding. There are times when a teenager desperately needs focused attention and parents feel least like giving it. As parents of teenagers, we must make it a priority to give them this kind of attention. We must ask ourselves, "What are the priorities in my life? Where do my children fit in?" We must determine this; otherwise it is easy to let our children take a low priority and suffer from some degree of neglect.

No one else can decide for us what is important. If we believe that our children are truly important, we must take advantage of both planned and spontaneous opportunities to meet our teenager's needs. Opportunities will be fewer than you think. Children are teenagers for such a short time.

As you think about your priorities, evaluate whether or not you have made your relationship with God the top priority in your life. At the beginning of the course we talked about priorities. God must be first in the believer's life, and the family core (the husband-wife relationship) must also have a high priority. Your relationship with your children, while never taking precedence over your relationship with God or your spouse, must be among the highest of priorities. It is easy to say that our children are a high priority, but the proof is in our commitment to spend time with them and give them focused attention when we are with them.

How do you give focused attention? First, set aside some time to be alone with your teenager. Finding time to be alone with a busy teenager, when you can both be free from other distractions, is not easy, but it is essential to good communication.

How do we find time to be available to them in a very busy schedule? It may work best to set a specific time with your teenager to do something together, whether it is taking a walk, going on a picnic together, or going to a music recital together. Whatever the activity, the important thing is to be alone, just the two of you, to spend time together when you can talk without interruption.

Perhaps you can invite your son or daughter to come along when you have a tedious drive in the car. One family makes it a practice to read books together with their teenager and discuss what they have read. Teenagers need this time with us, and we need the time with them to focus our love and attention on them.

Sometimes your teenager may want to talk when it is not very convenient—at midnight, for example, when you are eager to get to bed. Yet it may be more important to sacrifice the sleep to show him that you are available and that you care. Perhaps you have tried to set aside time to be with your teenager, but he or she responded with silence and had little to say. Do not try to force communication; it seldom works. Be pleasant, be available, and remember that there may be other times when your child will open up to you if you allow him the freedom to be himself.

Because our teenagers are striving for independence, they may sometimes communicate to us that they do not want to spend time with us. Yet exactly the opposite is true.

Adolescents need parental time and attention as never before. They are facing strong influences daily and, unfortunately, many of these influences are unhealthy, unwholesome, and sometimes evil. If you want your teenager to be able to cope with today's world, you must spend constructive time with him; especially when he is going through adolescent turmoil. If you do take the time to meet these needs, your teenager will gain the confidence and personal integrity to think for himself about the kind of values he will live by. He will develop strength to stand up against divisive influences from people who have little or no regard for him, but simply want to use him.

It may not be easy to give focused attention to teenagers when they act as though they do not really want it. Yet by giving focused attention, we can communicate respect and love to our teenagers in a way that they can understand.

QUESTION 19

Which of the following are ways suggested in this lesson to communicate love and respect to your teenager? *(Select all that apply.)*

    A. Set a specific time to do something together

    B. Focus on ministry in your church

    C. Encourage your teenager to spend more time with friends

    D. Let your teenager know that you are available to talk

QUESTION 20

If you are the parent of a teenager, when was the last time you had a special time with your teenager, just the two of you? Ask your teenager to do something special with you, or communicate that you want to spend some time with him or her. Be prepared to share the results or response you noted at the next meeting.

Concentrating on the Positive

A teenager is like a tapestry that is about three-fourths completed. A design is gradually taking shape, but parents are often so busy concentrating on those threads that are still missing that they do not appreciate the lovely pattern that is coming together. Of course, we are not to ignore the gaps and the misplaced threads that we see in the tapestry, but God wants us to concentrate on the positive and appreciate the design and workmanship of the tapestry as it gradually unfolds.

Assignment

- Memorize Philippians 4:8.

- Please read the following article:

Focus on the Positive

When we concentrate only on the negative things in our teenager, we can devastate and even destroy him. One teenager wrote this letter about his parents.

> Dear _____
>
> I got one A, two Cs, and a D on my report card, which is great for a guy like me. My parents screamed their heads off about the D.
>
> I built a pretty good model plane. All they saw is the mess in my room. I babysat my little brother the other day (for free). Instead of thanking me, they yelled because Larry broke the peanut jar. If I'd grabbed it instead of Larry, he would have fallen off the counter.
>
> They tell me I'm clumsy, lazy, sloppy, and "can't you do anything right?" Then they lecture me on how I should change. I know I'm dumb and awkward. They don't have to rub it in. Sometimes I feel like I'm an eggshell—if I get one more knock, I'll crack.
>
> -About to Give Up

(Letter adapted from Botel, 21)

This letter shows how easy it is for parents to make negative statements that can hurt an adolescent deeply. Christian counselor Dr. Narramore tells parents that it takes about seven compliments to counteract just one negative comment (Narramore, 124). If you were to keep a record for the next twenty-four hours of the number of positive and negative statements you made to your teenager, would there be more positives or negatives?

> Parents need to emphasize the positive—to confirm the things the kid does well, and for the most part, ignore the things he does poorly. It is far better to put the accent on the positive rather than to bandage up the negative. (Kesler and Beers, 285)

Look at the matter this way: If we parents do not build up our teenagers, who will? His or her friends? Probably not. Who will praise him? His teachers? Perhaps some teachers will encourage, build up, and praise their students. But there are also those who motivate students by criticizing, offering negative comments such as, "Can't you do better than that? Are you stupid? Your writing looks like a five-year-old's! How do your parents put up with you?"

Parents, we are the ones who care. Through the power of Christ we can love a sometimes unlovable, often irrational teenager.

> We have the potential to be one of the most positive reinforcing agents in our child's life. …Praise is affirming what your teen is becoming. Goethe, the great German philosopher, said, "If you treat a man as he is, he will stay as he is, but if you treat him as if he were what he ought to be and could be, he will become that bigger and better man." (Arp, pp. 58-59 [emphasis in original omitted].)

How does Goethe's quote relate to our teenagers? When your teenager shows real maturity or good judgment, give him a sincere compliment. Say something like, "I think you're going to be an excellent Bible study leader," or "You are going to make a wonderful wife someday. You are so caring and sensitive to others' needs." "I'm proud of you for staying home and studying for your test when I know you would rather have gone with your friends. It shows that you really are learning to make wise choices." These are not examples of flattery, which is insincere praise and without basis, but they are encouraging statements of sincere praise.

Philippians 4:8 is a key verse on the subject of dwelling on the positive.

> Finally, brethren, whatever is true, whatever is honorable, whatever is right, whatever is pure, whatever is lovely, whatever is of good repute, if there is any excellence and if anything worthy of praise, let your mind dwell on these things.

Sadly, too many of us have taken this passage and retranslated it. Instead of dwelling on the positive about our teens, this verse reads for us:

> Finally, brethren, if there is anything wrong, if there is anything that is not just the way we want it, if there is anything that is ungracious, if there is anything that is impure or unlovely, if there is anything that is not excellent, if there is anything that is not praiseworthy, think on these things.

When we think on these negative things, that is exactly what comes out of our mouths to our teenagers.

God instructs us to dwell on the positive. Notice that He does not say, "if **everything** is excellent, and if **everything** is noteworthy and praiseworthy." He says, if there is **any** excellence, if there is **anything** worthy of praise, think on these things. We need to think on the positive things in our teens and then let them know what we think is positive.

Praise and encouragement must be verbalized. We can have all kinds of nice thoughts about our teenagers, but thoughts have little effect unless we put them into words that can build someone up.

A group of mothers was studying how to praise their families better and they sadly admitted that they lacked the habit of encouraging their teens. They committed to God and to each other to make praise a habit and began by praising their children five times the first week. One mom at the end of the first week said, "It felt so strange to hear the words of encouragement and praise come out of my lips." It may seem strange at first, but let's do it anyway. Praise needs to become a daily verbal habit (Arp, p. 60).

You may want to praise your teenager in special ways at times. Some parents have done things like making a special plaque for a child on her birthday. One mother sewed a picture for her daughter's room, using each of the letters of the daughter's name to depict a good quality her parents noticed in her life.

Another idea is to write a child a birthday letter. On their son's sixteenth birthday, one family wrote a letter that said:

> On the occasion of your sixteenth birthday, we want to share with you sixteen things we admire about you.
>
> 1. Pleasing personality
>
> 2. Sensitivity to others
>
> 3. Commitment to our family
>
> 4. Inquisitive mind
>
> 5. Boldness in sharing your faith
>
> 6. Spiritual sensitivity to God
>
> 7. Wittiness and good sense of humor
>
> 8. Neatness and organization
>
> 9. Leadership ability
>
> 10. Willingness to stand alone in the midst of peer pressure
>
> 11. Academic excellence
>
> 12 Athletic ability
>
> 13. Good sportsmanship
>
> 14. Honesty and truthfulness
>
> 15. Commitment to God
>
> 16. Being a good model for others to follow

We want you to know we love and appreciate you. Happy Birthday!

> Love,
> Mom and Dad (Arp, 64)

How do you think the teenager felt when he received that letter? One seventeen-year-old girl whose father wrote her a letter of praise like this on her birthday was so excited that she framed the letter and put it on her wall herself. She still treasures it.

Giving a special gift of praise can encourage your teenager to think, "My parents think I am full of positive qualities. Maybe I really am."

Our lives are sprinkled with disappointments, hurts, and frustrations. The adolescent years are times that are especially vulnerable to hurts and hard knocks. If we are willing to sprinkle our adolescents' lives generously with encouragement and concentrate on their good points, we can be positive reinforcing agents who say, "You are very special. You are a person of value. I'm so glad I'm your mom [or dad]!"

Focusing on the Lovely

QUESTION 21

Give your teenager one honest compliment each day this week. List things for which you can compliment your teen. Plan and write down one special thing you are going to do this week, such as writing a note of praise, or something else meaningful to your teen. Record how he or she responded in your Life Notebook.

Topic 3: The Pillar of Discipline

Just as God's love involves discipline, so our expression of love toward our teenager should include discipline. God is not afraid to discipline us when we need to be redirected for our good (Heb 12:6). As our children move into adolescence, it is important to realize that they still need discipline. But our methods of discipline must change as our children mature. In Lesson 7 we will look at the subject of discipline in more detail, but at this point let us consider some of the issues involved in the discipline of adolescents.

Parents often raise the question of whether adolescents need discipline. The answer is yes. Discipline provides security for a teenager. Firm, fair, and reasonable discipline gives teenagers the knowledge that they belong to the family. They know that someone cares enough to set some limits for them. Defining limits demonstrates love and concern. The real question we should be concerned with is not whether to discipline adolescents but how to discipline them.

Assignment

- Please read the following article:

Increasing Privileges and Responsibilities

As our children mature, physical discipline becomes not only difficult but ineffective. It is important, though, that our teenagers experience consequences for their behavior—positive consequences for responsible behavior and negative consequences for irresponsible behavior. This is the way that young people learn to be responsible. Recall that the goal of discipline is to prepare our teenagers to live responsible lives on their own.

A parent's goal then should be to move gradually from restrictiveness toward independence. We can gradually allow more independence as our teenager shows responsibility in handling more freedom and as he or she earns our trust.

As the maturing child demonstrates he can be trusted to behave responsibly, parents can increase certain privileges and decrease the amount of control that they exercise over the adolescent. As a child proves trustworthy, your response should be to trust him more. In general parents will begin the early adolescent years using fairly restrictive discipline and gradually add privileges as a child shows that he can be trusted. Keep in mind that it is difficult to rescind a particular freedom once you have granted it to your child, even if he acts irresponsible at times. If this happens, you can temporarily restrict the privilege, but the teenager will always feel that he has that particular right because initially you granted it, even if you did grant it prematurely.

Most teenagers are in desperate need of being treated with respect and dignity. They are struggling with low self-esteem and trying to develop a sense of personal identity. They are also at an age when they are keenly aware of what is fair and just. Your disciplinary methods should reflect your desire to treat your adolescent with dignity and fairness.

You can demonstrate respect and dignity by communicating clearly with your young adolescent. He needs to know that you realize he wants more freedom in making decisions and fewer restrictions. Choose a time to talk with your child, to address the conflicts he might be experiencing, and periodically to clearly define the boundaries and limits for him. Tell your child you respect him and love him and desire for him to come to a point where he no longer needs parental control. But let him know that in the meantime you must be obedient to God in your responsibility to prepare him for such a day.

It would also be good to explain that your methods of discipline from now on will not include physical punishment or spanking but will be in the form of restrictions when irresponsible behavior demands a response. Most children will view this as fair but will still push against those limits at times to see if they really stand. Adolescents need to discover for themselves if the boundaries are really there or if they can be moved under pressure. This is where consistency on our part is important.

An important point to keep in mind is that punishment should suit the crime. A negative consequence or restriction should fit the violation. For instance, if a teenager fails to carry out his home responsibilities, such as cleaning his room or taking out garbage, restricting him from going out after school for six months is overreacting. This would discourage a child completely and possibly provoke open rebellion. On the other hand, some parents routinely nag and argue with their child but never deny a privilege or restrict him in order to curb his irresponsible behavior. This cycle of nagging accomplishes nothing, except to encourage further irresponsibility.

The simple approach is to say, "Son, until your room is cleaned (or your chores or school work are finished), you will be denied outside social activities." When the chores are finished, the restrictions should be immediately lifted. This is far more motivating for a teenager than being confined for six months whether he does his chores or not. It is also much easier for the parent to be consistent in applying the restriction. If you confined him for six months, you would surely be tempted to give in "just once" to his request to go out. It is important to use good judgment and fairness as you choose discipline to match the offense.

As Christian parents we should never use spiritual weapons as punishment. Never assign Scripture memorization or take away church activities as a form of punishment. The child who is forced to memorize verses pertaining to a particular offense that he has committed may learn to hate Scripture rather than love it and to view God in very negative terms. Encourage your child to memorize helpful verses during your times of family devotions when the memory work is not tied in with some wrong he has done.

As an adolescent grows, his responsibilities at home should increase. The adolescent may have responsibilities such as keeping a clean room, doing chores, finishing school work, or taking care of a younger sibling. The older adolescent can take on more adult decisions, such as deciding how he wants to spend his money, choosing appropriate friends, and establishing a reasonable curfew. Parents should think through how they plan to reward and discipline the adolescent when he violates the boundaries set up for him or acts irresponsibly. To ensure fairness and be sure that the teenager will learn from discipline, it might even be helpful to put the guidelines into writing; spell out the positive and negative consequences of a given course of action.

Let us say that the curfew hour you have established for your sixteen-year-old is ten o'clock. You can indicate that, if the teenager is consistent in obeying this and if he contacts you to ask for special permission on occasions when he cannot get home on time, then you will move the curfew to eleven o'clock when he is seventeen. You might also convey to him that, if he violates the curfew without permission, he will have to miss a social evening with his friends.

The important thing is communicating both firmness and fairness to the teenager. If he sees that you earnestly desire to give him more freedom, he will be more inclined to cooperate rather than lose privileges. Do all you can to keep communication open; discuss problems as they arise rather than letting tensions build until you or your teen explodes.

Lastly, but probably the most important, remember to immerse your child and yourself in prayer. Ask God for wisdom. His discipline is always fair; He never disciplines us more than we can bear, nor does He ignore discipline when it is needed for our good, as we saw in Hebrews 12:6. Ask God to help you find the proper balance between control and freedom with your adolescent. Do not be discouraged if you are experiencing problems in discipline, but lay out before God all your fears and questions.

Raising a child is not an easy task, particularly now when you are in the transition stage of releasing all rights of ownership to him. The Bible encourages us with these words: "And let us not lose heart in doing good, for in due time we shall reap if we do not grow weary" (Gal 6:9).

Let us summarize what we have said about discipline.

1. As children move into adolescence, physical discipline is ineffective, and we need to change our methods to suit the age of the child.

2. Defined limits and fair disciplinary actions provide security as well as guidance.

3. Positive consequences are as important for reinforcing responsible behavior as negative consequences are for irresponsible behavior. They teach our children that freedom requires responsible behavior.

4. Show respect and dignity to your adolescent in the process of discipline.

5. Communicate and clearly define the positive privileges that go with responsible behavior and the negative consequences that must be imposed as a result of irresponsible behavior.

6. Be fair and consistent. If you overreact, admit it, and apologize to your child.

7. The goal of discipline is to prepare our children to live responsibly without us.

8. Pray for wisdom.

QUESTION 22

Think through your present approach to disciplining adolescents or the approach of your parents when you were a teen. How does this approach compare with the approach outlined in the article? Discuss with your spouse what changes you might like to make. If you have no adolescents at home, reflect on how this approach to discipline compares with the approach your parents used when you were a teenager. Write your responses in your Life Notebook.

Lesson 6 Self Check

QUESTION 1

The physiological changes of adolescence are the basis for many of the personality changes and problems that teenagers experience. *True or False?*

QUESTION 2

An adolescent should be discouraged from expressing doubts about his faith. *True or False?*

QUESTION 3

The hormonal changes associated with puberty can upset one's entire emotional balance, causing some teenagers to go through rather lengthy periods of emotional upset. *True or False?*

QUESTION 4

Feelings of inferiority are often characteristic of the adolescent years and it is important that adolescents realize that they are not alone. *True or False?*

QUESTION 5

Emotional support from an adolescent's peer group is very important. *True or False?*

QUESTION 6

Parents need to emphasize the positive, to confirm the things the teenager does well, and for the most part, focus much less on the things he does poorly. *True or False?*

QUESTION 7

Which of the following is a key verse on the subject of dwelling on the positive that every parent should memorize and apply to relationship to their adolescent?

    A. John 3:16

    B. Romans 8:28

    C. Philippians 4:8

    D. Colossians 1:23

QUESTION 8

As the maturing child demonstrates he can be trusted to behave responsibly, parents can increase privileges and decrease the amount of control. *True or False?*

QUESTION 9

As our children mature, physical discipline is still a very effective method of changing bad behavior. *True or False?*

QUESTION 10

Unconditional love means you love your teenager, even when you detest his behavior. *True or False?*

Lesson 6 Answers to Questions

QUESTION 1: *Your answer*

QUESTION 2
    A. For a girl, being exceptionally tall
    B. Clumsiness in physical activities

QUESTION 3: *Your answer*

QUESTION 4: *Your answer*

QUESTION 5: *Your answer*

QUESTION 6: *Your answer*

QUESTION 7: *Your answer*

QUESTION 8
    B. Treat the teenager with respect.
    D. Love and accept the teenager during this stage.

QUESTION 9: *Your answer*

QUESTION 10: *Your answer*

QUESTION 11: *Your answer*

QUESTION 12: *Your answer*

QUESTION 13: *Your answer*

QUESTION 14: *Your answer*

QUESTION 15: *Your answer*

QUESTION 16
    A. It is quick to forgive.
    C. It brings restoration.
    D. It is extravagant.

QUESTION 17: *Your answer*

QUESTION 18: *Your answer*

QUESTION 19
    A. Set a specific time to do something together
    D. Let your teenager know that you are available to talk

QUESTION 20: *Your answer*

QUESTION 21: *Your answer*

QUESTION 22: *Your answer*

Lesson 6 Self Check Answers

QUESTION 1: True
QUESTION 2: False
QUESTION 3: True
QUESTION 4: True
QUESTION 5: True
QUESTION 6: True
QUESTION 7
    C. Philippians 4:8
QUESTION 8: True
QUESTION 9: False
QUESTION 10: True

Unit 3: Disciplining in Love

The area of discipline is often uppermost in parents' minds when they think of training their children. This is right and good if discipline is properly viewed as a positive means used to effect positive behavior. Regardless of the discipline used, the child still retains a freedom of choice. He can accept discipline and align his behavior and attitudes with it, or he can reject it. This choice is his, not ours, but it is clearly the parents' responsibility to discipline, and to do it in love.

This unit examines the Pillar of Discipline and its application. Various methods of discipline are presented, and emphasis is placed on shaping the child's will without breaking his spirit. In Lesson 7 we will study biblical principles of discipline, a biblical definition of discipline and how to implement discipline. Lesson 8 deals with the problems peculiar to children who are what we have termed strong-willed and who often challenge parental authority. Lesson 9 shows what can happen when an adolescent determines to reject his parents' authority and values, choosing instead a path of rebellion. The emphasis in all three lessons is twofold:

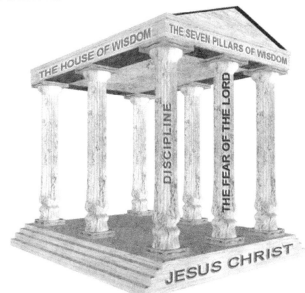

1. The parent's responsibility is to train and discipline is part of the training process

2. The child's responsibility is to respond to training

In other words, both parent and child share the responsibility for the child's development to maturity.

Unit Outline

Lesson 7: Discipline

Lesson 8: The Strong-Willed Child

Lesson 9: The Rebellious Adolescent

Unit Objectives

By the end of this unit, you will be able to do the following:

- Take steps to apply proper discipline, administered in love, in the effective training of children

- Evaluate your application of discipline and discern specific areas you need to work on

- Suggest some ideas on how to maintain good communication with, and demonstrate love and respect toward, children

- Describe the ways in which strong-willed children provide a special challenge to parents

Lesson 7: Discipline

Some parents mistakenly equate spanking with discipline. There are many ways of disciplining a child other than spanking. Each method of discipline has its advantages and its advocates. How is the average parent to decide which method to use in a given situation? What do I do when my eighteen-month-old throws a tantrum, when my three-year-old refuses to eat, when my eight-year-old dawdles about doing his homework, or when my thirteen-year-old comes home late? Obviously, all of these situations do not call for the same type of discipline.

In this lesson we will look at the nature of discipline and its application. We will deal with questions such as:

- What is discipline?
- How can I determine what type of discipline to apply?
- When do I spank?
- How do I discipline without breaking the child's spirit?

Lesson Outline

Topic 1: The Nature of Discipline

Uses of Discipline

The Goal of Discipline

Punishment Differs from Discipline

Break the Will, Not the Spirit

Topic 2: The Application of Discipline

Begin Early

Control Without Nagging

Support Your Spouse in the Discipline Process

Distinguish Willful Defiance from Childish Irresponsibility

Distinguish Defiance From Emotional Problems

Characteristics of Correction

Topic 3: The Rod

Topic 4: A Summary of Discipline

Topic 5: Project

Lesson Objectives

By the end of this lesson, you will be able to do the following:

- Explain the difference between corrective discipline and punishment
- Distinguish between willful defiance and childish irresponsibility
- Take steps to correct your children with confidence
- Make plans to improve your communication with your children, developing attitudes of love, acceptance, and respect

Topic 1: The Nature of Discipline

Parents generally think of discipline as meaning correction or punishment. But discipline involves much more than punishment. The English word "discipline" comes from the same root word as the word "disciple," that is, a learner or follower. The New Testament Greek word *paideia* denotes the general upbringing and handling of a child while he is growing toward maturity. Because the child has not reached maturity, he needs direction, teaching, instruction, and a certain measure of correction or even chastisement.

While we often think of discipline in terms of punishment, discipline should more accurately be associated with the concept of guidance. A "disciplinarian" is one who teaches or guides, promoting self-control, character, orderliness, and some measure of efficiency in the disciple.

Children need discipline for several reasons. Proverbs 1:4 implies that a child lacks knowledge and discretion. This means that, as he gradually learns about the world and his place in it, he must be guided or disciplined in order to develop thought patterns characterized by good judgment and discretion. Psalm 51:5 indicates that a child is born in iniquity or sin; his natural state is one of rebellion against God. This rebellion needs to be conquered through Jesus Christ. One of the goals of discipline is to help a child learn self-control, to gain self-discipline.

Uses of Discipline

In Lesson 2 we mentioned that the Hebrew word for discipline, *musar*, included the idea of instruction as well as correction. A goal throughout this course has been that of instructing and training a child to grow up to behave and live as a wise, godly individual. We are striving to create thirst in the child to do what is right and thereby to prevent serious problems later on. Part of discipline involves guidance.

For guidance to be effective, it is important for the child to develop a strong relationship with the guide. If you were setting out for the first time on a mountain climbing expedition, your faith in the guide would be a very important aspect of your willingness to go. Similarly, children need to be able to trust and rely on the guide who walks with them through life. A parent needs to cultivate a relationship of trust and mutual respect with his children. This involves spending time with his children and staying in constant communication with them.

QUESTION 1

Check yourself on the current level of your communication with your children by answering the following questions:

1. When was the last time I played with my children?

2. When was the last time I just sat and listened to my children?

3. When was the last time I showed physical affection to my children?

4. When was the last time I did something individually with each child?

5. When was the last time I helped my children work through a personal problem or decision?

If your answers were mostly negative, make plans to change your relationship for the better. Write down some specific ideas on what you plan to do with your children to improve your relationship. Describe one concrete step you took to accomplish this in your Life Notebook.

While parents are responsible to God to guide their children using instruction and modeling, such training may be ignored or rejected by the child at times. A parent's response will then be to correct their child's behavior; this is also a use of discipline.

QUESTION 2

The book of Proverbs was written for parents to help them raise their children. Read the following passages and match the Scripture with the command to children.

Scripture	Command to Children
Proverbs 2:1	Pay attention
Proverbs 3:1	Keep my words
Proverbs 4:1	Do not forget my teaching
Proverbs 7:1	Receive my words

Phrases like "pay attention" and "do not forget" make it apparent that a child is likely to forget the discipline and instruction of his parents at times and that he may reject it at others. When this happens, how should parents respond? We should correct.

The goal of discipline used to correct is the same as discipline used to guide: to create a thirst or desire for doing what is right and to inculcate the self-motivation to do what is right. The emphasis in correcting is eliminating unacceptable behavior in order to draw forth acceptable behavior. Thus, it is both punitive and instructive in nature. It is punitive in that it often inflicts a necessary penalty for unacceptable behavior; it is instructive in that its goal is to promote positive behavior and attitudes.

The Goal of Discipline

Discipline should have a positive end in view. This is consistent with the way in which God deals with us as His children. He does not simply lash out at us when He has had enough, as some parents do.

QUESTION 3

We should view discipline of our children in a manner similar to how our Heavenly Father disciplines us. Based on Hebrews 12:10 what would you say the ultimate goal should be for the discipline of our children?

Punishment Differs from Discipline

In view of these goals, discipline can be seen in a new light. Discipline should properly be seen as more than simply punishment. The differences between discipline and punishment are summarized in the chart below.

	Punishment	Corrective Discipline
Purpose	To inflict penalty for an offense	To train for correction and maturity; to correct unacceptable behavior and promote positive growth
Focus	On the past: on the misbehavior	On the past: on the misbehavior or poor attitude On the future: On anticipated change in behavior and attitude
Attitude of Parent	May be one of anger and frustration	Righteous indignation combined with love and concern
Resulting Emotion in Child	Fear and guilt, possible hostility or desire for revenge	Security: a sense of self-worth in being loved and forgiven

QUESTION 4

Two-year-old Liling Chen has just pulled all the pots and pans from the kitchen. Discovering the mess, her mother yells angrily, "How many times have I told you to stay out of there? You deserve a spanking!" She gives Liling a few good swats on her bottom and sends her to her room. Head down and teary-eyed, Liling goes to her room. Mrs. Chen _____ Liling for her actions.

    A. Encouraged

    B. Disciplined

    C. Ignored

    D. Punished

QUESTION 5

Raj Safou has just emptied the contents of mother's cupboard onto the floor. Arriving on the scene, Mrs. Safou says in a calm but firm voice, "Raj, Mother has told you not to put her pans on the floor. I will have to spank you so you will remember not to do it again!" With that she gives Raj a swat on his bottom and says lovingly, "Now let's help Mother pick them up." Raj cries a little, and his mother assures him that she loves him. In a few minutes Raj is ready to help his mother pick things up. Mrs. Safou _____ her child.

    A. Disciplined

    B. Ignored

    C. Punished

    D. Encouraged

These situations are similar; both children were physically spanked. But there were several differences. Mrs. Chen spanked Liling as a penalty for misdeeds. She was angry and frustrated at the moment of punishment. Liling went to her room obediently, but she may be sitting there pouting and thinking dark thoughts about Mommy. Mrs. Safou also spanked Raj as punishment for his misbehavior, but by taking time to explain to her son, she made it clear that her motive was that he learn correct behavior from this experience. She remained calm and in control of herself, not punishing in anger. She invited him to help her pick things up—a constructive way of redirecting his behavior and restoring his dignity by helping. She was training him to be obedient for his own good.

Mrs. Safou's example of discipline parallels the way God deals with us as His children. God does not punish us to even the score for our disobedience, but that we might learn and grow.

QUESTION 6

Read Proverbs 3:11-12. These verses indicate the father's loving motive in correction and the son's proper response—not despising correction but receiving it. This is the essence of corrective discipline: its focus is on instruction, and its motivation is love and desire for the good of the child. Discuss with your spouse how you and your spouse have succeeded or failed in following this pattern. Reflect on a plan of action that you will implement together. Record your ideas in your Life Notebook.

Break the Will, Not the Spirit

Babies come into the world with a will, which varies in strength from one child to the next. Parents need to shape the will of the child gently but firmly, while protecting the child's spirit. The child needs to learn discernment and gain the ability to make wise decisions. These abilities are the result of the shaping of the child's will. At the same time he needs to gain a proper perspective of who he is, understanding his value as a child of God and his dignity as a person created in God's image.

Wounding a Child's Spirit

QUESTION 7

Read Ephesians 6:4. This is a very important passage on child discipline. Discuss with your spouse in what ways you both have provoked your children. Also, what would it mean in your household to implement the two positive aspects of discipline mentioned in this verse? Record your thoughts in your Life Notebook.

It is very important to understand the difference between breaking the **spirit** of the child, and breaking his **will**. The human spirit is exceedingly fragile at all ages and must be handled with care. It involves a person's view of himself and his personal worth. A parent can damage his child's spirit very easily—by ridicule, disrespect, threats to withdraw love, and by verbal rejection. Anything that depreciates his self-esteem is costly to his spirit.

QUESTION 8

Look up the following verses related to a broken spirit, and summarize what they say: Proverbs 12:25; 15:4; 17:22; 18:14; Psalm 143:3-4. How did David deal with his crushed spirit in Psalm 143:5-12? Record your thoughts in your Life Notebook.

When Scripture speaks of the spirit of an individual being broken (Prov 15:13), it means that his inner life is in despondency or despair. Self-confidence is shattered; the person is discouraged, and his mind can find no pleasant thought. It is sad to think that parents can break the spirit of a child and bring him to such a point, but it happens.

Read the following passages and match the passage on the left with the family situation to which it applies on the right.

Scripture	*Situation*
Matthew 7:3-5	When forgiveness is unattainable
1 Corinthians 13:1	When words tear down instead of build up
Ephesians 4:29	When those in authority can never admit to being wrong
Ephesians 4:32	When obedience is demanded but love is withheld
Philippians 4:8	When failure is accentuated over success
Colossians 3:8	When harshness and anger replace gentleness, humility, and patience

When we as parents remember to demonstrate the fruit of the Spirit as we carry out our parental responsibilities, we will guard against destroying the fragile flower of our child's spirit. In a climate of love, joy, peace, patience, and gentleness, that flower will be nurtured and grow until it blossoms in beauty.

Topic 2: The Application of Discipline

No two situations involving corrective discipline are exactly alike. There is always some extenuating circumstance or some new twist to the problem that demands a different response from the parent. Our purpose in this topic is to develop a general philosophy of corrective discipline to use as a basis for case-by-case treatment.

Begin Early

It is important to begin disciplining children during the early years. As soon as a child begins to crawl or walk, he is old enough to begin to learn that there are limits or boundaries to life.

There is a critical period during the first four or five years of a child's life when he can be taught proper attitudes. These early concepts become rather permanent. When the opportunity of those years is missed, however, the prime receptivity usually vanishes, never to return.

> I believe that if it is desirable for children to be kind, appreciative, and pleasant, those qualities should be taught—not hoped for. If we want to see honesty, truthfulness, and unselfishness in our offspring, then these characteristics should be the conscious objectives of our early instructional process. …We cannot expect the coveted behavior to appear magically if we have not done our early homework. (Dobson, *The New Dare to Discipline*, 14-15)

Proverbs 19:18 says, "Discipline your son while there is hope, and do not desire his death" (NASB). Proverbs 22:15 says further, "Foolishness is bound up in the heart of a child; the rod of discipline will remove it far from him" (NASB).

QUESTION 10

Proverbs captures the many sides of a fool. Match the Scripture with the characteristic of a fool.

Scripture	Characteristic
Proverbs 10:23	He is perverse in speech.
Proverbs 12:15	Wickedness is a sport to a fool.
Proverbs 14:16	He rejects his father's discipline.
Proverbs 15:5	He thinks his way is the right way of living.
Proverbs 19:1	He brings shame to his mother.
Proverbs 20:3	He is quarrelsome, striving, and snarling.
Proverbs 29:15	He is overbearing and confident.

QUESTION 11

Think of an example of someone you know whose foolish behavior was not curbed in childhood. How has this person developed in later life? What struggles has he or she experienced as a result of a lack of training in childhood? Honestly consider your own children. Do any of them have the characteristics of the fool? Record your thoughts as prayers in your Life Notebook.

Control Without Nagging

Many parents resort to yelling and nagging in an effort to get a child to obey. Yet nagging is seldom effective as a means of control. An example illustrates this:

> Henry is sitting on the floor, playing with his games. Mom looks at her watch and says, "Henry, it's nearly nine o'clock (a thirty-minute exaggeration) so gather up your toys and go take your bath." Now Henry and Mom both know that she didn't mean for him to *immediately* take a bath. She merely wanted him to start *thinking* about taking his bath. She would have fainted dead away if he had responded to her empty command.

> Approximately ten minutes later, Mom speaks again. "Now, Henry, it is getting later and you have school tomorrow; I want those toys picked up and then I want you in that tub!" She still does not intend for Henry to obey, and he knows it. Her real message is "We're getting closer, [Henry]." Henry shuffles around and stacks a box or two to demonstrate that he heard her. Then he settles down for a few more minutes of play.

> Six minutes pass and Mom issues another command, this time with more passion and threat in her voice, "Now listen, young man, I told you to get a move on, and I meant it!" To Henry, this means he must get his toys picked up and meander toward the bathroom door. If his mother rapidly pursues him, then he must carry out the assignment posthaste. However, if Mom's mind wanders before she performs the last step of this ritual, or if the phone miraculously rings, Henry is free to enjoy a few more minutes' reprieve. (Dobson, *Dare to Discipline*, 37-38)

It is easy to see what is happening here. Henry's mother progresses through graduated steps, from polite commands to empty threats to real anger. Henry knows he does not need to obey until his mother reaches the stage where she is ready to take action, and he learns to wait until she builds up to that point. The result is that his mother seems to stay angry all the time because that is the only time Henry responds to her. Her relationship with Henry is plagued by a sense of frustration and irritability at her inability to get him to obey.

QUESTION 12

Remember the law of the harvest and the four key questions from Lesson 5, Topic 5. How would you answer those in regard to Henry's situation? Record your response in your Life Notebook.

Returning to the example of Henry at bedtime, Henry's mother could tell him at 8:30 that he has fifteen minutes more to play. Then she could set the alarm clock to ring in fifteen minutes. This gives Henry time to finish up what he is doing, for no one likes a sudden interruption to his activity. When the alarm rings, mother should quietly tell Henry to go get in the bath. Then, if he does not respond immediately, she should use action. She should take him by the shoulder or apply her hand to the seat of his pants or march him to the bathtub. If Henry learns that his mother means what she says and that this procedure is consistently followed, he will also learn to move promptly, before the consequence is applied. This is using action to produce action, and it is one way to break the cycle of nagging that exists in many homes.

Parents often hesitate to use physical means to motivate a child, but the alternative, which is constant nagging, often ends in physical punishment anyway. Nagging becomes a series of empty threats that the child learns to ignore until his parent is so angry that he responds.

Meanwhile, the parent-child relationship has been strained, and the parent's nerves are frayed, so that he may tend to swing wildly at the child instead of administering discipline in a calm, judicious manner. The situation could end very differently if parents learn to use action to produce action.

Henry's mother will have to prove several times that she will carry through with action, and occasionally Henry will continue to "check to see if she is still at the helm." But this approach involves much less pain and hostility between parent and child.

Support Your Spouse in the Discipline Process

There will be many times when you do not agree with how your spouse is handling a situation with the children. Discuss it privately with him or her later, when the children are not able to hear you. Try to come to an agreement beforehand as to how you want to handle the children in general. When disagreements arise about discipline, be supportive of the one who is handling the situation at the moment. Present a consistent and united front as mother and father. Studies have shown that this single factor, the lack of agreement between spouses over discipline, has a very negative outcome in the life of the child, who learns to respect neither parent "because each has assassinated the authority of the other" (Dobson, *The New Dare to Discipline*, 51). Some of the most hostile aggressive teenagers emerge from homes where parents act to contradict each other.

QUESTION 13

Do you and your spouse usually support each other in the discipline process, or do you frequently disagree on how discipline should be handled? Discuss this area with your spouse, and agree to disagree in private. Record your thoughts in your Life Notebook.

Distinguish Willful Defiance from Childish Irresponsibility

Corrective discipline can sometimes be difficult because the boundaries between childish irresponsibility and willful defiance are not always clear. For example, a child plays ball in the house and breaks a window. To deal with the situation, we must consider several factors. How old is the child? Was the child specifically told that ball playing is not permitted in the house? If so, does his action appear to be one of willful defiance or simply childish forgetfulness and carelessness?

QUESTION 14

With your spouse, take some time to discuss how this issue might apply to some specific instances in which you may have disciplined incorrectly. Was he irresponsible or defiant? Record your thoughts in your Life Notebook.

Distinguish Defiance from Emotional Problems

There are times when a child behaves rebelliously, not because he is being defiant but because he feels acute frustration, disappointment, or rejection. By a sudden show of bad behavior Jun may be saying, "I feel unloved now that I'm stuck with that screaming baby brother. Mom used to care for me; now nobody wants me." We need to understand our child, be able to see what he sees, and feel what he feels in order to tell what he is really communicating, for he may not be able to express his feelings in words.

A two-year-old screaming at bedtime may be afraid of the dark rather than merely protesting going to bed. As parents we need to ask ourselves, "What is my child thinking and feeling? What emotional need is he expressing by his behavior?" Asking ourselves these questions will give us a few moments to think before we respond to him.

QUESTION 15

With your spouse discuss whether or not your child was being willfully defiant or emotionally upset in some recent instances when you disciplined him. Record your thoughts in your Life Notebook.

Characteristics of Correction

Once you think you have established what happened and you believe the situation requires corrective discipline, it is important to act in a decisive manner. We would suggest a simple procedure to follow:

1. **Correct in private when possible.** While many situations will permit this, there will be times when you must decide whether immediate steps must be taken or whether the situation can wait until privacy is obtainable. When you choose to wait, the key is to follow through at the earliest possible time. Correcting in private will also protect the child from excessive and needless embarrassment, and immediate follow-through lets the child know that public displays of unacceptable behavior and attitudes will also be dealt with.

2. **Correct in love**. As truth should be spoken in love (Eph 4:15), discipline and reproof should be carried out in love (Prov 3:12; 13:24). Remember, discipline is most effective when it is done in the context of loving relationships. Correcting in love will help preserve the child's sense of self-worth, as he perceives that his wrongs do not cause you to withdraw your love.

3. **Correct with self-control and humility.** Galatians 6:1 says, "Brethren, even if a man is caught in any trespass, you who are spiritual, restore such a one in a spirit of gentleness; each one looking to yourself, lest you too be tempted" (NASB). Ephesians 4:26 says, "Be angry, and do not sin; do not let the sun go down on the cause of your anger." Parents will be angry at times, but it is possible to gain control of ourselves. We need to recognize that we too are capable of mistakes. Correcting a child when we are out of control is not true correction.

4. **Administer the appropriate discipline.** Generally speaking, it is desirable that fathers administer the majority of the correction in the home. This affirms the father's role as the moral and spiritual leader in the house. When he is not present, however, mother must often take the responsibility of correcting a child. A wife should avoid making her husband seem like the mean old ogre to the child by saying things like, "You just wait until your father gets home. You are really going to get a spanking from Daddy." For discipline to be most effective, it is better to

handle the matter soon after it occurs, unless you feel you would prefer to discuss it first with your spouse.

Topic 3: The Rod

It is one thing to say that the Scriptures support the use of the rod. It is another to know how to use it appropriately and effectively in the process of discipline. Please review "The Rod" from the Pillar of Discipline article. As discussed in Lesson 2 and the article you just read, the rod is not the first method of discipline to employ when training your child. The rod should be used only with young children—after the child begins to walk or crawl and until the age of seven. The rod does not work with every child even in cases of willful defiance.

Before

Recall that in Lesson 2 we suggested asking yourself several questions before you spank:

1. Did I train previously?

2. Did I reprove previously?

3. Is there a natural consequence I could apply?

4. Is there a logical consequence I could apply?

5. Is the child being rebellious or simply childish? Is this willful defiance or not?

6. Am I in control of my emotions?

During

When you administer the rod, we would recommend the following:

1. Use a light rod or switch to avoid any physical harm to the child.

2. Spank a child only on the bottom. It may be necessary to remove heavy outer clothing because you do want the child to feel the spank. Limit the number of swats—no more than four or five should ever be used. This should be sufficient for him to feel the impact and hopefully to learn to avoid this punishment in the future.

3. Allow the child to cry, but do not permit him to go on wailing or screaming for a long time. If he does this, put him in a room by himself until he calms down.

After

After a spanking it is good to spend time with the child, explaining again why the spanking was necessary, reassuring the child of your love, and letting him confess or repent if he desires. Express your affection to the child, taking him in your arms or hugging him or sitting him on your lap. Let him know you still love him. Praying together and confessing to God at some point also help show the child that restoration between God and the child is necessary. Assure the child that you forgive him when he says he is sorry. If restitution is needed, it is best if it follows shortly after the incident.

QUESTION 16

Discipline with the rod is always a last resort. If you carefully think about the things to consider before using the rod listed above, you may find that you never use it. Certainly, in our opinion, it should not be used after age six or seven. Take a moment and reflect on the before, during, and after suggestions mentioned above regarding using the rod. Discuss this with your spouse and record your observations and any changes you feel you need to make in your Life Notebook.

Topic 4: A Summary of Discipline

We have summarized below the key elements that are essential for effective discipline of the young child:

1. Begin discipline early in the child's life
2. Define the boundaries for the child
3. Control without nagging
4. Seek a balance of control and love
5. Support your spouse in the discipline process
6. Distinguish willful defiance from childish irresponsibility
7. Be sensitive to the child's feelings
8. Correct with confidence: in private, lovingly and consistently, with self-control
9. Consider legitimate appeals by the child
10. Seek repentance in the child
11. Reinforce appropriate behavior and attitudes
12. Use the rod appropriately, reassuring the child of your love afterward

QUESTION 17

Take time to reflect on your methods and practice of discipline. Have you established clear-cut boundaries for your children? Do they know what the rules are? Write them out on paper to be sure you have communicated them. Are there times when you punish your child for being childish and irresponsible, rather than for defiance? Discuss the summary of discipline with your spouse. Try to come to an agreement on how you want to handle your children. Write down a summary of the points you agree on in your Life Notebook. Pray together for unity and consistency in parenting.

Corrective discipline is a long-range process. The methods change as the child matures, but the ultimate goal of discipline remains the same. Our desire is to train up a child to Christian maturity, to the measure of the stature of the fullness of Christ.

This is a goal, however, and growth is a process. It does not take place overnight. Ephesians 5:8-10 says that as children of light we are trying to learn what is pleasing to the Lord. This is a daily process, and sometimes we learn by trial and error, but we keep pressing on toward that ultimate goal.

Hebrews 12:10 says regarding earthly parents, "For they disciplined us for a short time as seemed best to them" (NASB). We must work hard and work at being consistent in discipline. As we seek God's wisdom in the process of discipline, we make decisions that seem best to us at the time. Later, with the benefit of hindsight, a decision may not seem to be the right one. We press on from there, seeking always to right the wrongs and to do what is pleasing to God.

We have the assurance that God will work through us, and even in spite of us, toward the goal of sanctifying, of making His children holy. We are reminded again of Hebrews 12:10: "He disciplines us for our good, that we may share His holiness" (NASB). The process of disciplining may be painful for parents at times, but the final result, the prospect of seeing our children come to maturity as godly individuals, encourages us to dedicate ourselves afresh to the process of discipline.

Topic 5: Project

QUESTION 18

Below are some case situations in which corrective discipline is needed. We would like you and your spouse to read through them on your own and determine what your individual response would be. Afterwards, discuss with each other what each of you would do in this situation and why. Where you differ in your handling of a situation, try to resolve your disagreement and come to a consensus.

1. Your nine-month-old refuses to lie still when you diaper him. He squirms and kicks you throughout the process.

2. Your two-year-old daughter throws herself down in the supermarket and has a tantrum.

3. Your two-year-old is in the habit of biting other children.

4. Your three-year-old refuses to take your hand when it is time to cross the street and runs away from you.

5. Your four-year-old son whines the entire time you are visiting with a friend.

6. Your five-year-old daughter refuses to share her toys with another child who has come over to your house to play.

7. At bedtime you tell your seven-year-old that it is time to stop playing to get ready for bed. He ignores you and goes on playing.

8. Your nine-year-old dawdles when it comes to doing his school assignments. At bedtime he has not completed his work for the next day.

9. Some money has been stolen from where you left it in the bedroom, and you had seen your twelve-year-old coming out of your room a little while earlier.

10. Your wife asks your fourteen-year-old son to carry out the garbage on his way to school. Late in the day you notice that the garbage can is still full.

11. Coming home from work, you notice your fifteen-year-old son in a neighbor's yard smoking and drinking with other young people.

12. Your seventeen-year-old ignores her curfew repeatedly.

When you have finished this, take the latest major case of discipline in your own family, and discuss how it was handled, what the results were, and how you would handle the discipline differently if you had to do it all over again.

Lesson 7 Self Check

QUESTION 1

The primary meaning of discipline is punishment. *True or False?*

QUESTION 2

Discipline involves guidance, which is built on trust. *True or False?*

QUESTION 3

What is the desired outcome of corrective discipline according to Hebrews 12:10?

    A. A holy life

    B. Punishment

    C. To demonstrate that parents need to be strict as well as merciful

    D. To force children to obey

QUESTION 4

Punishment and discipline are not the same thing. *True or False?*

QUESTION 5

What is the most important outcome of corrective discipline?

    A. The child will conform to the parent's wishes.

    B. The child will stop what he is doing create havoc in the home.

    C. The child will learn instant obedience so the parents do not have to ask a second or third time for him to stop what he is doing wrong.

    D. The child will develop a sense of self-worth in being loved and forgiven.

QUESTION 6

After two-year-old Liling Chen pulled all the pots and pans from the kitchen cupboard, her mother yells at her and gives her a spanking. Liling, with tears in her eyes, goes to her room as her mother instructed. This is an example of properly applied discipline. *True or False?*

QUESTION 7

Parents often hesitate to use physical means to motivate a child, but the alternative, which is constant nagging, often ends in physical punishment anyway. *True or False?*

QUESTION 8

Ephesians 6:4 speaks of the danger of breaking the spirit of a child when we only want to break his will. *True or False?*

QUESTION 9

The father alone is the one who decides what kind of discipline is needed. *True or False?*

QUESTION 10

When viewing a child's bad behavior, it is important to distinguish between defiance and childishness before you administer discipline. *True or False?*

Lesson 7 Answers to Questions

QUESTION 1: *Your answer*

QUESTION 2

Scripture	Command to Children
Proverbs 2:1	Receive my words
Proverbs 3:1	Do not forget my teaching
Proverbs 4:1	Pay attention
Proverbs 7:1	Keep my words

QUESTION 3: *Your answer should be similar to the following:*

Discipline should result in righteous conduct, or a holy life. Our efforts to discipline our children should all have this goal in mind: a desire to see our children draw closer to the Lord and please Him in their actions and attitudes. Note: For younger children parents can have practical goals like obedience, respect, and self-control. As the child grows, he should gradually become accountable to God for his actions and attitudes so that he is able to make wise choices without the need for his mother and father to be there to tell him what to do.

QUESTION 4

D. Punished

QUESTION 5

A. Disciplined

QUESTION 6: *Your answer*

QUESTION 7: *Your answer*

QUESTION 8: *Your answer*

QUESTION 9

Scripture	Situation
Matthew 7:3-5	When those in authority can never admit to being wrong
1 Corinthians 13:1	When obedience is demanded but love is withheld
Ephesians 4:29	When words tear down instead of build up
Ephesians 4:32	When forgiveness is unattainable
Philippians 4:8	When failure is accentuated over success
Colossians 3:8	When harshness and anger replace gentleness, humility, and patience

QUESTION 10

Scripture	Characteristic
Proverbs 10:23	Wickedness is a sport to a fool.
Proverbs 12:15	He thinks his way is the right way of living.
Proverbs 14:16	He is overbearing and confident.
Proverbs 15:5	He rejects his father's discipline.
Proverbs 19:1	He is perverse in speech.
Proverbs 20:3	He is quarrelsome, striving, and snarling.
Proverbs 29:15	He brings shame to his mother.

QUESTION 11: *Your answer*

QUESTION 12: *Your answer*

QUESTION 13: *Your answer*

QUESTION 14: *Your answer*

QUESTION 15: *Your answer*

QUESTION 16: *Your answer*

QUESTION 17: *Your answer*

QUESTION 18: *Your answer*

Lesson 7 Self Check Answers

QUESTION 1: False
QUESTION 2: True
QUESTION 3
    A. A holy life
QUESTION 4: True
QUESTION 5
    D. The child will develop a sense of self-worth in being loved and forgiven.
QUESTION 6: False
QUESTION 7: True
QUESTION 8: True
QUESTION 9: False
QUESTION 10: True

Lesson 8: The Strong-Willed Child

Parents who have several children can quickly point out the differences among their offspring. While one child is sweet and gentle and slow-moving, another is a high-energy, ornery little rascal that moves at the speed of light, destroying all that lies in his path. Dr. Dobson describes these two types of children in a humorous account as follows:

> Some kids seem to be born with an easygoing, compliant nature that makes them a joy to raise. As infants they don't cry very often; they sleep through the night from the second week; they goo at the grandparents; they smile while being diapered; and they are very patient when dinner is overdue. And, of course, they never spit up on the way to church. During later childhood, they love to keep their room clean and they especially like doing their homework. There aren't many of these supercompliant children, I'm afraid, but they are known to exist in some households (though they didn't in ours).

> Just as surely as some children are naturally compliant, others seem to be defiant upon exit from the womb. They come into the world smoking a cigar and yelling about the temperature in the delivery room and the incompetence of the nursing staff and the way doctors are running things. …In infancy, these children fairly bristle when their bottle is late and demand to be held throughout the day. Three o'clock in the morning is the favorite "playtime." Later, during toddlerhood, they resist all forms of authority and their greatest delights include "painting" the carpet with Mom's makeup or trying to flush the family cat down the toilet. (Dobson, *The New Strong-Willed Child*, ix-x)

Perhaps you have a strong-willed child like the one described above at home. He is God's gift to you, although at times you might like to return the gift. Yet this child is precious in the eyes of God and in need of a special kind of understanding and discipline. In this lesson we are going to discuss the particular problems involved in raising a strong-willed child.

Lesson Outline

Topic 1: Characteristics of the Strong-Willed Child

Topic 2: Parents of the Strong-Willed Child

    Recognize Feelings Common to Parents of Strong-Willed Children

    Distinguish Between a Goal and a Desire

Topic 3: Dealing with the Strong-Willed Child

    Do Not Let the Child Win Direct Confrontations to Your Authority

    Be Consistent in the Application of Discipline

    Be Selective in Your Choice of Battles

    Do Not Let the Child's Persistence Change Your Mind

    Teach Self-Control

    Provide a Proper Emotional Outlet

    Be Positive

    Teach, Model, and Pray

Lesson Objectives

By the end of this lesson, you will be able to do the following:

- Define several temperaments that tend to shape a child's behavior, regardless of the circumstances of childhood
- Define the characteristics associated with the strong-willed child
- Explain the reasons why feelings of guilt, failure, fear, and frustration are common among parents of strong-willed children
- Discover and describe the corresponding strengths and weaknesses of each of your children

Topic 1: Characteristics of the Strong-Willed Child

Many parents may never have to deal with a strong-willed child. They find it difficult to understand the frustration some parents experience because they have never really experienced it. They seem to have raised perfect children. Each of them is respectful of adults, makes good grades in school, keeps their rooms clean, and loves Jesus. Some of those parents may take the credit for raising well-behaved children and offer advice on how to raise children like they do.

A family with several children may have compliant kids who never caused their parents difficulty, but have one child who always questioned why things are done a certain way. If that strong-willed child was the youngest child, the parents may have mistakenly thought that their mild mannered children were a result of their parenting and be quick to offer advice to other parents before their strong-willed child was born. If that strong-willed child was their firstborn, they would know that all kids do not respond to the same instruction the same way.

Assignment

- Please read the following article:

Types of Children

Let's look at some typical households. As you survey your friends you probably see several different types of children represented in various families: the strong-willed child, the easy child, and the shy child.

The Strong-Willed Child

Children possess certain temperaments at birth, according to evidence compiled over three decades by researchers Chess and Thomas. In their study they observed three broad categories or patterns of temperaments into which the majority of children can be classified. The first they called "the difficult child," who is characterized by "negative reactions to people, intense mood swings, irregular sleep and feeding schedules, frequent periods of crying and violent tantrums when frustrated" (Chess and Thomas, quoted by Dobson, *The New Strong-Willed Child*, 46-47). Such a child is more prone to lose control of his emotions, to have trouble adapting to new situations, and to be overly sensitive to sensory stimulation.

Many parents have been surprised to discover that their job suddenly got tougher: one of their children proved to be a hard-headed youngster much like the one described above. Such a child is inclined to test, challenge, resist, and blatantly defy authority. What sets this child apart from his more compliant siblings is the strength of his will.

The Easy Child

The second pattern Chess and Thomas termed "the easy child," who tends to have a positive approach to people, adapts quietly to new situations, has regular sleep and feeding schedules, and is willing to submit to the authority of others. Parents and teachers alike described such a child as a joy to be with.

The Shy Child

The third category of children the researchers describe might be titled "shy," or "slow-to-warm-up." These children respond negatively to new situations and adapt somewhat slowly. They are less intense, however, than difficult children, and they tend to have regular sleeping and feeding schedules. When they are upset or frustrated, they typically withdraw from the situation and react mildly, rather than exploding with anger and rebellion.

Characteristics of the Strong-Willed Child

Not every child fits into one of these categories, but most do. The characteristics of strong-willed children can be seen when they are babies. Those babies who were labeled "difficult" usually tended to display greater strength of will than the easy or compliant children. This tendency, present at birth, tends to persist throughout childhood. Thus, there are certain children whom we may refer to as "strong-willed" children.

One characteristic of a strong-willed child is an unhealthy desire for power, for control over his world. All children feel gratified when they gain a measure of control over their environment. When an infant is hungry, he cries, and he finds that his crying is successful—mother feeds him. He learns that his crying brings results, and he likes the feeling of it. Later, as he grows older, he learns other ways to bring about positive results for himself, and his confidence grows in this way.

But some children, because of the strength of their will, have a desire for control that is greater than that of others. A strong-willed child has great strength of will and an intense desire for power. Unless this strong will is dealt with the child can become extremely difficult.

Being "strong-willed" is part of one's genetic makeup

Some children obviously have a much stronger drive for power than others. They constantly fight their parents' wishes, while their siblings usually submit; they are compliant children and want to please their parents. So why is one child in the same family so different? Did his parents make him that way? Did they create a tyrant by treating him differently? Research seems to indicate that he was just born that way. His difficult temperament and strong will are part of his genetic make-up.

As we mentioned in an earlier lesson, in the twentieth century, behaviorism has emphasized the role of environment in molding children, teaching that children are born as blank slates and that their environment completely determines the outcome of their lives. If this is true, the logical conclusion would be that parents are largely to blame for whatever goes wrong with a child. Child-rearing books seem to substantiate this claim. Experts accuse parents of errors in feeding, toilet-training, or disciplining their children, and many parents, particularly mothers, have accepted a heavy load of guilt for "creating" their children's problems. Christians are not exempt from this. Many Christian parents feel guilty and responsible for the troubling behavior of a child with a strong, rebellious temperament, even though they may have done nothing to make the child that way.

Recent studies prove what parents have suspected all along, that children are born with different temperaments. From the moment of birth some children tend to be very strong-willed, exhibiting a high drive for power and control. Other children are very compliant; they tend to be cheerful, eager to obey and to please. Actually, most children are somewhere in between these two extremes. They exhibit a mixture of two characteristics, the desire to control and the desire to please. So we must be careful not to label our children too quickly and develop too narrow a view of their temperaments.

Normal development vs. a strong-willed temperament

We must be careful not to confuse normal development with a strong-willed temperament. Most toddlers go through a very assertive and negative stage around two years of age. This is a necessary part of their growth process as they develop a sense of their personhood and gain in independence. Parents may quickly conclude that their toddler is strong-willed, but it may be best to wait until this stage of development is over before you make up your mind. Many "strong-willed" toddlers turn out to be fairly compliant in another year or two.

When we use the labels "strong-willed" and "compliant" to describe the temperaments of some children, we must exercise caution. We do not want to suggest in any way that strong-willed children are "bad" and compliant children are "good." The strong-willed child may be more prone to outward disobedience and more difficult for the parents to handle, but he is not more evil or sinful in God's eyes. He is not a "bad" child. But he will be more of a challenge to you as parents.

In every personality there are corresponding strengths and weaknesses. For example, a child who has a lot of energy and enthusiasm may find it difficult to sit and concentrate, or a child who is very artistic and creative may also be a perfectionist who sets very high standards for himself and others. It is too easy to focus only on the negative aspects of the strong-willed child's temperament. He argues more with his parents than a compliant child; he may disobey more; he is generally more difficult to handle.

But his positive personality traits may be overlooked because he is so difficult for his parents to manage. It is important for the parents of a strong-willed child to recognize and reinforce their child's positive traits, while at the same time attempting to eliminate undesirable behavior.

QUESTION 1

Summarize the three categories of temperaments described in the article. Which of these categories, if any, best describes each of your children? Is the description inaccurate for your children on some points? Record your thoughts in your Life Notebook.

QUESTION 2

What do you think are some positive personality traits that are likely to be found in the strong-willed temperament?

QUESTION 3

Determine whether you think each of your children is very compliant, compliant, average, somewhat strong-willed, or very strong-willed. Make a list of the strengths and weaknesses of each of your children. If you do not have children, perhaps you can do the same exercise for yourself and your siblings. How can you reinforce the positive traits of each of your children? Write down some of your ideas.

Topic 2: Parents of the Strong-Willed Child

The job of being the parent of a strong-willed child is difficult enough without adding burdens to the task that need not be there. Two of these unnecessary weights could be the thought that you are alone in the battle and the assumption of responsibilities you do not need to bear. Here are a few thoughts along those lines to encourage you.

Recognize Feelings Common to Parents of Strong-Willed Children

Studies show that frustrated parents are often those who have strong-willed children. If you have felt great discouragement and fear that you are failing as the parent of a strong-willed child, perhaps it will comfort you to realize that your feelings are normal. Your feelings about your performance as a parent may not be entirely objective. In fact, they are probably greatly influenced by the temperament of your child. If your child were naturally more compliant and cooperative, you would probably feel more confident as a parent.

We want to offer encouragement and hope to parents who may be struggling with feelings of failure because of the behavior of a difficult child.

Parental Response to Strong-Willed and Compliant Children	Total Joy	Generally Pleasant	Average	Difficult	Unpleasant
Parents of very compliant children	44%	51%	4%	1%	0%
Parents of very strong-willed children	1%	10%	17%	55%	17%

Based on what we see in the chart above, a parent's feelings of success or failure as a parent are directly related to the difficulty of the task he faces. Parents of strong-willed children consistently feel more frustration and more guilt because their children are by nature more difficult to handle.

QUESTION 4

Look at the chart above, and take a few minutes to rate your own response to the task of being a parent. Is your own response one of total joy, or do you find the task generally unpleasant? How does your response relate to the presence of a strong-willed child or compliant child?

Parents of strong-willed children not only feel resentment, frustration, weariness, and a sense of failure, but they also struggle with guilt. They are prone to think, "Perhaps I have not done a good job of parenting. I could have spent more time in personal devotions. I must be doing it all wrong, or why else would he be responding this way?"

Unfortunately, others can add to the guilt feelings of a struggling parent. Many times other parents who have not had strong-willed children do not really understand the special problems associated with raising a strong-willed child. They may blithely assume that the parent is simply not handling the child correctly. Family members or friends may be quick to offer advice or criticism.

Parents of strong-willed children need support and encouragement, rather than criticism and a judgmental attitude. We can encourage these parents by showing sympathy for their situation, refraining from criticism, and offering advice only when we are asked.

- Abijah (1 Kgs 15:1-3) - Asa, his son (1 Kgs 15:8-11)

- Asa (1 Kgs 15:11-15) - Jehoshaphat, his son (1 Kgs 22:41-50)

- Jehoshaphat (1 Kgs 22:41-44) - Jehoram, his son (2 Kgs 8:16-18)

- Jehoram (2 Kgs 8:16-18) - Ahaziah, his son (2 Kgs 8:25-27)

- Ahaz (2 Kgs 16:1-4) - Hezekiah, his son (2 Kgs 18:1-8)
- Hezekiah (2 Kgs 18:1-8) - Manasseh, his son (2 Kgs 21:1-6)
- Amon (2 Kgs 21:19-22) – Josiah, his son (2 Kgs 22:1-2)
- Josiah (2 Kgs 22:1-2) - Jehoahaz, his son (2 Kgs 23:31-32)

QUESTION 5

Look up the pairs of Scripture above concerning various kings of Israel and Judah and their sons. What correlation do you notice between the quality of spiritual life of the father and that of his son?

QUESTION 6

As a result of the study above, "If the children turn out poorly, it is obviously the fault of the parents." *True or False?*

Distinguish between a goal and a desire

Assignment

- Please read the following article:

Distinguish Goals and Desires

Training our children is one of the most important assignments that we as parents will ever be given by God. As Christian parents, of course we care very deeply about the results of that training. We expend great energy in the task of nurturing and training our children, desiring to see them grow up to maturity in faith. But in considering our task to train our children we must be careful not to assume responsibility for things over which we have no control. In this regard it is helpful to keep in mind the difference between goals and desires. Christian psychologist Lawrence Crabb explains the difference:

> A goal is an objective that is under my control.

> A desire is an objective that I may legitimately and fervently want, but cannot reach through my efforts alone. To fulfill a desire requires the uncertain cooperation of another. (Crabb, 72)

Crabb goes on to say:

> We must never assume responsibility for fulfilling our desires. All we can do is pray that the One who is in control will allow our objectives to be realized.

> The proper response to a desire, then, is **prayer**. To a goal, the appropriate response is a set of **responsible actions**. …**Pray for your desires and assume responsibility for your goals**. (emphasis added)

Let us apply this distinction between goals and desires to the task of training our children. First, as parents we need to ask ourselves, what are my desires and what are my goals? Two examples are listed below, indicating the way in which a desire of our heart can translate into a goal which is possible to achieve.

Desire: That my children become Christians

Goal: To teach my children what the Bible says about God, salvation, and the Christian life

Desire: That my children learn to live in a loving way that honors God

Goal: To demonstrate to my children the love of God through my daily attitudes and actions

We run into trouble as parents when we confuse our desires with our goals, which leads us to assume burdens that God never intended for us to bear. It is our responsibility to be the best Christian parents we can be. It is our responsibility to be an example of Christlike character in our speech and in our actions. It is our responsibility to curb sin in our own life and to provide an atmosphere of love, security, and forgiveness in our home. These things translate into goals: as we rely on God's strength, we can work on curbing our weaknesses, we can work on being more Christlike, and we can work on making our home a loving and secure place.

We run into problems when we try to fulfill the desires of our heart for our children. When our child does not respond to Christian teaching or when he fails to act in a way that pleases God, we may be overwhelmed at times by feelings of guilt and a sense of failure. Parents cannot assume responsibility for their desires. Our proper response in this area is to pray.

If we have been reasonably consistent in upholding our responsibilities yet our child fails to respond to our training and discipline, what then? The Bible teaches that each person is responsible for his own—and only his own—choices and actions. The Lord made this very clear in Ezekiel 18:2-4:

> What do you people mean by quoting this proverb about the land of Israel: "The fathers eat sour grapes, and the children's teeth are set on edge"? As surely as I live, declares the Sovereign Lord, you will no longer quote this proverb in Israel. For every living soul belongs to me, the father as well as the son—both alike belong to me. The soul who sins is the one who will die (NIV).

Ultimately, your child must answer to God for his own behavior. Accept the fact that you are responsible for training your child in the way he should go. At the same time, recognize that you cannot take responsibility for how your child responds to training. Commit your desires to the Lord (Ps 37:4-5), and trust the Lord to help you in the daily task of training your child.

QUESTION 7

Based on the article, it would be correct to say that a goal is an objective under my control. *True or False?*

QUESTION 8

Review the distinction between goals and desires. What are some of your desires for your children? How can you translate these into practical, attainable goals for yourself as a parent? Examine yourself to see if you have been guilty of assuming responsibility to try to fulfill the desires of your heart for your children. Commit yourself to pray for your desires and to work on achieving your goals. Record your reflections in your Life Notebook.

Topic 3: Dealing with the Strong-Willed Child

There is no simple ten-step program that can guarantee success for parents in dealing with a strong-willed child. How you handle him will depend in part on your own values, convictions, and personalities as parents. But some general principles for dealing with a strong-willed child can guide you in this challenging task. The ideas in this section are designed to be adapted to your own family situation.

Although we are not responsible for the temperaments with which our children are born, we are certainly responsible under God to teach, train, and discipline our children. If your child is strong-willed and more rebellious by nature, your job as a parent will be more challenging and difficult. But this does not in any way lessen your responsibility. In fact, godly training and discipline are crucial for a child with a strong-willed nature. If he does not learn at an early age to restrain his will and submit to authority, the consequences could be disastrous. We are responsible to put forth our best efforts in teaching, training, and disciplining our children. Let us look at some helpful guidelines for parents of strong-willed children.

Do Not Let the Child Win Direct Confrontations to Your Authority

In the previous lesson we discussed the tendency of every child to test the boundaries and the authority of his parents. A strong-willed child will often challenge and defy his parents' authority. It is crucial that his parents respond with finesse and maintain control in their home, winning the direct confrontations initiated by the child. As we discussed in Lesson 7, it is also crucial to begin early, letting the young child know what is expected of him and enforcing the rules that have been established.

A strong-willed child can be very persistent in trying to get what he wants. You can say no to him, but he will come back again and again with new approaches, trying to wear you down until you give in to him. Many parents do eventually give in, allowing the child to win the direct confrontation with authority. When the child wins one such battle, you can be sure it is not the last. He will vie for power in many areas, and life can become a perpetual battleground.

Dealing With a Strong-Willed Child

QUESTION 9

If you have children, list any areas you can identify where your children are defying your authority. Resolve to pray about each issue with your spouse and then discern proper discipline as outlined in Lesson 7 to win the confrontations.

Be Consistent in the Application of Discipline

Consistent, proper discipline cannot be emphasized enough regarding the strong-willed child. Take a moment to read the summary of the discipline principles at the end of Lesson 7 listed below.

- Begin discipline early in the child's life
- Define the boundaries for the child
- Control without nagging

- Seek a balance of control and love
- Support your spouse in the discipline process
- Distinguish willful defiance from childish irresponsibility
- Be sensitive to the child's feelings
- Correct with confidence: in private, lovingly and consistently, with self-control
- Consider legitimate appeals by the child
- Seek repentance in the child
- Reinforce appropriate behavior and attitudes
- Use the rod appropriately, reassuring the child of your love afterward

Check yourself to see how you are doing in applying discipline with your children. Consistent discipline is essential for the welfare of the strong-willed child, and for the well-being of the entire family as well.

When an incident occurs with the strong-willed child, choose the method of discipline most appropriate for the situation and the age of the child. Decide whether a spanking is appropriate. Spanking can often make the situation worse with a strong-willed child. Other methods, such as rewards for good behavior or time-out alone, may prove to be more effective in channeling the child's behavior.

QUESTION 10

What advice do James and Paul give to help prepare yourself before you discipline your child (Eph 4:2; Jas 1:20)?

Be Selective in Your Choice of Battles

Since a strong-willed child tends to challenge his parents' authority almost continuously, it is quite easy to get in the habit of always saying no to the child and trying to control him too much. The atmosphere in the home can become very negative when you attempt to control the child's every move. A good guideline to keep in mind is this: Have as few rules in your home as possible, but require that the child keep the rules you do have.

If you are a strong-willed person yourself, it may be especially difficult for you to resist trying to control everything your child does. Save confrontations, however, for the issues that are the most important to you. When it is possible, let the child do what he wants so that he gains a measure of confidence.

For example, if the child wants to play in an area that you feel is dangerous, such as a busy street, then you certainly should say no, and discipline him if he fails to obey. But let us suppose the child wants to play in an area of your home that is not dangerous but merely inconvenient for you. You know there is a good chance that he will mess up the room or be very noisy. At such times, if you do not have a very good reason to say no, you may want to permit the child to do what he wants. There are so many times that you must say no to this child; try to say yes whenever it is possible, as long as the child is not breaking any of the rules of the home.

QUESTION 11

With your spouse discuss some battles you are fighting that you really do not feel are worth fighting. Which battles are worth it? Agree together on this so there is no difference of opinion before the child and so the child can see a united front from the parents. Record your reflections in your Life Notebook.

Do Not Let the Child's Persistence Change Your Mind

We have noted that strong-willed children can be very persistent when they are trying to get what they want. A child who does not get what he wants may act in a very unpleasant way, using every means to wear down his parents' patience and resolve. His behavior may greatly annoy or embarrass his parents, particularly when it takes place in the presence of others. A parent may be tempted to finally give in and give the child what he wants just so that the unpleasant behavior will stop.

This is a huge mistake! Giving in to persistent demands actually teaches the child that, if he cries long enough or loudly enough or if he asks frequently enough, eventually he will get his way. The next time the child will cry, beg, or scream twice as long to get what he wants. If you have a good reason for telling your child no, determine not to change your mind, no matter how your child acts. Teach him that it is not effective to cry, beg, or scream. When he sees that you remain firm, he will eventually stop trying to control you in this way.

If your child's will tends to be much stronger than yours, it may be difficult for you to stand firm in situations like these. It may be helpful for you to remember two things.

First, you do not need to be intimidated by your child's apparent unhappiness. Of course, as loving parents we all want our children to be happy. We work for their happiness and pray for their happiness and make sacrifices for their happiness. But it is not our job to keep our children happy constantly. It is our job to care for them and to train them in a way that pleases God.

QUESTION 12

Read Proverbs 23:13 and Hebrews 12:11. What counsel do Solomon and the writer to the Hebrews give regarding our concern about making our child unhappy if we discipline him?

Second, do not let embarrassment influence your response to your child. Children often act in ways that embarrass their parents, in spite of the loving attention and firm discipline they may have received. When you are around other family members or friends or in a public situation, try not to let fear of embarrassment influence how you treat your child. It may be wise to take your child aside (to another room or outside, for example) to administer discipline. But if this is not possible, you can do one of two things:

1. Discipline him right then and there
2. Warn him that he will be disciplined the moment you get home, and be sure to follow through

In every situation ask yourself, "How can I best train my child now? What is the best response in this situation?" Then follow through, and do what you think is right, regardless of your child's response or the opinions of others. Particularly when you are the parent of a strong-willed child, you must learn not to worry about what others are thinking.

QUESTION 13

Recall an example of a situation where you observed a parent discipline his child in public. How did the parent handle the situation? What was your response as an observer? What facts may have been unknown to you in this situation?

Teach Self-control

A strong-willed child often expends great energy trying to control other people in his world in order to get what he wants. He wants to control not only his parents but his grandparents, siblings, and friends. While he is usually very good at controlling others, he is often poor when it comes to controlling himself. He may be easily frustrated and given to emotional outbursts or tantrums.

As the child grows, he needs to be taught that God values self-control much more than He values controlling others (Gal 5:22-23). The world values power: having control over others. Jesus taught us to regard others as more important than ourselves and to be the servant of others. Teach your child what the Bible says about how we should treat others, as well as what the Bible says about self-control. Help him to recognize areas in his life where he needs to learn self-control. Pray with him that God will help him to grow in these areas. Then reward him with praise and encouragement when you see him demonstrate self-control.

QUESTION 14

Look up the following verses on self-control: Proverbs 25:28; Galatians 5:22-23; 1 Timothy 3:2; 2 Timothy 1:7; Titus 2:2, 5-6, 12; 1 Peter 1:13; 4:7; 5:8; 2 Peter 1:5-9. Summarize what these verses teach. List some specific areas that may apply to each of your children and record your thoughts in your Life Notebook.

Provide a Proper Emotional Outlet

Strong-willed children often have very intense emotions that are easily fanned into flames. They may have a tendency to react with angry emotional outbursts when they do not get their way, and they need to be taught self-control. In teaching self-control, we must be careful to allow some outlet for their intense emotions. A child should not be allowed to speak disrespectfully to his parents or to use bad language, but he should be allowed to tell his parents how he feels in an appropriate way.

For example, a child should not be allowed to scream, "I hate you!" at his parents or to throw an object at someone in anger. This is certainly disrespectful behavior: it does not honor the parent (Eph 6:2), and it displays a lack of self-control. The first time a child acts in this way he should be told that his behavior is not acceptable and why. The next time he acts in such a way he should be disciplined. It is dangerous to allow a child to show disrespect to his parents in such a way.

The child should, however, be permitted and even encouraged to express his feelings in an appropriate way. For example, he should be permitted to say things like, "I don't think it is fair that you won't let me do this. It makes me very upset because all my friends are doing it and you won't let me do it." A wise parent will take time to listen to his child's feelings and teach his child to express himself in a way that is acceptable and respectful. When you listen to your child this way, you communicate to him that you value his thoughts, opinions, and feelings, even if you do not agree with him or change your mind.

Letting a child express his feelings in an appropriate manner is one way that you can obey the command not to exasperate your child (Eph 6:4). It will lay the groundwork for a lifetime of communication and friendship with your child. After the child has expressed his feelings, explain your own position as clearly as possible, in a way that the child can understand. If you understand how he feels, be sure to tell him you do and assure him that you will take his feelings into consideration when you make your decision.

QUESTION 15

Think of a recent example of a time when your child expressed his feelings. Did he do so respectfully? What did you learn from this experience? What was the outcome of the interaction between you and your child? Write out several questions you might use to encourage your child to express his feelings in an appropriate way.

Be Positive

Given the nature of the strong-willed child, you as his parent are likely to have a great many negative interactions with him, frequently telling him no and disciplining him. Some days it may seem like you have had numerous skirmishes in an ongoing war. Many of these negative interactions are simply unavoidable. This is why the parent of a strong-willed child should be especially careful that his relationship with the child does not consist solely of these negative interactions. We need to make a special effort to balance conflicts with as much positive interaction as possible.

We learned in Lesson 7 about the importance of shaping a child's will while at the same time protecting his spirit. The parents of the strong-willed child should be especially attentive to this. A child who receives only negative feedback from his parents will begin to develop very bad feelings toward himself, which may tend to color his self-concept throughout life.

Discipline the wrong behavior, not the child's character

One way to avoid these feelings of unworthiness in a child is to focus on the wrong behavior during discipline instead of on the person. For example, the parent should say: "What you did was wrong because…" or "I didn't like the way you spoke to me just now." But it is very unwise for a parent to make statements such as "You are a bad child," "You are mean and selfish," or "Why do you act so stupid?" Avoid ridiculing or condemning your child when he disobeys you.

Avoid comparing with other children

It is also wise not to compare your child with other children, especially his or her siblings. For example, do not say to your child: "Why do you cause me so much trouble? Why can't you be sweet and helpful like your sister?" This will not motivate the child to change, but it will cause him to question whether you really love and accept him as he is, and it may cause him to resent or dislike his "sweet" sibling.

Tell the child you love him

Verbal affirmation from a parent can do much to boost a child's spirit, even when the parent is locked into a battle of wills with the child. Regardless of how much your child disobeys you or how unpleasant he may make your life, tell him regularly how special he is and how much you love him. Every child is a unique creation, made in God's image, and has infinite worth in God's eyes (Ps 139:13-18). If parents do not communicate this to their child, then who will?

Praise the good character qualities

It is also good to tell your child specific things about him that you like. At times it may be difficult to think of anything positive to say about your strong-willed child. If you pray and observe your child carefully, you will find some very positive traits to praise. Praise can be very simple, but it should be honest and sincere. For example, a parent could say: "I like the way you laugh all the time. It is fun to have such a happy person in our family."

Praise good behavior

Praise can also reinforce the child's good behavior. When a parent has been trying to train a child to improve his behavior in a certain area, it is good to provide positive reinforcement for any improvement.

For example, a parent could say, "I noticed that you played with your brother for a whole hour today without one single fight or argument. I'm so proud of you!" It may be helpful occasionally to give a child a small treat to reward his good behavior.

Spend time with the child

Taking time to be with your child, just to enjoy him, is giving him a great gift. Positive time to play with, talk with, read to, and show affection to a child is very important. It may not be easy to find an hour or two to enjoy your child. But even a few minutes of special attention each day can make a difference to a child. The parents of a strong-willed child should be careful not to withhold this special attention and affection from their child as a punishment for his disobedience. Withholding love is very dangerous to a child's emotional health. Time with your child should not be a reward for good behavior but a regular part of your daily schedule.

As you are striving to apply the principles we have discussed with your strong-willed child, remember that it may take a very long time to see positive results. Skill and dedication do not shorten the amount of time needed to effect change in your child's life.

> It may take several years to bring such a youngster to a point of relative obedience and cooperation within the family unit, and indeed a strong-willed child will be a strong-willed individual all her life. ...Don't try to "fix" your tougher boy or girl overnight. Treat your child with sincere love and dignity, but require him or her to follow your leadership. Choose carefully the matters that are worthy of confrontation, then accept her challenge on those issues and win decisively. Reward every positive, cooperative gesture she makes by offering your attention, affection, and verbal praise. (Dobson, *The Strong-Willed Child*, 12)

Teach, Model, and Pray

It has been said that there are three ways to influence someone—teach, model, and pray. Teaching our children to live in a way that pleases God is important. The way we teach and train them certainly influences their behavior. We often place most of our emphasis on training or teaching a child, while ignoring our own example and giving too little time to prayer.

While we often give prayer a low priority in our lives, praying for each of our children is the most effective way to influence our children for good. James assures us that "the prayer of a righteous man is powerful and effective" (Jas 5:16). James further says, "If any of you lacks wisdom, he should ask God, who gives generously to all without finding fault, and it will be given to him" (Jas 1:5). God can and will give us wisdom as parents. He cares about our families and can show us creative solutions to problems if we ask Him. We sometimes lack wisdom because we give up asking, yet we need God's help daily to be consistent as parents.

As Christian parents we all want our children to grow to become men and women of God. For this to happen, God must work in their lives. No matter how effectively and consistently we may train and discipline our children, we cannot make them men and women of God. Only God can do that. "Unless the Lord builds the house, its builders labor in vain. Unless the Lord watches over the city, the watchmen stand guard in vain" (Ps 127:1). As we pray for our children, we indicate our desire to cooperate with God in carrying out His purposes in their lives.

The goal of parenting is not for us to decide what we want our children to become and then ruthlessly teach, train, squeeze, badger, and cajole them into that mold. Instead, we must recognize that God has already designed them. God already has a mature person and a long-range purpose in mind. Our job is to see our children as God does—and to involve ourselves in God's plans for them. Like a sculptor, we must try to see the final form straining to break out of the uncut stone.

This cannot be accomplished without prayer.

Praying for our children should be a priority in our lives. Many parents call on God only when it seems that they are unable to handle a situation without Him. God is approached as if he were merely a great vending machine in the sky. If we simply insert a prayer, we can get a bottle of wisdom or a package of peace in return for our effort. This is not an accurate picture of prayer. God's desire is that we communicate with Him in prayer, intimately and frequently, about everything that concerns us about our children, and that we learn to desire His will as we discern it through His Word.

Listed below are some suggestions on praying for your children:

Pray kingdom prayers.

Pray for them to have a place in the kingdom—pray for each child's salvation.

Pray that they would be a credit to the kingdom—that each child will develop a godly character.

Pray that they would be used to promote the kingdom—that each child will become a servant of others.

Use the prayers of the Bible as your model.

Read the prayers of Moses, David, Hannah, and many others in the Old Testament, and the prayers of Paul for his spiritual children in the New Testament.

Use men and women of faith as models for your children in prayer.

For example, pray that your child, like Daniel, would courageously resist pressure to compromise his standards.

Ask God to build qualities that honor Him in your children's lives.

Several good lists of character qualities to pray for in your children are found in 1 Corinthians 13 and Galatians 5:22-23.

It is very important that you hold your children before the Lord in fervent prayer throughout their years at home. This will become a major source of wisdom that you will need to be the parent you desire to be.

When you are discouraged, frustrated, or just plain weary, take some time to meditate on God's infinite love for your strong-willed child, and draw on His resources to replenish you for the task of being the parent of this special child.

QUESTION 16

Take a moment to pray for each of your children right now. With your spouse identify several requests, record and date them in your Life Notebook, and pause for some prayer together. Here are some suggested guidelines:

Acknowledge that God's hand was on your child in the way he or she was formed before birth, according to God's good plan.

Admit any areas you resent in the way God put your child together.

Accept God's design for your child. Thank God for making the child the way he is.

Affirm God's purpose in creating your child for his glory.

Ally yourself with God in his plans for your child's life.

QUESTION 17

Write down what you feel this lesson has contributed to your understanding of dealing with the strong-willed child. What do you plan to do differently? What aspects of your parenting have been affirmed by this lesson? Write down several goals to work on in the next month.

Lesson 8 Self Check

QUESTION 1

Strong-willed children are more sinful than compliant children. *True or False?*

QUESTION 2

The shy child typically reacts negatively to people, has irregular sleep and feeding schedules, and intense mood swings. *True or False?*

QUESTION 3

The pattern of child-raising in the Bible is that good parents normally produce godly children and bad parents produce bad children. *True or False?*

QUESTION 4

All children are inclined to challenge the authority of their parents. *True or False?*

QUESTION 5

The tendency to display greater strength of will is present at birth and tends to persist throughout childhood. *True or False?*

QUESTION 6

When the child wins one confrontation with parental authority, he will be satisfied. *True or False?*

QUESTION 7

Strong-willed children are bad and compliant children are good. *True or False?*

QUESTION 8

It is important to balance the many negative interactions with the strong-willed child with as many positive interactions as possible. *True or False?*

QUESTION 9

One way to avoid producing a poor self-esteem in a child is to focus on the behavior during discipline instead of on the person. *True or False?*

QUESTION 10

A goal is an objective that is under my control. A desire is an objective that I may legitimately and fervently want, but cannot reach through my efforts alone. *True or False?*

Lesson 8 Answers to Questions

QUESTION 1: *Your answer*

QUESTION 2: *Your answer*

QUESTION 3: *Your answer*

QUESTION 4: *Your answer*

QUESTION 5: *Your answer should be similar to the following:*

None! Time after time a godly king had an evil son and an evil king had a godly son.

QUESTION 6: False

QUESTION 7: True

QUESTION 8: *Your answer*

QUESTION 9: *Your answer*

QUESTION 10: *Your answer should be similar to the following:*

Parents must be especially careful with the strong-willed child not to allow anger to influence their discipline. Take time to calm down before you respond to your child. Count to ten or quote a verse to yourself before you deal with the situation. Decisive, calm action is the best response to his disobedience. Anger will generally cause the situation to escalate. Parents frequently find that the number of confrontations with a strong-willed child causes the frustration to build up to a point where it tends to explode. Recognize this tendency if you have experienced it, and concentrate on dealing with each issue as an isolated case

QUESTION 11: *Your answer*

QUESTION 12: *Your answer should be similar to the following:*

Basically, they would counsel, "Don't worry about it; it is the child's problem. If he wants to be happy, he can start behaving properly."

QUESTION 13: *Your answer*

QUESTION 14: *Your answer*

QUESTION 15: *Your answer*

QUESTION 16: *Your answer*

QUESTION 17: *Your answer*

Lesson 8 Self Check Answers

QUESTION 1: False
QUESTION 2: False
QUESTION 3: False
QUESTION 4: True
QUESTION 5: True
QUESTION 6: False
QUESTION 7: False
QUESTION 8: True
QUESTION 9: True
QUESTION 10: True

Lesson 9: The Rebellious Adolescent

Mark is seventeen. He lives at home with his parents, but they hardly ever see him. He is out most of the time with his friends, of whom his parents strongly disapprove. He started drinking and smoking several years ago, against his parents' wishes. He knows that his lifestyle violates their religious convictions. "I don't care what you think," he has shouted, too many times to recall. "It's my life, and I'll live it the way I please!"

For the past several years that is what he has done. He does what he wants to do, and his parents have little success in controlling him or communicating with him. Weary of the frequent battles with their son, they admit sadly, "He is such a rebellious boy that we don't know what to do with him."

A rebellious two-year-old can be difficult to handle, but a rebellious adolescent is another matter. While a parent has more control over the small child, a rebellious adolescent cannot be spanked or made to stand in a corner. The scope of rebellion in the teenage years can make this a frustrating and anxious time for the parents of a rebel.

This lesson is written particularly for those of us who may be experiencing the pain of having a rebellious adolescent. Often these are parents who have tried to center their families in Christ and train their children to live according to God's Word. But despite their best efforts their teenager has determined to reject what he or she has been taught. This lesson will discuss some of the problems encountered and suggest some helpful approaches to dealing with rebellion.

Lesson Outline

Topic 1: Some Causes of Rebellion

    The Prodigal Son Rebels

    Our Responsibility as Parents

Topic 2: Help for the Wounded Parent

    Breaking the Downhill Slide

    Coping with Rejection

    Recognizing the Limits of Parental Responsibility

    Learning to Wait on the Lord

    Committing Yourself to Prayer

    Relinquishing Your Child

    Launching a Campaign of Love

Lesson Objectives

By the end of this lesson, you will be able to do the following:

- Discuss the scope of rebellion and its basic cause

- Discuss the limits of parental responsibility and the importance of allowing a teenager to accept the natural consequences of his rebellion

- Define what it means to relinquish your child to God

- Formulate a plan to try to ward off adolescent rebellion before it develops

Topic 1: Some Causes of Rebellion

Rebellion in adolescence takes many forms, and it varies greatly from one individual to the next and from one family situation to another. One situation may involve a mild form of rebellion. The child ignores parental curfews, dresses in wild fashions, or listens to hard rock music. In another home, an adolescent may develop chronic habits of lying or stealing. In still another family, a teenager may use alcohol or drugs. Another teenager may rebel in the sexual area, becoming involved in premarital sexual relations or homosexuality. Some families face situations in which a son or daughter runs away from home, throwing the family into weeks or months of pain and turmoil. For many different reasons, some adolescents experience a particularly difficult and rebellious time, characterized by a negative attitude toward their parents and their parents' values.

The Prodigal Son Rebels

Ultimately it is true that young people themselves are responsible for their attitudes and behavior. Some may rebel no matter what the parents do. Let's take a look at a profound story in the New Testament about the rebellious adolescent and see if we can find some principles to help us.

Assignment

- Read about the prodigal son in Luke 15:11-32 before continuing.
- Please read the following article:

The Parable of the Prodigal Son

The very title by which this parable is known in the church declares the parable's clear intent. This is the story of a son who has wandered away from his father!

There is a problem of interpretation that deserves brief comment. Some have suggested that the rebellious son represents the unbeliever who is lost and condemned to hell, and is found by a loving father. However, the New Testament never suggests that unregenerate people may be considered as "sons of God." That honor is granted only to "those who have received him" (Jn 1:12-13). It follows, therefore, that the reference is to a Christian who has gone astray, just as the lost sheep and the lost coin have exactly the same reference.

Viewed in this light, it applies directly to the situation of the rebellious adolescent.

The Rebellious Son

In Luke 15:11-12 the younger son requests his inheritance while his father is still alive and in good health. In traditional Middle Eastern culture, this means, "Father, I am eager for you to die!"

Ken Bailey notes that for over fifteen years he has talked with people in the Middle East from Turkey to the Sudan about the implications of the son's request for an inheritance while the father is still alive (Bailey, 161-62).

The conversation goes like this:

"Has anyone ever made such a request in your village?"

"Never!"

"Could anyone ever make such a request?"

"Impossible!"

"If anyone ever did, what would happen?"

"His father would beat him, of course!"

"Why?

"This request means – he wants his father to die!"

If the father is a traditional Middle Eastern father, he will strike the boy across the face and drive him out of the house. Surely anywhere in the world this is an outrageous request. The prodigal is not simply a young boy who is "off to the big city to make his fame and fortune." Rather, this young son makes a request that is unthinkable, particularly in Middle Eastern culture. The father is expected to refuse if he is an oriental patriarch! In fact, he does not, which brings us to the second point.

The Father's Gift

In Luke 15:12 we read, "And he divided his wealth between them."

Remarkably, the father grants the young son's request, gives him his inheritance, and the right to sell it for cash. In the Middle Eastern milieu the father is expected to explode and discipline the boy for the cruel implication of his demand. It is difficult to imagine a more dramatic illustration of the quality of love that grants freedom even to reject the lover, than is given in this opening scene.

The inheritance is substantial. This is a wealthy family that has a herd of fatted calves and a herd of goats. House servants appear.

QUESTION 1

According to the article, are any reasons given for what the father may have done wrong in raising such a son?

Our Responsibility as Parents

The above study indicates that sometimes, through no fault of the parents at all, children make their own incorrect choices in spite of having received godly instruction and observing a godly model in the parents' lives. That said, let us leave the story of the prodigal son for a moment and consider some factors from the parents' side that might contribute to rebellion.

QUESTION 2

Read Ephesians 6:4. Consider the possible causes and possible effects below. In a discussion with your spouse, consider these items and in your Life Notebook record your reflections on your possible contribution to the conflict in your home.

Cause	Effect
When a father does not fulfill his promises	His children get a wounded spirit
When a father does not admit he is wrong	His children lose confidence in his leadership
When a father refuses to ask forgiveness	His children reject his pride
When a father does not have correct priorities	His children feel he is too busy for them
When a father is too strict with his discipline	His children have their spirits broken
When a father does not love his wife	His children begin to defend their mother against him
When a father neglects God's word	His children may do likewise
When a father disciplines in anger	His children develop bitterness
When a father focuses on outward beauty in others	His children may feel inferior and reject themselves
When a father lets his wife assume spiritual leadership	His children may regard religion as a female motivation when they grow older
When a father does not have personal convictions	His children accept situational ethics and excuse sin
When a father is impatient with his children	His children may seek approval from friends
When a father tries to warn his children only of the consequences of sin	His children learn to be successful in avoiding the consequences of sin and not the sin itself

Topic 2: Help for the Wounded Parent

We can draw one obvious conclusion about rebellion: rebellion hurts. It hurts everyone involved. It hurts the child, who faces a sense of alienation from those he loves as he rejects their values, and it deeply hurts the parents.

In this lesson we want to offer hope and encouragement to the hurting parent and also help for you in loving, accepting, and disciplining your wayward child. The healing process must begin in you, the hurting parent, before you can help your child.

Breaking the Downhill Slide

Often parents ask, "What can we do when we see our child begin to turn away from us and make wrong choices?" Often this occurs in the early teenage years. One of the first signs of problems can be poor communication. Communication between parents and teenagers often becomes strained, or even nonexistent. As parents we need to work at maintaining good communication with our teenager, letting him know what is expected of him but also reaffirming our love and respect.

Once communication shuts down between parent and child, it is much more difficult to reestablish. It is a very difficult thing to pry open the door of communication with an angry adolescent. It can require more tact and skill than any other assignment in parenthood. Mothers and fathers who are determined to maintain communication may find themselves drawn into endless verbal battles that leave them exhausted and accomplish little.

Assignment

- Please read the following article:

Advice from Dr. James Dobson

Dr. Dobson suggests that parents use the following approach to help break the downhill slide toward full-blown rebellion. He uses the illustration of a fourteen-year-old boy named Brian, who seems to have entered a period of rebellion and defiance. Brian has started to break rules and seems to hate the entire family. He becomes angry when his parents discipline him, but even during tranquil times he seems to have a lot of resentment stored up. What course of action would be best for his parents to take at this point in early adolescence?

Let us assume that you are Brian's father. Dr. Dobson recommends that you invite him out for a man-to-man talk. Go for a walk or to some quiet place where you can leave the rest of the family at home and be alone with your child. It would be best if this event could occur during a relatively tranquil time, rather than when you are in the midst of a disagreement with him. Tell him that you have some important matters to discuss with him which cannot be communicated adequately at home, but do not tell him exactly what you are going to say before the time.

The following is what Dr. Dobson suggests that you share with him:

> Brian, I wanted to talk to you this morning because of the changes that are taking place in you and in our home. We both know that the past few weeks have not been very pleasant. You have been angry most of the time and have become disobedient and rude. And your mother and I haven't done so well either. We've become irritable and we've said things that we've regretted later. This is not what God wants of us as parents, or of you as our son. There has to be a more creative way of solving our problems. That's why we're here.

> As a place to begin, Brian, I want you to understand what is happening. You have gone into a new period of life known as adolescence. This is the final phase of childhood, and it is often a very stormy and difficult few years. Nearly everyone on earth goes through these rough years during their early teens, and you are right on schedule. Many of the problems you face today were predictable from the day you were born, simply because growing up has never been an easy thing to do. There are even greater pressures on kids today than when we were young. I've said that to tell you this: We love you as much as we ever did, even though the past few months have been difficult in our home.

> What is actually taking place, you see, is that you have had a taste of freedom. You are tired of being told what to do. Within certain limits, that is healthy evidence that you are growing up and becoming your own man. However, you want to be your own boss and make your own decisions without interference from anyone. Brian, you will get what you want in a very short time. You are fourteen now, and you'll soon be fifteen and seventeen and nineteen. You will be grown before we know it, and your mom and I will no longer have any responsibility for you. The day is coming when you will marry whomever you wish, go to whatever school you choose, select the profession or job that suits you. We will respect your adulthood. Furthermore, Brian, the closer you get to that day, the more freedom we plan to give you. You have more privileges now than you had last year, and that trend will continue. We will soon set you free, and you will be accountable only to God and yourself.

> But, Brian, you must understand this message: You are not grown yet. During the past few weeks, you have wanted your mother and me to leave you alone—to let you stay out half the night if you choose, to fail in school, to carry no responsibility at home. And you have blown up whenever we have denied even your most extreme demands. The truth of the matter is, you have wanted us to grant you a twenty-year-old's freedom during your fourteenth year, although you still expect to have your shirts ironed and your meals fixed and your bills paid. You have wanted the best of both worlds with none of the responsibilities or limitations of

either. It doesn't work that way. So what are we to do? The easiest thing would be for us to let you have your way. There would be no hassles and no conflict and no more frustration. Many parents of fourteen-year-olds have done just that. But we must not yield to this temptation. You are not ready for that complete independence, and we would be showing hatred (instead of love) for you if we surrendered at this time. We would regret our mistake for the rest of our life, and you would soon blame us too. And as you know, you have two younger sisters who are watching you very closely, who must be protected from the things you are teaching them.

Besides, Brian, God has given us a responsibility as parents to do what is right for you, and He is holding us accountable for the way we do that job. I want to read you an important passage from the Bible that describes a father named Eli, a priest in the temple, who did not discipline and correct his two unruly teen-age sons [Read the dramatic story from 1 Samuel 2:12-17, 22-25, 27-34; 3:11-14; 4:1-3, 10-22]. It is very clear that God was angry at Eli for permitting his sons to be disrespectful and disobedient. Not only did He allow the sons to be killed in battle, but He also punished their father for not accepting his parental responsibilities.

This assignment to parents can be found throughout the Bible: Mothers and fathers are expected to train their children and discipline them when required. What I'm saying is that God will not hold us blameless if we let you behave in ways that are harmful to yourself and others. The Bible also tells parents not to overcorrect and demoralize their children. We are going to try harder to conform to that Scripture too.

That brings us to the question of where we go from this moment. I want to make a pledge to you, here and now: Your mother and I intend to be more sensitive to your needs and feelings than we've been in the past. We're not perfect, as you well know, and it is possible that you will feel we have been unfair at one time or another. If that occurs, you can express your views and we will listen to you. We want to keep the door of communication wide open between us. When you seek a new privilege, I'm going to ask myself this question, "Is there any way I can grant this request without harming Brian or other people?" If I can permit what you want in good conscience, I will do so. I will compromise and bend as far as my best judgment will let me.

But hear this, Brian. There will be some matters that cannot be compromised. There will be occasions when I will have to say no. And when those times come, you can expect me to stand like the Rock of Gibraltar. No amount of violence and temper tantrums and door slamming will change a thing. In fact, if you choose to fight me in those remaining rules, then I promise that you will lose big-time. …I have the courage and the determination to do my job during these last few years you are at home, and I intend to use all of my resources for this purpose, if necessary. So it's up to you. We can have a peaceful time of cooperation at home, or we can spend this last part of your childhood in unpleasantness and struggle. Either way, you will arrive home when you are told, and you will carry your share of responsibility in the family, and you will continue to respect your mother and me.

Finally, Brian, let me emphasize the message I gave you in the beginning. We love you more than you can imagine, and we're going to remain friends during this difficult time. There is so much pain in the world today. Life involves disappointment and loss and rejection and aging and sickness and ultimately death. You haven't felt much of that discomfort yet, but you'll taste it soon enough. So with all that heartache outside our door, let's not bring more of it on ourselves. We need each other. We need you, and believe it or not, you still need us occasionally. We're going to be praying for you every day and asking the Lord to lead and guide you. I know He will answer that prayer. And that, I suppose, is what I wanted to convey to you this morning. Let's make it better from now on.

Do you have things that need to be said to me?

(Dobson, *The New Strong-willed Child*, 192-196)

The content of this message should be modified to fit individual circumstances and the needs of particular adolescents. Furthermore, the responses of children will vary tremendously from person to person. An "open" boy or girl may reveal some very deep feelings at such a moment of communication, permitting a priceless time of mutual sharing and expression of love. On the other hand, a stubborn, defiant, proud adolescent may sit immobile with his head down and give no response at all. But even if your teenager remains stoic or hostile, at least he knows what you expect of him and what your intentions are.

QUESTION 3

You may not be struggling with a rebellious child at this time, in which case this lesson will have little importance in your family. However, if this is your situation, please open your Life Notebook after reading the letter and write a short letter that summarizes what you would say to your teenager, using Dobson's letter to give you some ideas. If you have a teenager and if you feel the time is appropriate, use your letter as a basis for a personal talk with your son or daughter. What response did you observe in your teenager? You may know some other parents who have this problem. Perhaps this discussion could help them as well.

Coping with Rejection

The father in the parable of the prodigal son must have been terribly hurt. Furthermore, because the son's behavior was public, the father was no doubt embarrassed that his son's behavior may have created gossip in the town.

Assignment

- Please read the following articles:

The Hurried Sale

Read Luke 15:13. The prodigal "gathered all he had." This means that he is selling his part of the family farm. He "turns it into cash" (NEB). However, according to local law at the time of Jesus, the son did not have the right to sell the property until his father died. Yet, he does it anyway.

As that happens, this horrendous family breakdown becomes public knowledge, and the family is shamed before the entire community. Jewish law of the first century provided for the division of an inheritance (when the father was ready to make such a division), but did not grant the children the right to sell until after the father's death.

In a departure from the expected norm, the father grants the inheritance and the right to sell, knowing that this right will shame the family before the community.

Read in Luke 15:13 of the younger son's quick departure.

The prodigal sells quickly ("a few days later"). He is probably obliged to do so; since he shamed his father and his extended family, the villagers are angry and would most likely rise up against him. According the Jewish law, a healthy father may continue to farm the land during his lifetime. As a result he has to conclude the sale and get out of town as quickly as possible. As mentioned above, Jewish law did not permit such a sale. The prodigal does not care.

The Qetsatsah Ceremony

Shameful behavior such as that of the younger son made it certain that he would face what was called a *qetsatsah* ceremony if he dared to return to his home village. What was the *Qetsatsah*? The villagers would bring a large earthenware jar, fill it with burned nuts and burned grain and break it in front of the guilty individual. While doing this, the community would shout, "So-and-so is cut off from his people." From that point on, the village would have nothing to do with the wayward lad.

QUESTION 4

Read the parable of the prodigal and with your spouse think for a moment about the feelings of the rejected father. The text says nothing about his feelings but put yourself in his place. What was he thinking? What were his hurts? Then reflect on your own situation. Record your feelings. In what ways do you as a parent feel rejected and like a failure?

One thing that hurts deeply when your adolescent rebels is the sense of growing alienation from your child and rejection by him. One father spoke openly about his feelings of rejection:

> After giving to my child for so many years, now he is rejecting me, and I don't know why. I feel as though my son and I are divorced. He ignores the training we have given him in morality and the Christian convictions we thought he had developed.

This type of emotional divorce between parent and child is an especially painful form of rejection.

Rejection can take many forms:

- Rejection of the parents' love
- Rejection of the parents' moral code
- Rejection of the parents' lifestyle
- Rejection of the parents' church and all that it stands for
- Rejection of God

Coping with Rejection

To watch your own child pursue a path of rebellion against God is to wade in the very depths of pain as a Christian parent. This kind of pain is chronic; it does not subside. How do we cope with this? The resources of Scripture are ours as believers, along with the assurance that God's hand will hold us. Some have found particular comfort reading the Psalms, perhaps because the Psalmist openly expresses his feelings in times of deepest distress and often finds his way back from the brink of despair to a reaffirmation of faith in God.

QUESTION 5

Read Psalm 73. What change takes place in the speaker as the Psalm progresses? Do the circumstances surrounding the speaker change? What are some of the factors which cause the speaker (Asaph) to reconsider his thinking? In which verse do you note the change?

In the Psalms we often note that the speaker faces discouragement, despair, and even destruction, and he speaks openly of his feelings to the Lord, pouring out his pain and his disappointment. Whether the speaker is David or Moses or Asaph, he has learned the lesson of bringing his grief to the only One who has balm to soothe the pain and strength to lift up the fallen.

For parents of a rebellious adolescent, the act of coming to God with our grief and hurt is a repeated one. Daily we need the balm of His comfort and assurance; daily we need His strength renewed in us so that we may face the future with hope. We may find practical help in Christian books and methods. We find solace and strength only in Christ and in those who encourage us to walk with Him.

Recognizing the Limits of Parental Responsibility

One of the hardest things for parents of a rebellious child to deal with is the "why" of rebellion. Parents simply do not understand why their child has chosen to walk a different road in life, a road that they know can lead to destruction. They look at other parents who apparently have not been consistent in following godly principles of child-rearing, yet their children seem to be following the Lord and living an upright life, while one of their own children is choosing to walk away from God.

When a child becomes rebellious, the human tendency is to look for reasons. Many parents seek a place to lay the blame. In past generations, parents and grandparents often said of a wayward child, "Well, that's just the way he is" or "He is just like his father" (or some other relative). Today many Christian parents tend to blame themselves for their child's mistakes. Today's parents have been made more aware of their responsibilities as parents and are consequently more aware of their shortcomings and failures as well. Thus, when a teenager rebels, a parent is likely to begin a process of examining all his own shortcomings, and it is not difficult to find some evidence that he has been less than a perfect parent.

Dr. Guy Greenfield, professor of Christian ethics, experienced the pain of having a rebellious child. He writes:

> When your son or daughter has rebelled against your Christian beliefs and values, it is normal to look back over the years and ask yourself, "What went wrong? I don't understand." But instead of asking who is to blame or whose fault was it, it is much more productive to ask, "What can I learn from this? How can I best relate to my child now that all of this has happened? How can my husband or wife and I work together in building a new relationship with our child?" (Greenfield, 67)

Dr. Greenfield and his wife struggled with guilt, recognizing that they did not measure up to all their expectations of what a parent should be. Ultimately, they accepted God's forgiveness for their failures and began to concentrate on building a new relationship with their child, rather than wallowing in guilt over past failures.

Dr. Dobson also deals with the question of parental responsibility for wayward children. He returns to the question of the interpretation of Proverbs 22:6:

> Those who believe Proverbs 22:6 offers a guarantee of salvation for the next generation have assumed, in essence, that a child can be programmed so thoroughly as to **determine** his course. The assignment for them is to bring him up "in the way he should go." But think about that for a moment. Didn't the great Creator handle Adam and Eve with infinite wisdom and love? He made no mistakes in "fathering" them. They were also harbored in a perfect environment with none of the pressures we face. They had no in-law problems, no monetary needs, no frustrating employers, no television, no pornography, no alcohol or drugs, no peer pressure and no sorrow. They had **no excuses!** Nevertheless, they ignored the explicit warning from God and stumbled into sin. If it were ever possible to avoid the ensnarement of evil, it would have occurred in that sinless world. But it didn't. God in His love gave Adam and Eve a choice between good and evil and they abused it. Will He now withhold that same freedom from your children? No. Ultimately, they will decide for themselves. (Dobson, *Parenting Isn't for Cowards,* 186)

We touched on this subject in our study of Proverbs 22:6. We pointed out the need to recall that proverbs are generalizations, not promises. In other words there are general rules. Good parents are less likely to produce problem children than bad parents. Stable homes are more likely to produce stable children than unstable homes, but that is as far as it seems to go. There are no steel-reinforced rules which say:

Good parenting always produces good children.

Bad parenting always produces bad children.

In fact, there is evidence that good parenting can produce bad children at times, while bad parenting has been known to produce good children. This is contrary to common thinking, but a look around your neighborhood will probably yield examples that verify this. Some of the best parents have rebellious children because God gives every individual the right to choose. The influence of peers during adolescence sometimes leads them in the wrong direction. Individual temptation is another factor, the strength of their will is another. Parents have a vitally important role to play but they merely influence the outcome. They do not determine it. That is why it is unfair for parents to blame themselves completely when children rebel. There are many factors which affect the outcome such as genes, school and social environment, and the child's own decisions.

QUESTION 6

In Lesson 8, you studied the pattern of success or failure in parenting by the kings of Judah. Let's take another look. Please open your Life Notebook and after reading the following verses, record your observations about the various kings of Judah and their sons. This time see if you can identify any issues in the lives of the good kings which may have led to successful or failed outcomes with their children. Do you see any automatic relationship between the quality of the parent and the quality of the son?

1. Abijah (2 Chron 13:10)
2. Asa son of Abijah (2 Chron 14:2-5)
3. Jehoshaphat son of Asa (2 Chron 17:3-6; 20:34-35)
4. Jehoram son of Jehoshaphat (2 Chron 21:4-6)
5. Ahaziah son of Jehoram (2 Chron 22:1-4)
6. Jehoiada son of Ahaziah (2 Chron 23:16-18; 24:16)
7. Joash son of Jehoida (2 Chron 24:2, 20)
8. Amaziah son of Joash (2 Chron 25:1-2; 25:27)
9. Uzziah son of Amaziah (2 Chron 25:3-5; 26:16)
10. Jotham son of Uzziah (2 Chron 27:2, 6)
11. Ahaz son of Jotham (2 Chron 28:1-4)
12. Hezekiah son of Ahaz (2 Kgs 18:5; 2 Chron 29:1; 30:1; 31:20-21)
13. Manasseh son of Hezekiah (2 Chron 33:1-3)
14. Amon son of Manasseh (2 Chron 33:21-33)
15. Josiah son of Amon (2 Chron 34:1-4, 31-33)
16. Jehoiakim son of Josiah (2 Chron 36:5)

The point we make here is that we are not totally responsible for all that our child is or does. We are responsible to do the best we can to train our children in the way they should go. Yet all of our best efforts do not preclude the possibility that our child will reject our teaching and choose a wayward path instead. Our parental responsibility has limits which we must recognize and accept, and we cannot go beyond them. If we insist on taking all the blame, we will spend the rest of our lives living with a crushing sense of failure and remorse.

Of course we make mistakes; all parents do. When we recognize our mistakes and our shortcomings as parents, we need to deal with them. We must seek God's face in prayer, confessing our sins against our children, both past and present, and asking forgiveness. We may also need to ask forgiveness from our child.

Once we have dealt with any sin in our lives, God does not want us to continue to wallow in guilt and despair. We need to accept God's forgiveness and put our past sins behind us. If feelings of guilt arise again over the same sins, we should ignore them, for this is false guilt, a tool of Satan to keep us mired in despair. If our sin is confessed, 1 John 1:9 assures us that our hearts are washed by the blood of the perfect Lamb slain for sin. Guilt that continues to arise over the same sin is not from God.

Learning to Wait on the Lord

One family had a daughter who had a serious problem with dishonesty. The parents never knew for certain when she was telling the truth. Each time an incident occurred they wondered if the daughter was lying again. They tried to love her and to listen. They tried everything they knew to do to encourage their daughter to change her habit of lying. They pleaded with God repeatedly to intervene, but all they experienced was silence.

After some time the parents began to realize that God was providing them the opportunity to come into a marvelous understanding of Himself. The lesson they saw in this experience was that God's silence in this instance was not meant to produce hopelessness, but patience, faith, and quiet confidence. When God is silent, when the answer we had hoped for does not come, we can still be confident that God has listened carefully to our pleas and that in His sovereignty He will reveal His answer in His time.

The psalmist encourages us to wait for the Lord, to be strong, and to let our heart find courage and rest in Him (Ps 27:14; 37:7). As we learn to do this, He promises that we will gain new strength, so that we may mount up with wings as eagles (Isa 40:31).

Does this poem express the concerns of your heart?

Waiting on the Lord

Desperately, helplessly, longingly, I cried.

Quietly, patiently, lovingly God replied.

I pled and I wept for a clue to my fate,

And the Master so gently said, "Child, you must wait!"

"'Wait?', you say, wait!" my indignant reply.

"Lord, I need answers, I need to know why!

Is your hand shortened? Or have you not heard?

By FAITH I have asked, and am claiming your Word.

"My future and all to which I can relate

Hangs in the balance, and you tell me to WAIT?

I'm needing a 'yes,' a go-ahead sign,

Or even a 'no' to which I can resign.

"And Lord, you promised that if we believe

We need but to ask, and we shall receive.

And Lord, I've been asking, and this is my cry:

I'm weary of asking! I need a reply!"

Then quietly, softly, I learned of my fate

As my Master replied once again, "You must wait."

So, I slumped in my chair, defeated and taut

And grumbled to God, "So, I'm waiting. . .for what?"

He seemed then to kneel and His eyes wept with mine,

And he tenderly said, "I could give you a sign.

I could shake the heavens, and darken the sun.

I could raise the dead, and cause mountains to run.

All you seek, I could give, and pleased you would be.

You would have what you want—but, you wouldn't know ME.

"You'd not know the depth of my love for each saint;

You'd not know the power that I give to the faint;

You'd not learn to see through the clouds of despair;

You'd not learn to trust just by knowing I'm there;

You'd not know the joy of resting in me

When darkness and silence were all you could see.

"You'd never experience that fullness of love

As the peace of my Spirit descends like a dove;

You'd know that I give and I save. . .(for a start),

But you'd not know the depth of the beat of my heart.

"The glow of my comfort late into the night.

The faith that I give when you walk without sight,

The depth that's beyond getting just what you asked

Of an infinite God, who makes what you have LAST.

"You'd never know, should your pain quickly flee,

What it means that 'My grace is sufficient for thee.'

Yes, your dreams for your loved ones overnight would come true,

But, oh, the loss! if I lost what I'm doing in you!

"So, be silent, my child, and in time you will see

THAT THE GREATEST OF GIFTS IS TO GET TO KNOW ME.

And though oft may my answers seem terribly late,

My wisest of answers is still but to WAIT."

(Kelfer)

Often we do not want to wait on the Lord. We want solutions to our problems now. But God's perspective on time is often different from ours. Think of Mary and Martha, waiting for Jesus after sending word that their brother Lazarus was severely ill. The Bible says that when Jesus heard that Lazarus was sick, He stayed two days longer in the place where He was. Imagine the agony of those three siblings as they waited anxiously for the Lord to come. At times we may agonize in this way, wondering, has Jesus received the message we sent? Will He come in time? What if this or that happens? "Oh, Jesus," we cry out, "where are You? Why don't You do something now?"

QUESTION 7

Record your responses to the following questions in your Life Notebook. In what ways am I allowing God to be sovereign in the situation with my child? How am I trusting Him for what I cannot see? How am I standing firm in my conviction of His goodness?

Committing Yourself to Prayer

We can deepen our reliance on God and stand firm in Him as we spend more time in prayer. Even when your heart wells up with nothing but requests, remember to praise Him. God desires our praise for who He is. We do not have to praise Him *for* the circumstances; it would be wrong to praise God that our child has fallen into sin. But we can praise Him *in* the circumstances.

Make a commitment to pray consistently for your child, as we discussed in Lesson 8. We need to pray for ourselves also, so that we can respond with faith in the midst of this trial with our child. Like the father of the demon-possessed boy, we may say to the Lord at times, "I do believe; help my unbelief" (Mk 9:24). This is a response of faith, acknowledging at the same time that our faith is weak and needs to grow.

It may encourage you to find a friend to pray with you regularly. When you are hurting, it is important to let other Christians share your hurt. Many wounded parents are embarrassed and fearful of what their Christian friends in the church may think. They try to hide the problems they are having with their children. It may not be advisable to share details that might embarrass your teenager, but it can be so comforting to find a friend with whom you can share openly and pray, knowing that this friend will keep your confidences. We need one another, particularly when we are hurting.

One mother who was going through a deep struggle with her teenager sought out another mother, and these two parents covenanted together to meet once a week to pray for their teenagers. They experienced a time of deep fellowship, mutual encouragement, and a uniting of spirits as they prayed together regularly.

Perhaps you and your spouse can covenant together to pray for your child. Pray that God delivers your child from overwhelming temptation. Pray that He gives that child every opportunity to return to Him, that He reveals His tenderness and His forgiveness toward that child. At the same time, recognize that God will never force a person to bow the knee against his will. Your child must respond to God's love. If he refuses to respond, God is not to be blamed. He desires our child's salvation and sanctification even more earnestly and consistently than we do as parents, and He is grieved when our child chooses a wayward path.

Relinquishing Your Child

We do not know how long the father in the parable of the prodigal son had to wait. It may have taken years for his son to come to his senses. However, there is one lesson we can learn from this father.

QUESTION 8

How did the father in the parable respond to his son's request?

    A. He reasoned with him about the foolishness of his decision.

    B. He allowed him to make his own choice and experience the consequences.

    C. He explained to him how this would embarrass the family.

    D. He warned him of the Qetsatsah ceremony that would forever keep him away from the village.

In a word, the father relinquished his son to God.

What is relinquishment? It involves four things.

    1. It is an attitude that says it is better to be godly parents even though we may fail to produce godly children.

    2. It is allowing our children to face the consequences of their own rebellious decisions.

    3. It is the abandonment of the desire to be proud of our children.

    4. It is giving our children up to God and allowing Him to work in their lives in His own way and timing.

If relinquishment were merely a giving up it would be relief enough. But it is giving up to God.

Being Godly Parents

Our focus is to be on our walk with God and not on the outcome that all our efforts may produce. God's desires for all His creatures have not always been fulfilled and ours for our children will not be satisfied either. We are called to move beyond pragmatism to a walk before God. We are to choose what is right without demanding that the right shall always gratify our vanity, satisfy our carnal longings or even the yearnings of our least selfish loves. If God wept over a rebellious humanity, then we at times may have to grieve over rebellious children.

Consequences

Relinquishment also means to allow your children to face pain, by allowing them to experience the consequences of their own actions. Too often the parents of troubled adolescents continually enable the rebellious behavior by paying their children's debts, making excuses for them, and refusing to face the reality of what they have become. By continually protecting their children, particularly when they are older, they are actually preventing their children from learning valuable lessons. Wealthy parents of alcoholics are known for their mistakes in this regard. They pay their children's debts, bail them out when they await trial, hire expensive lawyers for them, go out on a limb arranging employment for them. Some never seem to learn. Relinquishment means to trust God about your children rather than your own ability to manage their lives. It means recognizing that wise counsel to older children is just that—wise counsel. It cannot be forced on them. It may, and often will, be refused by them.

Right to be Proud

Relinquishment means to forsake the right to be proud. We all want to be proud of our children and their rebellious attitude conflicts with that desire. Parents think about all they have done for their children. Did I not give them birth? Did I not feed them? Did I not make it possible for them to get extra training in sports or music, etc.? It is painful to listen to other parents describe how their children are moving on with the Lord, when you own are totally indifferent to Him. Instead, like the younger brother in the parable, the child brings humiliation and embarrassment. To counter this, many parents nag their children or scream at them. Who would not want to hear others praise their children? "He is such a godly young man." "My daughter is going on a mission trip this summer." Yet some parents get no accolades. Instead they grieve as their hopes burst one by one.

To them it seems that every effort they put into raising their children was wasted. They swallow their shame as they mingle with the parents of successful children. Give up your right to be proud.

QUESTION 9

Review each of the four aspects of relinquishment above. Ask yourself how you are doing in the matter of relinquishing your child to God in these areas. Make these items a matter of prayer this week. Go over these areas with your spouse, and pray together about relinquishing your child to God.

QUESTION 10

Think again about the parable of the prodigal son. How did the father respond to his son's request to have his inheritance now? Why did he respond this way?

QUESTION 11

What lessons do you learn from the way the father dealt with his son's failure? What would you have done if the prodigal was your son and he was wallowing in a pigsty? Open your Life Notebook and record your thoughts.

The father in this story must have experienced all of the emotions we discussed earlier. He knew the anguish of his son's rejection of his moral values, of his lifestyle, and of his love. He had to face the fact that his son was determined to leave and was probably going to take the money he was given and squander it.

His decision to let the son go was not made because he did not care what happened to him. He cared very deeply, yet he also realized that he could not force his son to accept either his values or his love. He reached a point where it seemed there was nothing to do but to physically let the son go. We as parents may reach such a point where we must let our son or daughter go. Our hope lies in the fact that, as we let our child go, we give him to God.

Read the comments by John White from his book *Parents in Pain* called "Letting Go."

Letting Go

Letting a child go is never easy. One parent tried to make a mental picture of this process to help him gain the proper perspective. The parent pictured in his mind putting his son into a gift box, wrapped with beautiful paper and ribbon. Then he imagined the glorious throne of God, situated at the top of a flight of celestial stairs. In his mind he walked up those stairs with his gift-wrapped package and put it down at the feet of Jesus, who was sitting on the throne. He waited as Jesus then picked up the package, put it in His lap, removed the wrappings, took off the lid, and lifted the child out. After he had seen Jesus holding his child, he walked back down the stairs. He turned midway to look back and assure himself that Jesus was still holding his child. He continued to the bottom of the stairs, thanking God for taking control.

The parent used this mental image to remind himself that he had totally given his prodigal to God and had taken his hands off. When we have released our child into God's keeping, we can ask God to do all that is necessary to bring our child to Himself. Only after truly relinquishing our children to God's care can we pray such a prayer. Circumstances may unfold that will tear at our heart, but God will undertake to reach the rebel, to convict of sin, and to draw the child back to Himself. When we are tempted to take control again, we can point to a definite time when in our mind we walked up those stairs and gave the gift of our child to God and our child was received by a faithful, loving Father.

Giving the child up to God does not mean that things will get better. Whether the child leaves home or not, if he continues in rebellion, life may become more difficult for him, as it did for the prodigal son. As parents we may be tempted to try to right all our child's wrongs or to help him by removing all obstacles from his path or by paying for his mistakes. If our son steals something, we pay for it. If our daughter misses school, we tell a lie to cover for her so that she will not be expelled. By actions such as this, we let the child know that we will always be there to get him or her out of trouble. Consequently, he or she fails to learn from mistakes. We cannot and should not always deliver a child from experiencing the natural consequences of his actions.

We cannot always go before our son to smooth the way or follow behind our daughter to sweep up the debris left behind. We cannot be running in to cleanse the stench of the pigpen or to remodel it and make it homey. The pigpen is what it took to drive the prodigal home. If we clean it up, our child may make it his permanent dwelling!

When we repeatedly try to keep our child from experiencing pain or loss as a result of his choices, we may be unknowingly fighting against what God Himself is faithfully trying to do in the young person's life to bring him to the end of himself. Make it clear to your child that, if he wants to make his own decisions, he must also bear the responsibility for those decisions. If he refuses your counsel, he must bear the full impact of the consequences alone.

By allowing his son to bear the consequences of his wrong actions, the father in Luke 15 allowed his son to learn a very painful lesson. It grieved the father greatly, but it also proved to be the tool that was used to goad the son to return to his father. John White writes:

> The father of the prodigal son let his son go. And God the Father of us all does likewise. He who could coerce our wills refuses to. There is a limit even to his pleading. He does not block the doorway as we try to leave him, flooding us with a thousand arguments. Nor does he pursue us pestering us with, "I told you so." He gives us the full dignity of choice.

> There is wisdom as well as justice in what he fails to do. There are times when our wills are so set on disastrous courses that disaster alone will teach us. There is nothing like a belly full of husks to teach a man that he's a fool. (White, 219)

White advises parents:

> Do not feel guilty about allowing your children to reap what they have sown for this is how God deals with all of us. He does not enjoy letting us pursue our stubborn way until we live with pigs, but faced with a choice between giving us the full dignity of personhood with all its attendant risks or enslaving us to involuntary servitude like the beasts, he chooses the former. He could not make us a little lower than the angels without facing the possibility that we might choose to become little better than demons. Love says, "I will give you the high dignity of choice, even though you choose to fling my gift back in my face."

> Clearly, letting go is a matter of degree, and the degree to which I let go will increase over the years. In fact our hand may often be forced by realities which wrest control from us. Yet if we adopt an attitude of relinquishment, we may save ourselves and our children some needless frustration. Moreover, we will be giving our children the same high dignity that God gives us.

> All is not lost when our children make foolish choices. It will be painful for us to watch them eat hog's food, but there is hope that when that happens they will learn from experience what they never could have learned from precept.

When we relinquish our child, mentally and emotionally, we are not giving up on him. We are giving him up to God. We place him in the very best hands, capable of keeping him, caring for him, and goading him to return to the fold.

(White, 219-35)

QUESTION 12

As you discuss "Letting Go" with your spouse, what part of his discussion seems particularly relevant to your situation? Record your thoughts in your Life Notebook.

QUESTION 13

Read the story of Hannah as she left her tiny Samuel in the charge of old Eli at Shiloh (see 1 Sam 1:1-28; 2:1-11). Samuel was not a rebel; he was a child but Hannah gave him up to God. She had relinquished much—her right to possess, to enjoy, to be proud before her rival Peninnah, to control Samuel's development, to be repaid for all her tears. She did not know her son would change the destiny of Israel, towering above the nation's history as the founder of two dynasties of kings, setting the moral tone of the nation for generations to come. The fashioning of such a man was the work of God Himself. This may be the time for your to write out your own prayer of relinquishment in your Life Notebook, giving your child over into God's hands.

Launching a Campaign of Love

Assignment

- Please read the following articles:

The Prodigal Becomes a Pig Herder

Please read Luke 15:14-15. The young son wastes his inheritance and faces famine.

There were apparently ten recorded famines in and around Jerusalem from 169 BC to AD 70. A lone Jew in a Gentile country would be particularly desperate during such a time. Now his inheritance has ended up in the hands of Gentiles. The *qetsatsah* definitely awaits him should he ever attempt to return home. Normally, after spending everything, a son would return home, but the prodigal cannot until he pays back the lost inheritance. To avoid the *qetsahtsah* ceremony, he must get back the money he has wasted and pay it back. So he makes two unsuccessful attempts to find employment. The first attempt is working at feeding pigs.

So he attaches (Greek *kollao*) himself to a citizen of that country. The Greek word is quite strong. He "glues" himself to this citizen. He is now an indigent and looks for any benefactor who will take care of him. Having come to the community with money and then losing it in reckless living, he has lost the respect of his new community. The normal way a polite Middle Easterner gets rid of unwanted "clingers" is to assign them a task he knows they will refuse.

For a Jew, no fall from favor could be more catastrophic. Becoming a pig herder was the extreme opposite of enjoying the father's favor and blessing. The Jews did not like pork! But his money is spent, and even though he naturally desires to return home, he has broken the rules. As he sinks further into psychological and spiritual despair and takes a despised job, he could not be more lost.

Read about his lost condition in Luke 15:16. Becoming a pig herder does not work. The text deliberately affirms, "No one gave him anything." As a pig herder, the prodigal is not fed. He was so hungry that he was willing to eat pig food, "pods" (Greek *keration*). This was a bitter, harsh tasting berry. He says in the next verse that he is dying of hunger.

Demonstrating Love in the Midst of Rebellion

After several years of severe difficulty in the home with a daughter, one father made a commitment that during that daughter's last year in secondary school, for the entire year, her last year at home, she was not going to hear one negative thing from her father. In fact, all she would hear for one year was words of encouragement and praise.

Another father and mother share a hurtful situation where their 16-year-old daughter did not come home at the expected time, 11:00 p.m. As the night wore on they became more and more worried ….and angry. "How can she do this to us?" They got in the car and drove all over town until 2:00 a.m., searching all the known places where young people visited. Exhausted, they finally returned and stayed awake the rest of the night in great worry. About 7:00 a.m. the daughter called and said, "Dad, I am OK, I will be home after school" and hung up! As the father thought about the Parable of the Prodigal Son, he wondered how he could demonstrate love, acceptance, and rejoicing. He bought a dozen roses and put them on her bed with the following note.

> Mary, I am so glad you are home. You do not have to explain anything to me about where you have been. I am just delighted you are back and safe.
>
> Love you,
> Dad

One parent described an "I love you campaign" she undertook. Her child was acting very unlovable; at times she even screamed, "I hate you," at her mother and father. The mother began to conscientiously express affection toward her child, giving her a hug or a gentle touch on the arm or rubbing her back. Her daughter often shrugged off her touch. "I had to learn not to give up after a rejection or two," the mother said. She began to leave little notes expressing her love for her daughter, not gushing but simply stated expressions of love, such as, "I'm glad you are home," "You look nice today," or simply, "I love you." She frequently put a note on her daughter's pillow or in her lunchbox, somewhere the daughter would see it.

Another mother longed to express her love to her rebellious son, but he had left home, and she did not even know where to find him. So she began writing in a journal, one paragraph a day, dating each entry. She wrote about the things that were happening while he was gone, things that were once of interest to him. Each day she also wrote down some expression of her love for him. When he returned one day, she gave the journal to him. He read it, and she and her son were able to talk for the first time about deep-seated emotions that they previously could not discuss with each other.

At times expressing love for a rebellious teenager may simply mean listening. A Christian leader and his wife were forced to watch as their son went down the road of rebellion, step by step. The mother and father were hurt and embarrassed. They prayed, they tried everything possible to reach their son, and finally, they did not know what else to do.

At last the father decided, "I'm going to show love to my son just by sitting and listening, just by being there." His son would often come in at 3:00 in the morning, sometimes drunk or angry, yet this dear father would sit there and just say, "Tell me what you are feeling. I love you. I care."

This was the beginning of a change in their relationship. Night after night, the father was there when the son came home. The son eventually began to realize how much his father cared, and this was the turning point in the son's life. The young man saw that, instead of condemning him, his father was listening, wanting him to communicate. Somehow this conveyed love to him in a way that many other actions had not. He already knew what his father thought about what he did, but he began to see that his father could condemn his actions and still love him.

The rebellious child needs you more than ever. He needs extra care, extra love, extra patience, and extra protection, for he is weak and lost. He may lack the courage and the inner strength displayed by some of his peers that have enabled them to stay close to God. He needs you to encourage him and pray for him and love him.

Probably every parent who has ever agonized over a troubled child has asked the question, "God, why did you give me this child? I feel so helpless. I don't know what to do with him." Children too have asked at times, "God, why did you place me in this family?" It is not merely by chance that a child is placed in your family. It is by design. God had a purpose in placing that child in your family. God also knew that problems would come when he placed this child in your family. He has given you a divine commission to plead for this child's soul, for his safety, and for his salvation.

We do not know what kind of parent the father was before his son ran away, but we do know what he was like when he returned. He was filled with love and forgiveness.

Even when your adolescent is rebellious, he needs to hear that you love him, and he also needs to see your love in action. When things are at their worst, we are still called to love our children. You can love your child even when your child is very unlovable.

For most of us, the pain of a child running away from home is not likely. Yet, in a real sense, every time the child does something which severely shatters the family relationship, he has gone away. He needs to know that in spite of his behavior, you love and accept him even if you do not accept his attitudes.

God wants you as a parent to continue to demonstrate Christian love toward your rebellious child: to give extra love, an affectionate touch, a word of praise, a note of encouragement, and especially a listening ear. He wants you to learn to respond with a smile when your child knows that what he deserves is a frown. God is not finished with this child yet. He can do all things, and no purpose of His can be thwarted. Do not give up hope, and do not cast aside faith that a pigsty experience will draw your child back to the heavenly Father. Be waiting with open arms when that time comes.

QUESTION 14

After reading this article on demonstrating love, in what encouraging ways you can demonstrate love to your child?

Lesson 9 Self Check

QUESTION 1

When a father asks forgiveness and admits he was wrong, even if he really is wrong, his children may lose respect for his leadership. *True or False?*

QUESTION 2

How did the father in the parable respond to his son's request?

    A. He reasoned with him about the foolishness of his decision.

    B. He allowed him to make his own choice and experience the consequences.

    C. He explained to him how this would embarrass the family.

    D. He warned him of the Qetsatsah ceremony which would forever keep him away from the village.

QUESTION 3

Once communication shuts down between parent and child, it is much more difficult to reestablish. *True or False?*

QUESTION 4

Proverbs 22:6 offers a guarantee of salvation for the next generation and assumes that a child can be lovingly programmed so thoroughly as to determine his course. *True or False?*

QUESTION 5

The Scriptures indicate that there is not a definite correlation between godly parenting and producing a godly child. *True or False?*

QUESTION 6

What does relinquishment involve?

    A. Allowing your children to make their own decisions with no input from you

    B. Giving our children up to God and allowing Him to work in their lives in His own way and in His time

    C. Protecting our children from making decisions that will have negative consequences

    D. Focusing on our child's good behavior

QUESTION 7

In dealing with a rebellious child, one must be careful to not to give too much affirmation, praise, and encouragement lest you encourage the same behavior you are trying to modify. *True or False?*

QUESTION 8

In the parable of the prodigal son, his repentance is intended to illustrate the salvation of a lost man. *True or False?*

QUESTION 9

The father does not demonstrate love in response to his son's confession. Rather, out of his own compassion he empties himself, assumes the form of a servant, and runs to welcome his estranged son. *True or False?*

QUESTION 10

The story of Mary and Martha and the raising of Lazarus has direct application to the burden wounded parents feel when dealing with a rebellious adolescent. *True or False?*

Lesson 9 Answers to Questions

QUESTION 1: *Your answer should be similar to the following:*
As far as the text says, the father did nothing wrong. This becomes evident as the story unfolds. Just because an adolescent rebels, that does not necessarily mean the parents are at fault.

QUESTION 2: *Your answer*

QUESTION 3: *Your answer*

QUESTION 4: *Your answer*

QUESTION 5: *Your answer*

QUESTION 6: *Your answer*

QUESTION 7: *Your answer*

QUESTION 8
B. He allowed him to make his own choice and experience the consequences.

QUESTION 9: *Your answer*

QUESTION 10: *Your answer should be similar to the following:*
The father chose to let the son go. He chose to allow the child to bear the consequences of his wrong actions, until the son had fallen so low that he was reduced to eating pig's food. There is sometimes wisdom in this approach, which allows a child to learn from his mistakes and receive the natural consequences of his poor choices. There may be times when parents should come to a teenager's rescue, but it may be in God's plan to use failure to bring a child to the end of himself and show him his need of the Lord.

QUESTION 11: *Your answer*

QUESTION 12: *Your answer*

QUESTION 13: *Your answer*

QUESTION 14: *Your answer*

Lesson 9 Self Check Answers

QUESTION 1: False

QUESTION 2

    B. He allowed him to make his own choice and experience the consequences.

QUESTION 3: True

QUESTION 4: False

QUESTION 5: True

QUESTION 6

    B. Giving our children up to God and allowing Him to work in their lives in His own way and in His time

QUESTION 7: False

QUESTION 8: False

QUESTION 9: True

QUESTION 10: True

Unit 4: Teaching Your Child to Walk with God

Read the divine command given to Adam and Eve in the Garden in Genesis 1:27-28.

Man was to rule! This conquest of planet earth was to be achieved by being godly parents who trusted in Christ and manifested His way of life to their children.

Read what Moses said to fulfill this mandate in Deuteronomy 6:1-9.

These words give us our challenge. We are to lead our children to Christ and teach them God's ways. While it is true that each child makes his own decisions, our responsibility is specified in these verses.

In this unit we will focus leading our children to Christ, teaching them about God's way of life, and then trusting them to God by releasing them to Him.

Unit Outline

Lesson 10: Beginning with Christ

Lesson 11: Teaching our Children to Commit to God's Way of Life

Lesson 12: Releasing Your Child to God

Unit Objectives

By the end of this unit, you will be able to do the following:

- Clearly explain the gospel to your child
- Implement creative methods of teaching your child about God
- Release your child to God in a healthy manner

Lesson 10: Beginning with Christ

Lesson Introduction

Enoch was a man who walked with God. The Bible gives us very little information about Enoch. He was the father of Methuselah, of course, and he lived 365 years. The most important bit of information about Enoch is found in Genesis 5:24: "Enoch walked with God; and he was not, for God took him."

Enoch walked with God. We usually tend to think of Enoch as a wrinkled old man of 365 years, walking faithfully with the Lord. But the "walk" was a process that began much earlier in Enoch's life, so that at the culmination of his years people could look back and say, "Enoch really loved the Lord and served Him."

Teaching Your Child to Walk with God

"Walking with the Lord" is not confined to old age. Children can be trained to begin walking with the Lord while they are still young, with a whole life stretching ahead to serve Him. Many adults can point to a childhood experience that was the starting point of their walk with the Lord. Many children have made professions of salvation, and many learn to walk with God at a very early age. What a precious gift this is from God—the privilege of knowing Christ when we are very young and being with Him throughout our lives. As parents and teachers, let us encourage, let us welcome the little ones to come to Jesus and to spend their lives walking with the Lord.

Lesson Outline

Topic 1: Leading a Child to Christ

Christian Homes, Christian Children?

Preparing the Soil

Can Children Make Genuine Commitments?

When Can a Child Understand Salvation?

How to Communicate the Gospel

What to Tell a Child about Salvation

Topic 2: Helping a Child Grow Spiritually

Teaching Basic Truths

Teaching a Child to Feed Himself from the Word of God

Topic 3: Instilling Christian Character

Topic 4: Committing Our Desires to God

Lesson Objectives

By the end of this lesson, you will be able to do the following:

- Communicate the message of salvation clearly and make conscious steps toward preparing each child for salvation

- Counsel a child regarding assurance of salvation and a further walk with God

- Train your own children to further develop a relationship with God through regular Bible reading and prayer

- Give specific examples of how to build Christian character in a child's life

Topic 1: Leading a Child to Christ

Some parents seem to feel that if they love God, their children automatically will love Him too. But it does not always work that way.

What can parents do to see that their children know what it means to walk with the Lord? Is it enough to simply raise a child in a Christian environment? How can we grow a child for God, so that the young person's desire will be to please God and serve Him?

Christian Homes, Christian Children?

Someone has estimated that nearly eighty percent of the children brought up in Christian homes do not become Christians. This figure is somewhat startling. We may well ask why this is so. Certainly it is not because Christian parents have ignored spiritual training altogether. If we assume that parents have been training their children to walk with the Lord, then what has gone wrong? Why do so many children from Christian homes reject the faith of their fathers and mothers? What should parents do differently to nurture their children spiritually? How can we cultivate good soil in order to grow a child for God?

Preparing the Soil

A man who is planning to grow a vegetable garden would not simply toss the seeds at random onto a patch of mud. The soil must be prepared, and the right growing conditions, such as proper watering and fertilizing, must be attended to. We can think of growing a child for God in similar terms. The young shoot will thrive best in a climate where the right conditions prevail.

Some parents are so eager to train their children in the way they should go that they practically inundate their children with lectures on morality. We might compare this to overwatering a young plant. The motives are good, but the methods tend to kill the plant rather than help it to prosper.

Just as we can never force a plant to grow, so it is with children. Pressure seldom produces good results when it comes to growing a child for God. Putting too much pressure on children, particularly as they approach adolescence, only tends to increase children's resentment toward spiritual things. In particular, parents who have been too harsh and authoritarian in the early years may find that their children develop a dislike for authority of any kind. They can hardly wait to be free of the yoke of authority, and in their eagerness for independence they may reject the faith of their parents altogether.

How can we motivate children to become the persons God intends them to be? The answer is through love. Love is what motivates children to lead good lives. A climate of love at home, characterized by affection, forgiveness, patience, gentleness, and the other fruits of the Spirit, is the most effective climate for growing a child for God.

Another important condition for producing receptive soil in children is a consistent example. We have talked much about this in other lessons. What we are speaks more loudly than what we say. If we talk much about loving the Lord but do little to demonstrate it by our behavior, our children will not learn how love translates into action, and they will not be attracted to the Christian lifestyle. We need to live in such a way that we are examples of faith for our children. When we try to teach our faith to our children but fail to live it, our words will fall flat. The soil has not been properly prepared; it may even be hardened by our inconsistent example.

While our example is crucial to producing receptive soil, it is also vitally important to communicate our faith in words as well. That is what this lesson is about. In our study of Deuteronomy 6:1-9 we saw that we are to teach our children diligently and regularly. This instruction is to be as regular as getting up in the morning and going to bed at night; it is to take place in the home, under a variety of circumstances.

Parents need to teach their children spiritual principles, explaining why certain behavior is right and other behavior wrong, and consistently demonstrate godly behavior for their children in the things they do and say. They can explain the reasons for living as they do. They can talk about the principles from God's Word that they use in making decisions and establishing a guide for life. This process helps children build a biblical basis for their own choices and actions. As parents do this, children not only learn to follow the godly example of their parents but learn why they do what they do.

We might summarize the right conditions for growing a child for God as establishing a loving atmosphere at home where we both live out our faith and teach it to our children.

Can Children Make Genuine Commitments?

Some parents are skeptical about the sincerity of childhood commitments to Christ. Some Christians are persuaded that a child cannot even begin to understand the commitment involved in asking Christ to be his Lord. "A child is not capable of counting the cost of becoming a Christian," they say.

Can a child be a true believer? If so, at what age? And how can we be confident that a child's understanding of spiritual things is sufficient for salvation?

As adults we may think that a small child cannot really comprehend salvation because he or she has not fully comprehended the meaning of sin. Yet sin is very real to some boys and girls in their early years. A child may not be able to express himself clearly in words, but he may feel a genuine sense of guilt or sorrow for sin.

Children are sinners, both by virtue of having inherited a sin nature from Adam and by choosing to practice sin. Even an infant, having never deliberately sinned against God, has a sin nature. Therefore, it should not be surprising that children too must suffer the consequences of sin. Like us, they are subject to physical and emotional pain, and ultimately they face the reality of hell. This is a "hard saying," and one from which all who love children will naturally recoil. Matthew 18:10-14 makes clear it is not the Father's will that any of these little ones should perish, yet they can perish.

QUESTION 1

In terms of God's kingdom the Scriptures ultimately designate two groups of people. Study the following passages, and determine what characterizes each of the two groups: John 3:18, 36; 8:42, 44; 1 John 3:1. Do you think these verses include children also? Why or why not?

The Bible teaches that each individual who has believed in Jesus Christ as his Savior is justified before God. Those who have not believed are spiritually dead and must be condemned by God. The Bible allows for no exceptions to the conditions for salvation.

Children fall into the same two categories as adults—the saved and the unsaved. There is no indication in Scripture of a separate theology for children. Jesus' statement that no man can come unto the Father except through Himself includes children, so the child who has not believed in Christ tragically falls into the second group of those who are unjustified, outside of Christ.

Children need the Lord, and they need to hear about His saving grace from us. The biblical commands concerning evangelization are never prefaced with a specific age limit. Matthew 28:19 simply says "go and make disciples," teaching them to observe all that Jesus commanded. Romans 1:16 declares that the gospel is the power of God to "everyone who believes." Is a small child capable of such understanding that leads to faith?

A few examples found in Scripture should convince us that the answer is an unqualified yes. Luke 2:40 and Luke 2:52 record the spiritual growth of our Lord and Savior. Luke 2:40 says that the baby Jesus grew and became strong, increasing in wisdom; true wisdom is what comes from God. The Scripture says of Jesus at age twelve, "And Jesus kept increasing in wisdom and stature, and in favor with God and men." The young Jesus not only experienced physical growth, He also developed in discernment and understanding and grew in favor with men and God. We glean some idea of how this process of spiritual growth took place, as we read in Scripture, "They found Him in the temple, sitting in the midst of the teachers, both listening to them, and asking them questions." At age twelve Jesus already had a solid basis of wisdom. His spiritual awareness had been kindled and nurtured from earliest childhood.

Some would argue, "Yes, but Jesus was also God." So let us look at other examples. Read 2 Timothy 3:14-15. In this passage Paul exhorts the young man Timothy to continue in what he has learned and become convinced of. This passage indicates that Timothy knew the holy Scriptures from infancy and that the Scriptures were able to make him wise, leading to the knowledge of salvation. The passage does not make it clear at what age Timothy knew the Lord, but it clearly indicates that the foundation was laid at a very early age.

The witness of the Old Testament leads to the same conclusion. Samuel as a small boy was ministering before the Lord (1 Sam 2:18). In 1 Samuel 2:26 we read, "Now the boy Samuel was growing in stature and in favor both with the Lord and with men." Does this sound familiar? Note how 1 Samuel 3 records that, in a time when "word from the Lord was rare" and "visions were infrequent," the boy Samuel received a vision from the Lord regarding Eli's sons. Up until this point Samuel did not yet know the Lord (1 Sam 3:7). The implication seems to be that he met the Lord in this experience: "Thus Samuel grew and the Lord was with him" (1 Sam 3:19).

The list of faithful young servants of God continues. Daniel is another example of a boy who was trained very early to know and love the Lord. As a youth his faith, along with the faith of Shadrach, Meshach, and Abednego, was already firm, able to withstand the strongest tests (Dan 3:13-18). David the shepherd boy also loved the Lord from his youth and stood against Goliath with a slingshot in the name of the Lord. Jeremiah thought the Lord could not use him to speak to the nations as a prophet, "because I am a youth." But the Lord said, "I am with you" (see Jer 14–19).

"Adults tend to doubt a child's confession of faith in Christ," says a children's evangelist. He describes his own hesitancy when his four-year-old daughter informed him one night, "Daddy, I got saved tonight." While he and his wife were joyful, they also had doubts, and their child sensed this. The following day she waited on the steps for her father to come home, and her first words of greeting were, "Daddy, you and Mommy don't really believe that I got saved last night, do you?" The evangelist realized that he and his wife had discounted her profession of faith merely because she was a child. Subsequently, he and his wife saw genuine evidence of the reality of her conversion, little acts of kindness, an interest in pleasing Jesus, and a concern for people who do not know Jesus.

QUESTION 2

What has your own experience been regarding salvation experiences in children? Have any of your children made a personal confession of faith in Christ? Do you know others who have? What is your thinking at this point regarding salvation experiences in children?

When Can a Child Understand Salvation?

Many Christians know someone who came to a saving knowledge of Christ at the age of five or six, and occasionally even as early as age four. In each case the child had a clear understanding of Jesus' death on the cross to pay for sin, as well as a real conviction of personal sin. The child made a profession of faith in Christ and began to grow, demonstrating the fruit of the Spirit at a very young age. On the other hand, some children as old as eight or nine still do not fully understand the meaning of Christ's death for sin and are not ready to receive the Savior.

In Matthew 18 Christ called for "the little children" to come unto Him, specifically using the Greek word *paidion* (meaning little child) in Matthew 18:2-5 and *mikros* (meaning little one) in verses 6, 10, and 14. These children were probably small enough for Christ to take up into His lap. The meaning of Jesus' calling to a child to come to Him remains unclear. Did He mean that the disciples were to allow the children to come to Jesus merely in a physical sense or also in a spiritual sense?

Scriptures do not indicate exactly when a child is capable of understanding salvation. Some have established an arbitrary "age of accountability" for a child. By "age of accountability" we mean that age when a child commits sin consciously and deliberately and is therefore held accountable before God for it.

QUESTION 3

Read Isaiah 7:15-16 and Deuteronomy 1:35-39. What do these verses contribute to the idea of the age of accountability?

We cannot know the age of accountability with certainty. Indeed it may even vary with each child. But we can fulfill our responsibility as parents by preparing the child for the time when he reaches that "age." Though God is the one ultimately responsible to bring in the harvest, we must sow the seeds of salvation in our child by teaching the Word, presenting the gospel clearly, living consistent Christian lives, and praying for him. Others may also be involved in the watering process, but as Christian parents we are privileged to be able to plant the seed and watch it grow. God chooses to work through human instruments to prepare the soil to grow a child for God.

How to Communicate the Gospel

In speaking of the conversion of Lydia, the book of Acts uses the phrase, "and the Lord opened her heart to respond to the things spoken by Paul" (Acts 16:14). Every person who is born of the Spirit of God experiences the miracle of the redemptive work of God. This verse shows both sides of the coin: God's work in salvation and our participation in the process.

On the one hand, the Lord opened Lydia's heart; on the other hand, she responded to what she heard from Paul. She heard the truth of the gospel from another human being, was receptive to it, and the Lord opened her heart. As a Christian parent, God wants to use you, as He used Paul, to bring the message of salvation to your child and lead him to Christ.

Many parents have had this wonderful experience. A child who has heard the gospel comes to a point where he is ready to receive it. Blessed is the parent who has the opportunity of leading his or her own son or daughter to faith in Christ. Christian parents should rely on the Holy Spirit to speak to the heart of their child and draw him to faith in the Lord Jesus Christ. The Holy Spirit can use you to lead your child to the Lord Jesus Christ for salvation.

Some parents may ask, "How do I go about it? What do I say?" The material in this section is designed to be used by both parents and teachers in presenting the gospel to children in a simple way that they can understand. You may want to share this material with some of your church workers and Sunday School teachers.

If a child came to you with questions about salvation, would you be prepared to sit down and talk with him about the basic truths of salvation? In order to communicate the gospel to a child, you must have a clear understanding of the Bible's teaching on salvation. Since a child's comprehension is more limited than an adult's, you have to be able to explain these truths simply and clearly.

This section will set forth the biblical teaching on salvation in a clear way, so that both parents and teachers can make use of the material as they work with children. To be able to communicate well with children is an art. Those who work with children's ministries need a clear and comprehensive knowledge of Scripture. They also need to be able to talk to children on a child's level. Use a clear and simple vocabulary when you deal with a child, avoiding any biblical terms you have not carefully explained. Here are some other things to keep in mind as you train your children to love the Lord.

The work of salvation belongs to the Holy Spirit (Jn 3:5; Tit 3:5). As you talk to your child concerning salvation, you should be in an attitude of prayer, trusting the Holy Spirit both to guide you and to move in your child's heart. Since each child is different, we need guidance in each case. Always remember that God alone can save a soul. It is fairly easy for an adult to push a young child to make a decision, but we need to be sensitive to his receptivity, rather than forcing the issue.

> If the Holy Spirit convicts, the child can make a lasting decision. If the child's decision is because of someone's convincing, rather than because of the conviction of the Holy Spirit, it will not be genuine. Indeed this kind of decision—only because of pressure—may be harmful in the child's life, for he later wonders just what his standing with the Lord is. He may not want to admit his confusion because he knows others think he is a Christian; then he lives in turmoil and dissatisfaction. (Soderholm, 28-29)

The Holy Spirit uses the words of Scripture to speak to children as well as adults. When talking to a child about spiritual matters, use the Bible often. Read, refer to, or quote from the Bible as your source of truth (Heb 4:12). When a child indicates that he may be ready for salvation, show him specific verses in the Bible. If he can read, he should be encouraged to read the verses for himself; if not, the parent can read them to him. Keep it simple: read and talk about one verse at a time, and use only a few verses. If too many verses are used, the child will more than likely become confused or bored. Remember that a child's attention span is limited.

Present the gospel in clear and simple terms. When it comes to actually leading a child to Christ, concentrate on one or two basic salvation verses. You could choose between John 1:12; 3:16, 36, Acts 16:31, and Romans 3:23; 5:6-8 as they are all good verses to use as a springboard to discuss salvation. Memorize some basic Scripture verses such as these that will help your child see for himself what the Bible teaches. When a child has questions about a particular aspect of salvation, you will be able to turn to an appropriate verse in order to show him how Scripture answers his question.

Take enough time to talk with the child, to listen to what he has to say, to ask him questions, and to answer his questions. The object is not to hurry the child through certain motions but to help him understand the significance of Christ's death for him and to help him actually receive Christ as Savior.

QUESTION 4

Take time to write down a basic personal plan for presenting the gospel to a child. Decide which verse or verses you would use, and write out your main points for discussion.

Try to determine what the child understands. When you talk to a child about the Lord, remember to be a good listener as well. Keep eye contact or whatever is appropriate in your culture to communicate. Seek for opportunities to ask questions to ascertain the level of the child's comprehension, rather than simply lecturing. Helping the child think through issues and come to his own conclusions about salvation will ensure that he has a much more solid grasp of truth.

Your goal in communicating is not that the child can repeat back to you what you have told him, like a parrot, but that he or she understands the meaning of what you said. For this to happen usually takes some time. The child, like an adult, should have an opportunity to think through the truths you have communicated and draw some conclusions of his own. If he does not, his knowledge will be very superficial. He may not really understand what he is doing when he makes a decision.

Asking appropriate questions can help you determine how much he or she really understands. Questions can be used to encourage children to seek and discover answers for themselves. Allowing a child to ask questions and express his ideas also communicates to him, "I am interested in what you think and say."

Instead of telling Han, "Han, the Lord Jesus wants to wash away your sins," you can ask, "Han, what does the Lord Jesus want to do for you?" Tacking on a leading question like "Doesn't He?" only encourages a simple yes or no response. The child may merely nod or shake his head, sensing the response desired of him. A better approach is to encourage a child to say it in his own words or to find the answer directly from Scripture.

We can know that Han understands when we hear his reply, "Jesus wants to give me everlasting life," or "He wants to make me a child of God." If a child can articulate a clear understanding of what Scripture teaches, we know we are building a solid foundation for understanding what it means to be saved. This is more effective than asking, "Do you believe this, Han?" and Han nodding yes.

QUESTION 5

Based on the verses you selected to present the gospel to a child, write down some questions you might ask a child.

Probe gently to discern problems. After you have explained the plan of salvation clearly, your child may have further questions that need to be answered, or he may genuinely desire to put his faith and trust in the Lord Jesus Christ right at that point. Ask a few questions in order to discern what he is thinking and feeling in this regard. If he indicates a readiness to receive Christ, do not put off the discussion; ask the child if he would like to pray now to receive Christ as His Savior.

What to Tell a Child about Salvation

For some who have never led a person to the Lord, we have included a simple approach that a parent or teacher can use to explain the message of salvation in simple terms to children.

Be sure that it is clear to the child that Jesus Christ, the perfect Son of God, is the only Savior and that the child cannot save himself by doing good works (Tit 3:5).

QUESTION 6

Read Ephesians 2:8-9; John 14:6; Acts 4:12; 1 Timothy 2:5. Formulate some questions to be sure the child understands these verses. For example, "Can I earn my way to heaven by being very good?" or "Who is the only one who can wash away your sin?"

Discuss what the Lord Jesus did to save the child from sin. Make this very personal for the child. "The Lord Jesus never sinned, yet He was willing to die on the cross to take the punishment for your sins. He shed His precious blood, which alone can cleanse you from sin" (see 1 Jn 1:7).

Make it clear that Jesus rose again from the dead and lives forevermore. He is a living Savior. Do not go further until you are sure that the child understands that it is only the Lord Jesus who can wash away his sins, because the Lord Jesus loved him so much that He died on the cross and shed His blood for him.

Emphasize that salvation is by grace alone in Christ alone. Some make the mistake at this point of asking the child to repent or to commit to change his life. This can confuse a person and confuse the gospel offer. What should be emphasized here is the incredible grace of God.

QUESTION 7

Based on Revelation 21:6, what would it cost your child to believe in Christ?

QUESTION 8

Based on John 1:12; 3:16; 6:29; 8:24; 11:26; 20:31; Acts 16:31, what is the one condition a child needs to meet in order to become a Christian?

Emphasize a personal decision to receive Christ. Turn to one of the many verses in the New Testament in which God offers a promise of salvation and tells the child what to do to receive it. Examples are John 1:12; 3:16; 3:36, Acts 16:31. If the child is able to read, have him read the verse to you. Otherwise you can read the verse to him. In doing this, you are communicating to the child that the Bible is your authority; these are not your ideas but God's. A child will learn to face future storms with strong assurance if his young faith is firmly planted on the direct promises from God's own Word.

After you read the verse together, it may be helpful to offer a simple explanation of the verse. For instance, you may say, "Salvation is God's free gift to you. The Lord Jesus can wash away all your sin and make you clean in the sight of God." Then ask a question such as, "What is salvation?" or "What is God's free gift to you?" to reinforce and confirm the child's understanding of the verse.

Using a verse such as John 1:12 you might ask, "How can you become a child of God?" (Desired answer: "By believing in the Lord, or by receiving Jesus Christ.")

You might ask further, "What does it mean to believe in Jesus, or to receive Him?" (Desired answer: "To trust that He took the punishment for my sins and rose from the dead so that I can live forever with Him.")

Then you might follow with a question such as, "What do you want Jesus to do for you right now?" (Desired answer: "To save me; to make me His child; to come into my heart.")

Be thorough and yet simple in your explanation of the verse you have chosen, and if necessary, go over it again to be sure that the child understands. When you are satisfied that he understands the truth of the verse, remind him of the seriousness and importance of making a decision to trust in the Lord Jesus.

It is important that the time does come in your discussion when you ask him if he would like to receive the Lord Jesus into his heart and life right then. God has offered him the gift of eternal life and the forgiveness of his sins, but the gift will not be his unless he accepts it. You can use the example of a gift. If someone is given a gift but he does not receive the gift and open it, then it is not his. If at this point the child acts uncertain of what he wants to do or tells you that he does not want to believe and receive God's gift right now, make it clear that he can come again to you and discuss this at any time.

If the child indicates that he would like Jesus to be his Savior, encourage him to pray out loud. Of course praying does not make one a Christian and is not really necessary. However, a prayer can be a significant psychological point in a child's life where he declares his faith to the Lord. He might pray something as simple as this:

> *Lord Jesus, thank you for dying for my sins and I trust you now for forgiveness and for the gift of eternal life.*

If the child is very young or shy, he may prefer to say a prayer after you. Keep in mind that it is easy to persuade many children to repeat a simple prayer after you and then tell such children that they are now Christians. Try to be sure that the child you are dealing with really understands what he is saying.

After the child prays, give him the opportunity to express what the Lord has done for him. Ask him, "What did you just do? What did Jesus promise to do if you believe in Him?"

The basics of salvation should be clear in your own mind as you deal with the child.

The following five points may serve as a basic guide:

1. God loves you.
2. You have sinned.
3. Christ died to pay for your sin and then rose from the dead to give you eternal life.
4. You must admit to Him that you are a sinner, confess that you are trusting Jesus' death alone for the forgiveness of your sins, ask Him to forgive you, and believe that He has.
5. Then you are in God's family and you have everlasting life.

Always remember to avoid additions to the gospel such as baptism, repentance, submitting to Christ as Lord of one's life, promising God that you will be good and other items beyond mere faith. It will likely confuse the child.

Topic 2: Helping a Child Grow Spiritually

The child who has made a decision to receive Christ in his life is not finished at this point; he has only begun. He is a new creation in Christ, and he needs to know more about this new life (2 Cor 5:17). Like a newborn baby he needs to drink the milk of the Word in order to grow. To help a spiritually newborn boy or girl to grow in the Lord, we need to ground him in the truths of God's Word.

Teaching Basic Truths

The Christian life is based on truth as revealed in the Bible. As you spend time with your child, both in formal and informal teaching situations, help him to learn basic truths about the Christian life and to reinforce what he already knows.

Assurance of salvation. The child who has recently received Christ needs to know from the Word of God that the Lord Jesus has indeed come into his life as a result of his prayer for salvation. Assurance of salvation is not based on the child's feelings nor on the word of the one who leads him to Christ; it is based on God's Word. If the child does not have this assurance from the Word of God, Satan and others can easily tempt him to believe that his experience of being born again was not real.

QUESTION 9

Read John 6:37, 47; 10:27-30 and 1 John 5:11-13. Formulate some questions to ask a child based on these verses and write them in your Life Notebook.

Go back to the Bible verses you used earlier in discussing salvation, and ask the child, "How do you know you have everlasting life?" Be consistent in using the same term for salvation to avoid confusing him. We want our children to understand that, when they have believed in Jesus and asked Him to be their Lord, they can know they have eternal life simply "because the Bible says so."

If the child answers, "Because you said so," reread together the verses containing the promise of everlasting life. Then ask, "What did you ask God to do for you?" or "What do you believe He did?" When you ask, "How do you know?" the child will probably answer, "Because God said He would in the Bible." This is important, because time and again, when he has questions and doubts, he needs to learn to go back to God's Word for answers and assurance.

When the child understands that his salvation is sure, it would be good to encourage him to pray a short prayer of thanks. This could be a simple one-sentence prayer: "Thank You, Lord, for saving me from my sins and giving me eternal life." Encourage the born-again child to tell someone else right away that Jesus is now his Savior. This will strengthen and confirm his faith. Ask him, "Whom would you like to tell that you have asked the Lord Jesus to come into your life?"

Confessing sin. Explain that Christians still need to confess their sins to the Lord when they do something wrong. A simple explanation like this can help much:

> When you do something wrong, you do not need to be saved again. God does not want you to do bad things, but Christians sometimes do bad things anyway. When you sin, you should tell God right away whatever you have done. Tell him you are sorry, and ask Him to give you the strength not to do it again.

Explain that just as the child learns to say he is sorry to his parents when he has been disobedient or to his brother when he has wronged him, so sin is a wrong against God, and God needs to hear him say he is sorry. Use 1 John 1:9: "If we confess our sins, He is faithful and righteous to forgive us our sins and to cleanse us from all unrighteousness."

Some important steps involved in confession can be taught: (1) Tell the Lord Jesus what you have done wrong and that you are sorry for doing it; (2) ask Him to forgive you and thank Him for making you clean again, as He has promised in 1 John 1:9; and (3) ask Him to help you not to do it again.

Reading the Bible. Parents can begin to encourage a child, when he is able to read, to begin a regular practice of daily Bible reading. If he does not have his own Bible, make your Bible available to him at some time during the day. The gospel of Mark or John is a good place for a child to start reading. If your child is too young to read, select a time during the day, usually about five to ten minutes, when you or someone else in the family can read the Bible to him.

Prayer. Teach a child that it is important for him to talk to God, his heavenly Father, in prayer. The child can do this at any time and in any place, but he should also have a special time during the day he remembers to talk to God. The habit of taking things to the Lord can be learned as children see their parents bringing not only their petitions but their praise to the Lord. Children learn from our example to pray about everything.

A life pleasing to God. A child needs to learn that the moment a person believes in the Lord Jesus, God sends the Holy Spirit to live in that person. God places His Holy Spirit in the child to help him and give him power to live a holy life. Explain to a child that God expects him to live daily according to the teachings of His Word. God says to his children, "Be holy, for I am holy" (1 Pet 1:16). God wants the child to decide to live a life that pleases Him.

God tells us how He wants us to live in His Word, and He wants His children to obey His Word. Tell the child who has received Christ that God wants his or her life to be different now and that God will give him the strength to obey Him if he asks his heavenly Father.

The presence of Christ in the believer. Explain to the child that the Lord has promised, "I will never desert you, nor will I ever forsake you" (Heb 13:5). The Lord Jesus has promised that He will always be with each of His children, no matter what. That means a child who becomes a Christian always takes Jesus with him wherever he goes and whatever he does. Ask him to think about the fact that Jesus is always with him and to ask himself every day, as he makes choices and decisions, "What would Jesus do?"

Teaching a Child to Feed Himself from the Word of God

A child who receives Christ is a newborn babe in Him and needs, like any newborn baby, to learn how to eat (1 Pet 2:2). At first he will be very dependent on you to feed him spiritual food from the Bible. A child who cannot read will be totally dependent on you to tell him Bible stories. When he is older, however, you can teach him how to "feed" himself. This means teaching him how to have his own quiet time daily, reading God's Word and applying it to his life.

Encourage the child to have a daily time of devotion. Your child can be encouraged to have his own personal quiet time, particularly after the age of ten. Let the child choose the time and place that is best for him. Show him how to begin the time with prayer, asking God to enable him both to understand and to obey what he reads in God's Word. Encourage him to read his Bible at least five minutes daily (or longer, if he desires). You can suggest he begin reading in the gospel of Mark, followed by books such as Acts, John, Genesis, and Psalms.

Suggest that he read a short passage several times so that it may speak to him. Teach him to ask questions about the passage, learning to think about and reflect on the verses he has read. Five questions he can ask himself are:

1. Is there a promise to claim?
2. Is there a command to obey?
3. Is there a warning to heed?
4. Is there an example to follow?
5. Is there a truth to learn about God or myself?

Help your child learn to find the promise, command, warning, or truth, and teach him to translate what he finds in a passage into a prayer to God.

QUESTION 10

Read Joshua 1:1-9, and look for answers to the five questions above. Write these in your Life Notebook. Write a few simple questions you might use to help a child find the promise or warning or truth about God.

As your child becomes familiar with God's Word, encourage him to memorize specific verses that are appropriate to his age level. Children have remarkable capacities for memorization: in future years your child may draw on these verses many times to help him. Children get very excited about learning verses when they are motivated by a small reward for learning a certain number of verses. You can make a chart with stars to show his accomplishments in memorizing.

Encourage him to apply what he reads in the Bible to his day-to-day life. Setting up "what if" situations encourages a child to think through how he might respond in such a situation. When a similar situation occurs, he may see the parallel. For example, you can ask a child, "What would you do if you saw a friend cheating at school?" Or "what would you do if you accidentally broke your mother's favorite vase while she was at work?" Let him decide on a course of action, and then lead him gently to see if it is in line with Christian values and standards of conduct.

QUESTION 11

Write out a list of five "what if" situations appropriate for your children. If you have no children, write out five for a ten-year-old child. Try these out with a child, and see what responses you get.

Topic 3: Instilling Christian Character

We often see small children imitating their parents: little girls playing house and pretending they are mommies or little boys walking and talking like daddy. Our children learn many other things by imitation as well: they learn specific traits of character from us.

As Christian parents our desire is for our child to become more like Christ, to begin to demonstrate Christian character. A godly parent plants the seeds of righteousness in his children not only by his words but also by his actions. His entire life is a sermon for his child to read. It is good to teach a child the Scriptures so that he will build God's Word into his life, and to see that a child comes to church. But it is even better when a child can see Christian character in the lives of his parents on a day-to-day basis and when he observes that what his parents say is consistent with how they live. In other words, who we are is more important than what we say when it comes to teaching Christian character.

The book of Proverbs gives us seven character qualities Solomon viewed as essential for Wisdom. Let's review them briefly.

1. The Pillar of Discipline: learning to respond to those in authority (parents, teachers, bosses at work, etc). The parents may utilize disciplines of natural consequences, reproofs, or even the rod.

2. The Pillar of Discernment: learning from Scripture to understand the world's point of view and distinguish it from God's point of view in Scripture.

3. The Pillar of Wise Behavior: learning to obey God and deal fairly and honestly with other people and to do it in a gracious manner.

4. The Pillar of Prudence: learning how to navigate through life and avoid the traps that can harm our spiritual lives.

5. The Pillar of Knowledge: learning through experience to apply God's truth to life (for example, by recording life experiences of applied biblical truth in the Life Notebook). Knowledge is a "life related" knowledge and not only information. It is a "life message."

6. The Pillar of Discretion: learning to formulate and carry out wise plans.

7. The Fear of the Lord: learning to view ourselves as a subject in a kingdom and to obey the king. It involves a reverential awe, respect, and response of obedient service.

We will return to this subject in the next lesson (Lesson 11, Topic 3) when we discussion "Projects for Mature Independence."

QUESTION 12

Select one of the Pillars above and with your spouse, develop a project you think is appropriate for your child. Write it out in your Life Notebook.

Topic 4: Committing Our Desires to God

Most Christian parents have a sincere desire to see their children grow to become men and women of God. What are some things Christian parents desire to see happen in the lives of their children?

- They will believe in Jesus Christ as Savior and Lord and have a personal relationship with Him
- They will know the Bible and submit to its authority
- They will pray regularly and see God answer prayer
- They will live holy lives of obedience to God's Word, lives marked by love for and service to others
- They will tell their friends about Jesus Christ
- They will become active members of a local church
- They will worship and praise God as a routine of life
- They will choose a marriage partner who loves the Lord and who will share their commitment in the building of a Christian home

Earlier in the course we discussed the difference between desires and goals. The proper response to our desires, we said, is the response of prayer. As we bring these desires to the Lord and ask Him to work in the life of our child, we can be confident that He will do so, and that He will use us, as we commit ourselves to Him, as instruments to help grow our child for God.

QUESTION 13

Write your desires for your children in your Life Notebook, and commit yourself to praying regularly for your children for each of these desires.

Assignment

- Please read the following article:

Spiritual Training of Children

Dr. James Dobson, in his excellent book titled *Dr. Dobson Answers Your Questions*, deals with some common questions parents have in the spiritual training of their children.

Should a child be allowed to "decide for himself" on matters related to his concept of God? Aren't we forcing our religion down his throat when we tell him what he must believe?

Let me answer that question with an illustration from nature. A little gosling (baby goose) has a peculiar characteristic that is relevant at this point. Shortly after he hatches from his shell he will become attached, or "imprinted," to the first thing that he sees moving near him. From that time forward, he will follow that particular object when it moves in his vicinity. Ordinarily, he becomes imprinted to the mother goose who was on hand to hatch the new generation. If she is removed, however, the gosling will settle for any mobile substitute, whether alive or not. In fact, a gosling will become most easily attached to a blue football bladder, dragged by on a string. A week later, he'll fall in line behind the bladder as it scoots by him. Time is the critical factor in this process. The gosling is vulnerable to imprinting for only a few seconds after he hatches from the shell; if that opportunity is lost, it cannot be regained later. In other words, there is a critical, brief period in the life of a gosling when this instinctual learning is possible.

There is also a critical period when certain kinds of instruction are possible in the life of the child. Although humans have no instincts (only drives, reflexes, urges, etc.), there is a brief period during childhood when youngsters are vulnerable to religious training. Their concepts of right and wrong, which the psychologist Freud called the superego, are formulated during this time, and their view of God begins to solidify. As in the case of the gosling, the opportunity of that period must be seized when it is available. Leaders of the Catholic Church have been widely quoted as saying, "Give us a child until he is seven years old and we'll have him for life"; their affirmation is usually correct, because permanent attitudes can be instilled during these seven vulnerable years. Unfortunately, however, the opposite is also true. The absence or misapplication of instruction through that prime-time period may place a severe limitation on the depth of the child's later devotion to God. When parents say they are going to withhold indoctrination from their small child, allowing him to "decide for himself," they are almost guaranteeing that he will "decide" in the negative. If a parent wants his child to have a meaningful faith, he must give up any misguided attempts at objectivity. The child listens closely to discover just how much his parent believes what he is preaching; any indecision or ethical confusion from the parent is likely to be magnified in the child.

It is difficult for us to have meaningful devotions as a family because our young children seem so bored and uninvolved. They yawn and squirm and giggle while we are reading from the Bible. On the other hand, we feel it is important to teach them to pray and study God's Word. Can you help us deal with this dilemma?

The one key word to family devotions is brevity. Children can't be expected to comprehend and appreciate lengthy adult spiritual activities. Four or five minutes devoted to one or two Bible verses, followed by a short prayer, usually represents the limits of attention during the preschool years. To force young children to comprehend eternal truths in an eternal devotional can be eternally dangerous.

How is the concept of God established in the mind of the child?

It is a well-known fact that a child identifies his parents with God, whether or not the adults want that role. While yielding to their loving leadership, for example, children are also learning to yield to the benevolent leadership of God Himself.

We have the responsibility of reflecting the two aspects of divine nature to the next generation. First, our Heavenly Father is a God of unlimited love, and our children must become acquainted with His mercy and tenderness through our own love toward them. But make no mistake about it, our Lord is also the possessor of majestic authority! The universe is ordered by a supreme Lord who requires obedience from His children and has warned them that "the wages of sin is death." To show our little ones love without authority is as serious a distortion of God's nature as to reveal an iron-fisted authority without love.

What is the most critical period in the spiritual training of young children?

I believe the fifth year of a child's life is the most critical. Up to that time, he believes in God because his parents tell him it is the thing to do. At about five or six years of age he comes to a fork in the road: either he begins to reach out and accept the concept as his own, or he does not. At that point, he may "buy it" and put his feet down onto a more solid foundation—or he may start to doubt it, laying the basis for rejection.

I certainly don't mean to imply that parents should wait until the child is five or six to begin spiritual training. Nor are subsequent years unimportant. But I am convinced that our most diligent efforts in the home, and our best teachers in Sunday school, ought to be applied to the child of five or six years. There are crucial crossroads after that, but this is the first important one.

Many people believe that children are basically "good," and only learn to do wrong from their parents and culture. Do you agree?

If they mean that all children are worthy and deserving of our love and respect, I certainly do agree. But if they believe that children are by nature unselfish, giving, and sinless before God, I must disagree. I wish that assessment of human nature were accurate, but it contradicts scriptural understandings. Jeremiah wrote: "The heart is deceitful above all things, and desperately wicked: who can know it?" (Jer 17:9, KJV). Jeremiah's inspired insight into human nature is validated by the sordid history of mankind. The path of civilization is blotted by murder, war, rape, and plundering from the time of Adam forward. This record of evil makes it difficult to hold to the naive view that children are pure and holy at birth and merely learn to do wrong from their misguided parents. Surely during the past 6,000 years, there must have been at least one generation for whom parents did things right. Yet greed, lust, and selfishness have characterized us all. Is this nature also evident in children? King David thought so, for he confessed, ". . . in sin did my mother conceive me" (Psalm 51:5, KJV).

What meaningful difference, then, is made by the distinction between the two views of children? Practically everything, in fact. Parents who believe all toddlers are infused with goodness and sunshine are urged to get out of the way and let their pleasant nature unfold. On the other hand, parents who recognize the inevitable internal war between good and evil will do their best to influence the child's choices—to shape his will and provide a solid spiritual foundation. They acknowledge the dangers of adult defiance as expressed in 1 Samuel 15:23—"For rebellion is as bad as the sin of witchcraft, and stubbornness is as bad as worshiping idols" (TLB).

Parents have been commanded in the Bible to "train up a child in the way he should go." But this poses a critical question: What way should he go? If the first seven years represent the "prime time" for religious training, what should be taught during this period? What experiences should be included? What values should be emphasized?

You've asked an excellent question. It is my strong belief that a child should be exposed to a carefully conceived, systematic program of religious training. Yet we are much too haphazard about this matter. Perhaps we would hit the mark more often if we more clearly recognized the precise target.

Listed below is a "Checklist for Spiritual Training"—a set of targets at which to aim. Many of the items require maturity which children lack, and we should not try to make adult Christians out of our immature youngsters. But we can gently urge them toward these goals—these targets—during the impressionable years of childhood.

Essentially, the five scriptural concepts which follow should be consciously taught, providing the foundation on which all future doctrine and faith will rest. I encourage every Christian parent to evaluate his child's understanding of these five areas:

CONCEPT I: *"And thou shalt love the Lord thy God with all thy heart"* (Mk 12:30, KJV).

1. Is your child learning of the love of God through the love, tenderness, and mercy of his parents? (most important)

2. Is he learning to talk about the Lord, and to include Him in his thoughts and plans?

3. Is he learning to turn to Jesus for help whenever he is frightened or anxious or lonely?

4. Is he learning to read the Bible?

5. Is he learning to pray?

6. Is he learning the meaning of faith and trust?

7. Is he learning the joy of the Christian way of life?

8. Is he learning the beauty of Jesus' birth and death?

CONCEPT II: *"Thou shalt love thy neighbor as thyself"* (Mk 12:31, KJV).

1. Is he learning to understand and empathize with the feelings of others?

2. Is he learning not to be selfish and demanding?

3. Is he learning to share?

4. Is he learning not to gossip and criticize others?

5. Is he learning to accept himself?

CONCEPT III: *"Teach me to do thy will; for thou art my God"* (Ps 143:10, KJV).

1. Is he learning to obey his parents as preparation for later obedience to God? (most important)

2. Is he learning to behave properly in church—God's house?

3. Is he learning a healthy appreciation for both aspects of God's nature: love and justice?

4. Is he learning that there are many forms of benevolent authority outside himself to which he must submit?

5. Is he learning the meaning of sin and its inevitable consequences?

CONCEPT IV: *"Fear God, and keep his commandments: for this is the whole duty of man"* (Eccl 12:13, KJV).

1. Is he learning to be truthful and honest?

2. Is he learning to keep the Sabbath day holy?

3. Is he learning the relative insignificance of materialism?

4. Is he learning the meaning of the Christian family, and the faithfulness to it which God intends?

5. Is he learning to follow the dictates of his own conscience?

CONCEPT V: "But the fruit of the Spirit is . . . self-control" (Gal 5:22, 23, RSV).

1. Is he learning to give a portion of his allowance (and other money) to God?

2. Is he learning to control his impulses?

3. Is he learning to work and carry responsibility?

4. Is he learning the vast difference between self-worth and egotistical pride?

5. Is he learning to bow in reverence before the God of the universe?

In summary, your child's first seven years should prepare him to say, at the age of accountability, "Here I am, Lord, send me!"

My four-year-old frequently comes running home in tears because she has been hit by one of her little friends. I have taught her that it is not right to hit others, but now they are making life miserable for my little girl. As a Christian parent, what should I tell her about defending herself?

You were wise to teach your daughter not to hit and hurt others, but self-defense is another matter. Children can be unmerciful in their torment of a defenseless child. When youngsters play together, they each want to have the best toys and determine the ground rules to their own advantage. If they find they can predominate by simply flinging a well-aimed fist at the nose of their playmate, someone is likely to get hurt. I'm sure there are Christians who disagree with me on this issue, but I believe you should teach your child to defend herself when attacked. Later, she can be taught to "turn the other cheek," which even mature adults find difficult to implement.

I recently consulted with a mother who was worried about her small daughter's inability to protect herself from aggression. There was one child in their neighborhood who would crack three-year-old Ann in the face at the slightest provocation. This little bully, named Joan, was very small and feminine, but she never felt the sting of retaliation because Ann had been taught not to fight back. I recommended that Ann's mother tell her to return Joan's attack if Joan hits first. Several days later the mother heard a loud altercation outside, followed by a brief scuffle. Then Joan began crying and went home. Ann walked casually into the house with her hands in her pockets, and explained, "Joan socked me so I had to help her remember not to hit me again." Ann had efficiently returned an eye for an eye and a tooth for a tooth. She and Joan have played together much more peacefully since that time.

Generally speaking, a parent should emphasize the foolishness of fighting. But to force a child to stand passively while being clobbered is to leave him at the mercy of his cold-blooded peers.

How can I help my child develop wholesome, accepting attitudes toward people of other racial and ethnic groups?

There is no substitute for parental modeling of the attitudes we wish to teach. Someone wrote, "The footsteps a child follows are most likely to be the ones his parents thought they covered up." It is true. Our children are watching us carefully, and they instinctively imitate our behavior. Therefore, we can hardly expect them to be kind to all of God's children if we are prejudiced and rejecting. Likewise, we will be unable to teach appreciativeness if we never say, "please" or "thank you" at home or abroad. We will not produce honest children if we teach them to lie to the bill collector on the phone by saying, "Dad's not home." In these matters, our boys and girls instantly discern the gap between what we say and what we do. And of the two choices, they usually identify with our behavior and ignore our empty proclamations. . . .

How can I teach my children Christian attitudes toward possessions and money?

This is accomplished not only with words, but also by the way you handle your own resources.

It is interesting to me that Jesus had more to say in the Bible about money than any other subject, which emphasizes the importance of this topic for my family and yours. He made it clear that there is a direct relationship between great riches and spiritual poverty, as we are witnessing in America today. Accordingly, it is my belief that excessive materialism in parents has the power to inflict enormous spiritual damage on our sons and daughters. If they see that we care more about things than people . . . if they perceive that we have sought to buy their love as a guilt reducer . . . if they recognize the hollowness of our Christian testimony when it is accompanied by stinginess with God . . . the result is often cynicism and disbelief. And more important, when they observe Dad working fifteen hours a day to capture ever more of this world's goods, they know where his treasure is. Seeing is believing.

We've heard a lot about war toys. Do you think they are damaging to children?

Kids have been playing cowboys and Indians and other combat games for hundreds of years, and I'm inclined to feel that the current worry is unfounded. Young boys, particularly, live in a feminine world; they're with their mothers far more than their dads. The teachers of the nursery school, kindergarten, and elementary school are likely to be women. Their Sunday school teachers are probably female, too. In this sugar and spice world, I think it is healthy for boys to identify with masculine models, even if the setting involves combat. Two boys can "shoot" each other without emotional arousal. "Bang! Bang! You're dead," they shout.

On the other hand, parents should limit the amount of violence and killing their children view on television and in the movies. The technology of audio-visual electronics has become tremendously effective, and can be far more stimulating and damaging. Measurable physiological changes occur while a child is watching a violent movie; the pulse rate quickens, eyes dilate, hands sweat, the mouth goes dry, and breathing accelerates. If repeated often, the emotional impact of this experience should be obvious.

My husband and I are distressed because our teenager seems to be rejecting her Christian beliefs. She was saved at an early age and in the past has shown a real love for the Lord. My inclination is to panic, but before I do, can you offer a word of encouragement?

A small child is told what to think during his formative years. He is subjected to all the attitudes, biases, and beliefs of his parents, which is right and proper. They are fulfilling their God-given responsibility to guide and train him. However, there must come a moment when all of these concepts and ideas are examined by the individual, and either adopted as true or rejected as false. If that personal evaluation never comes, then the adolescent fails to span the gap between "What I've been told" versus "What I believe." This is one of the most important bridges leading from childhood to adulthood.

It is common, then, for a teenager to question the veracity of the indoctrination he has received. He may ask himself, "Is there really a God? Does He know me? Do I believe in the values my parents have taught? Do I want what they want for my life? Have they misled me in any way? Does my experience contradict what I've been taught?" For a period of years beginning during adolescence and continuing into the twenties, this intensive self-examination is conducted.

This process is especially distressing to parents who must sit on the sidelines and watch everything they have taught being scrutinized and questioned. It will be less painful, however, if both generations realize that the soul-searching is a normal, necessary part of growing up. . . .

You've indicated that seven deaths have occurred in your family during the past eighteen months. We have also had several tragic losses in our family in recent years. My wife died when our children were five, eight, and nine. I found it very difficult to explain death to them during that time. Can you offer some guidelines regarding how a parent can help his children cope with the stark reality of death—especially when it strikes within the immediate family?

Some years ago, I attended a funeral at the Inglewood Cemetery-Mortuary in Inglewood, California. While there, I picked up a brochure written by the president of the mortuary, John M. McKinley. Mr. McKinley had been in the funeral business for fifteen years before writing this valuable pamphlet entitled "If It Happens to Your Child." He gave me permission to reproduce the content here in answer to your question:

I knew Tommy's parents because they lived in the neighborhood and attended the same church. But I knew Tommy especially well because he was one of the liveliest, happiest five-year-olds it had ever been my pleasure to meet. It was a shock, therefore, when his mother became a client of mine at the death of her husband.

As a doctor must learn to protect himself from the suffering of his patients, so a funeral director must protect himself from grief. During the course of the average year I come in direct contact with several thousand men and women who have experienced a shattering loss, and if I did not isolate myself from their emotions, my job would be impossible. But I have not been able to isolate myself from the children.

"I don't know what I would have done if I had not had Tommy," his mother told me when I visited her in her home the morning she called me. "He has been such a little man—hasn't cried, and is doing everything he can do to take his daddy's place." And it was true. Tommy was standing just as he imagined a man would stand, not crying, and doing his best to take his daddy's place.

I knew it was wrong. I knew I should tell her so—that Tommy was not a man; that he needed to cry; that he needed comfort probably far more than she. But I am not a psychologist, and I said nothing.

In the two years since then I have watched Tommy. The joy has not come back in his face, and it is clear even to my layman's mind that he is an emotionally sick child. I am sure it began when his mother, unknowingly, made it difficult—impossible—for him to express his grief, and placed on him an obligation he could not fulfill; that of "taking daddy's place."

There have been few examples so clear cut as Tommy's, but I have seen so much that made me wince, and I have been asked so often: "What should I tell Mary?" or Paul, or Jim, that I finally decided to do something about it. I went to the experts, the men who know how a child should be treated at such moments of tragedy, and I asked them to lay down some guidelines that parents could understand and follow. I talked to several psychologists and psychiatrists and pediatricians, but principally to Dr. A. I. Duvall, a psychiatrist, and Dr. James Gardner, a child psychologist. Translated into my layman's language, here is the gist of what I learned.

When a child, like any other human being, experiences a deeply painful loss, not only should he be permitted to cry; he should be encouraged to cry until the need for tears is gone. He should be comforted while the tears are flowing, but the words "Don't cry" should be stricken from the language.

The need to cry may be recurrent for several days, or at widening intervals, several months, but when the need is felt, no effort should be made to dam the tears. Instead, it should be made clear that it is good to cry, and not "babyish" or "sissy" or anything to be ashamed of.

At times, the child may need to be alone with his grief, and if this feeling comes, it should be respected. But otherwise physical contact and comfort will be almost as healing as the tears.

The child should be told the truth; that death is final. "Mommy has gone on a vacation" or "Daddy has gone on a trip" only adds to the confusion and delays the inevitable. Children—particularly young children—have a very imperfect time sense. If "Mom has gone on a vacation," they are going to expect her back this afternoon or tomorrow. And when tomorrow and tomorrow comes and she does not reappear, not only will the hurt be repeated endlessly, but the child will lose faith in the surviving parent just at the time when faith and trust are needed most. It is hard to say "never" when you know it will make the tears flow harder, but it is the kindest word in the long run.

It is not necessary to explain death to a young child. It may even be harmful to try. To the five-year-old, "death" is absence, and explanations may only confuse him. If he has seen a dead bird or a dead pet, it may be helpful to make a comparison, but the important fact which the child must accept is absence. If he can be helped to accept the fact that father or mother or brother or sister is gone and will never return, then through questions and observations he will gradually build his own picture of "death" and its meaning.

A child should not be unduly shielded from the physical appearance and fact of death. If a father dies, the child should be permitted to see the body, so that with his own eyes he can see the changes, the stillness, the difference between the vital strength which was "daddy" and this inanimate mask which is not "daddy" at all. Seeing with his own eyes will help.

A child should be protected, however, from any mass demonstrations of grief, as from a large group of mourners at a funeral. Rather, the child should be taken in privately before the funeral to say goodbye.

If the child is very young—say two to five or six—great care should be used in explaining death in terms which are meaningful to adults, but which may be very puzzling to children. For example, to say that "Mommy has gone to Heaven" may make perfect sense to a religious bereaved father, but it may leave a five-year-old wondering why Mommy has deserted him. At that answer, "Heaven" is simply a far place, and he will not be able to understand why his mother stays there instead of coming home to take care of him.

Along with tears, a child is quite likely to feel sharp resentment, even anger at the dead parent, or the brother or sister who has "gone." This feeling is the result of the child's conviction that he has been deserted. If this feeling does arise, the child should be permitted to express it freely, just as in the case of tears.

More common, and frequently more unsettling to a child, is his guilt feelings when a death occurs. If he has been angry at his sister, and the sister dies, he is likely to think it is his fault, that his anger killed her. Or if his mother dies, and he is not told honestly and simply what has happened, he is likely to believe that his misbehavior drove her away. Guilt feelings in young children, reinforced by death, can lead to neurotic patterns which last throughout life.

But if a child is encouraged to cry until the need for tears is gone; if he is comforted enough; if he is told the simple truth; if he is permitted to see for himself the difference between death and life; if his resentment or guilt is handled in the same straightforward way as his tears, his sense of loss will still be great, but he will overcome it.

There is a positive side, too. If death is treated as a natural part of human experience, it is much easier for a loved one to live in memory. When the initial impact of grief is gone, it is a natural thing to remember and re-tell stories which evoke vivid recollections of the personality and habits which made the loved one a special person. Children take great delight in this, for in their rich world of imagination they can make the absent one live again. Such reminiscing does not renew or increase their sorrow. To the extent that it makes them free to remember, the cause for sorrow is removed.

Mr. McKinley's advice is excellent, as far as it goes. However, it has not included any references to the Christian message, which provides the only satisfactory answer to death. Obviously, I disagree with Mr. McKinley's reservations about heaven. We can say, "Your mother is gone for now, but thank God we'll be together again on the other side!" How comforting for a grieving child to know that a family reunion will someday occur from which there will never be another separation! I recommend that Christian parents begin acquainting their children with the gift of eternal life long before they have need of this understanding.

(Dobson, *Dr. Dobson Answers Your Questions*, 41-59)

QUESTION 14

What does Dobson say about allowing a child to decide for himself on matters related to his concept of God?

QUESTION 15

Review Dobson's "Checklist for Spiritual Training" (refer to this Article placed earlier in the lesson). Evaluate where your children are in terms of salvation or their Christian walk. Write down what you think are the specific needs of each of your children in this area. Outline three specific goals to work on with each child in the next two months, and begin working toward these goals.

Lesson 10 Self Check

QUESTION 1

The Scriptures indicate that most children cannot understand the gospel and believe in Christ until they are adolescents. *True or False?*

QUESTION 2

Children do not need to repent for salvation, because the only condition for receiving forgiveness and the gift of eternal life is to believe in Christ. *True or False?*

QUESTION 3

Which one of the following verses is correct to use in sharing the gospel with a child? (The others refer to how Christians should live, not to what a person must do to be saved.)

   A. Acts 2:38

   B. Romans 12:1,2

   C. John 3:16

   D. Matthew 7:21

QUESTION 4

All children reach the age of accountability at age twelve. *True or False?*

QUESTION 5

What are the two things you might do after your child has prayed to receive Christ suggested in this lesson? *(Select all that apply.)*

   A. Encourage him to tell someone about the step he has taken.

   B. Tell him that he cannot know for sure that he has really believed unless he begins to show good works in his life.

   C. Explain that now he is saved, he must continue in good works and not fail or he might lose his salvation.

   D. Give him the opportunity to pray and thank God for what He has done for the child.

QUESTION 6

Which of these verses would be a good passage to use to challenge your child to grow spiritually?

   A. 1 Peter 2:2

   B. Romans 6:23

   C. Hebrews 13:5

   D. Romans 5:8-9

QUESTION 7

What are some good ways to encourage application of the Scripture to daily life? *(Select all that apply.)*

   A. Write out five "what if" questions after reading a passage.

   B. Encourage your child to have a daily time of devotion with God.

   C. As he reads, ask key questions like, Are there promises to claim? Commands to obey? Examples to follow?

   D. Stress the importance of a life pleasing to God.

QUESTION 8

Children learn by observing their parents and imitating their behavior. *True or False?*

QUESTION 9

According to Dr. James Dobson, it is very important that we allow our children to decide for themselves and not force our religion on them at too early an age. *True or False?*

QUESTION 10

Parents should demonstrate unlimited love and authority to their children as they seek to reflect God's nature. *True or False?*

Lesson 10 Answers to Questions

QUESTION 1: *Your answer*
QUESTION 2: *Your answer*
QUESTION 3: *Your answer*
QUESTION 4: *Your answer*
QUESTION 5: *Your answer*
QUESTION 6: *Your answer*
QUESTION 7: *Your answer should be similar to the following:*
Nothing! Jesus says He offers eternal life to us "without cost."
QUESTION 8: *Your answer should be similar to the following:*
Believe in Christ for eternal life.
QUESTION 9: *Your answer*
QUESTION 10: *Your answer*
QUESTION 11: *Your answer*
QUESTION 12: *Your answer*
QUESTION 13: *Your answer*
QUESTION 14: *Your answer*
QUESTION 15: *Your answer*

Lesson 10 Self Check Answers

QUESTION 1: False
QUESTION 2: True
QUESTION 3
    C. John 3:16
QUESTION 4: False
QUESTION 5
    A. Encourage him to tell someone about the step he has taken.
    D. Give him the opportunity to pray and thank God for what He has done for the child.
QUESTION 6
    A. 1 Peter 2:2
QUESTION 7
    A. Write out five "what if" questions after reading a passage.
    B. Encourage your child to have a daily time of devotion with God.
    C. As he reads, ask key questions like, Are there promises to claim? Commands to obey? Examples to follow?
    D. Stress the importance of a life pleasing to God.
QUESTION 8: True
QUESTION 9: False
QUESTION 10: True

Lesson 11: Teaching Our Children to Commit to God's Way of Life

Lesson Introduction

As a child approaches maturity, his awareness of accountability continues to increase. In the previous lesson our focus was on leading our child to Christ, and establishing in him some basic spiritual disciplines. In this lesson we want to discuss biblical principles regarding how to lead your child into a deeper commitment to and relationship with God.

In this lesson we will address the needs of children from age thirteen to eighteen or the *Elem* (age thirteen to fifteen) and the *Naar* (age fifteen to eighteen).

As we continue to build our house of wisdom, we return again and again to the seven pillars—particularly the first one, the Fear of the Lord. In the lesson we will consider all of the pillars but especially the pillars of the Fear of the Lord, Prudence, and Wise Behavior.

Lesson Outline

Topic 1: The Life Journal

> Resolutions
>
> Insights from Scripture
>
> Recording Personal Experiences with God
>
> Projects

Topic 2: Peer Pressure: Learning to Stand Alone

> When to Stand Alone
>
> Standing Alone in the Classroom
>
> Standing Alone in Dating Relationships
>
> Fathers and Daughters
>
> Standing Alone in Friendships

Topic 3: Projects for Mature Independence

> The Pillar of Discipline
>
> The Pillar of Discernment
>
> The Pillar of Wise Behavior
>
> The Pillar of Prudence
>
> The Pillar of Knowledge
>
> The Pillar of Discretion (Wise Planning)
>
> The Foundation: The Fear of the Lord

Lesson Objectives

By the end of this lesson, you will be able to do the following:

- Encourage your child in the practice of using his own life journal
- Help your child to stand alone
- Introduce your child to some projects for mature independence

Topic 1: The Life Journal

Beginning around age ten to twelve, you might consider helping your child to begin a personal life journal.

According to Psalm 139 God has designed each child uniquely. How that child is designed by God needs to be discovered and developed. As his design is discovered, the child begins to understand his life message. This message is a personalized experience of biblical truth enabled by the Holy Spirit. Each message is unique to God's design. It is called a "message" because each life is intended by God to be a message to a lost world regarding His way of life and His character.

As the child records his experiences with God, his commitments, his insights from Scripture, and various practical projects in his life journal, he begins to understand the purpose for which God created him. Not only will this help him discern God's will for his life, it will also give him a sense of value, identity, and a life mission.

A life message is a personal experience of God's work in your life. It involves:

-resolutions you have made

-your insights from Scripture

-your personal experiences of biblical truth

-the personal projects you have done to help you grow in Christ

The child's life journal is a personal notebook in which he records his personal experiences with God and his insights about his life message. Many other items can be recorded in this journal and you may think of things you would like to include. Be sure to ask your child what he would like to incorporate.

We suggest you purchase an attractive notebook or journal and take your child out some place special and present the idea. Give him or her the notebook as a gift.

In this topic we will consider four aspects of his life message:

1. Resolutions
2. Personal insights from Scripture
3. Personal experiences with the Holy Spirit
4. Projects for mature independence

Resolutions

As we go through life, we realize we need to make certain commitments. Jonathan Edwards, a famous theologian and early American pastor in the 1700s, made this a lifelong practice. At various points in his life he realized the need to put in writing certain commitments he made. When he died, over one hundred commitments were recorded in his diary.

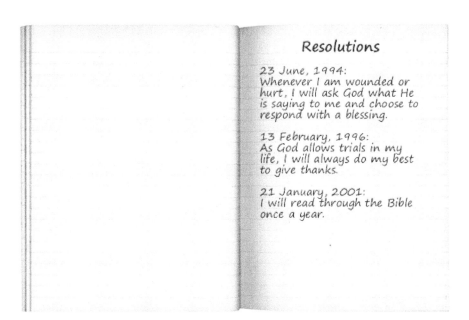

A life journal is the place to record these commitments. Men and women we have known have made and recorded such commitments in their journals. For example:

- Resolved (Jan 15, 1990) – I will be faithful to my wife in word and thought

- Resolved (June 1, 2001) – With the exception of a house and a car, I will not buy anything unless I can pay cash for it.

- Resolved (September 16, 1987) – By God's help, I will read through the Bible once a year.

- Resolved (September, 15, 1986) – I will never waste the pain. From now on whenever trial comes into my life, I will seek God's purpose and give Him thanks for how He will use this in my life.

Children can make these commitments as well. For example, they might record when they received Christ and the circumstances that led up to this event.

One 10-year-old girl wrote this after receiving Christ with her grandmother:

I, Laura Christians, dedicated my life to God, here at this desk in January of 2004. It changed my life forever.

Insights from Scripture

Christians throughout the ages have written what they believe God is saying to them when they prayerfully read the Scriptures.

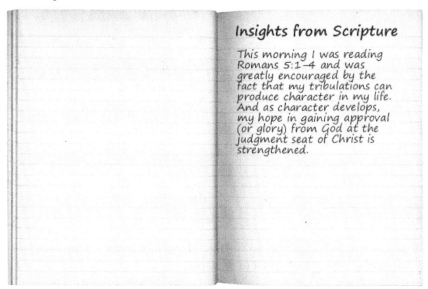

Recording Personal Experiences with God

As our children learn to walk with God, there will be many experiences which God will use to fashion them into the kind of person He can use. It can be very helpful to start a child recording these things when he is very young. They become a description of his life journey to be read and reread to encourage his faith.

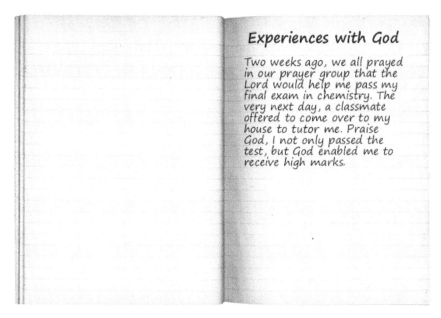

Projects

As your child continues to grow in his faith and invest in his relationship with Christ, he may want to use the life journal to record his study projects. Study projects may focus on a topic, person, or book of the Bible among other things. Recording the study and what he learns as a result will be a valuable way to document what God does in his life.

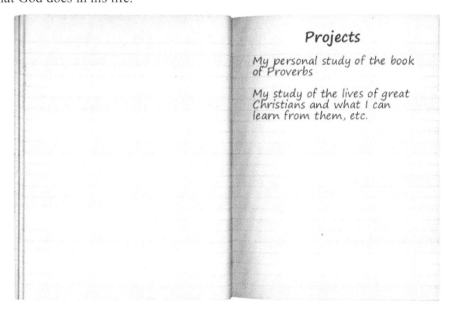

Topic 2: Peer Pressure: Learning to Stand Alone

Many of the questions in this lesson are designed not only for parents, but as projects that parents can suggest to their children. As you work on the following questions, think about how you might raise these questions and Scriptures with your children. You might consider going out with your child for a walk or to a restaurant to discuss each of these verses and talk about the kinds of situations which they may face in the future. Preparation is a good defense.

We noted in an earlier lesson that many of the values of the world are completely different than the values of the believer.

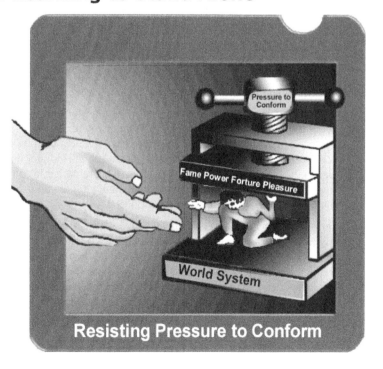

Resisting Pressure to Conform

The world system emphasizes at least four major objectives, which can be summarized in four words:

- Fortune
- Fame
- Power
- Pleasure

Furthermore, the world generally believes that these values are the keys to happiness.

Many adults, including many Christians, have accepted these values as legitimate. If adults are caught up in this syndrome, how much easier is it for children to be captivated by it? Many of our children, because they are placed in the middle of the world system with no help or preparation on how to handle it, inevitably think like, look like, sound like, and act like the system. They will be pressured to conform to the world, squeezed into its mold.

When to Stand Alone

The ability to stand alone for what Scripture says, no matter what others believe or what is happening around you, is a sign of maturity. A key to motivating your children to do this is to convince them that they have **a superior way of life.**

Assignment

- Please read the following article:

The Pressure to Conform

Dr. Dobson cites a striking example of how peer pressure works.

Psychologist Ruth W. Berenda brought groups of ten adolescents into a room for a test. Subsequently, each group of ten was instructed to raise their hands when the teacher pointed to the longest line on three separate charts. What one person in the group did not know was that nine of the others in the room had been instructed ahead of time to vote for the **second**-longest line.

Regardless of the instructions they heard later, once they were all together in the group, the nine were not to vote for the longest line, but rather vote for the next-to-the-longest line. The desire of the psychologists was to determine how one person reacted when completely surrounded by a large number of people who obviously stood against what was true.

The experiment began with nine teenagers voting for the wrong line. The one who did not know about the experiment would typically glance around, frown in confusion, and slip his hand up with the group. The instructions were repeated and the next card was raised. Time after time, the self-conscious stooge would sit there saying a short line is longer than a long line, simply because he lacked the courage to challenge the group. This remarkable conformity occurred in about seventy-five percent of the cases, and was true of small children and secondary school students as well (Dobson, *Parenting isn't for Cowards*, 225-226).

Dobson comments, "The moral and ethical implications that accompany such an experiment are frightening." This illustration points out the need to teach a child how to stand alone when surrounded by those who put him to the test. Without preparation the Christian child "will go through self-doubts, then uncertainty, and finally slump into complete conformity. If our kids are not given a good deal of practical help on how to handle peer pressure, chances are good they will fail when the tests come" (Dobson, *Parenting Isn't for Cowards*, 225-226).

Peer pressure can overwhelm our children. The movies, the culture, the pressure of friends, the non-Christian viewpoints represented in the classroom all are traps that can harm our children's growth in Christ.

QUESTION 1

There are many situations in which our children may be called on to stand alone. Match the Scripture with the corresponding situation.

Scripture	Life Situation
Proverbs 1:10-19	Participation in activities which would cause us to violate our own moral convictions
Daniel 1:8	Desire to conform to indecent dress and fashion
Colossians 2:8	To fulfill sensual school assignments such as reading or watching impure books, movies, or plays
Romans 13:1-5; Ephesians 6:1	To date someone who is not a growing Christian
Romans 12:2; 1 Peter 3:3-4	To adopt as friends those not committed to God's way of life in order to be popular
2 Corinthians 6:14; Ephesians 5:11,12	To defy authority in order to gain the approval of friends, e.g., curfew imposed by parents, regulations established by the school
1 Corinthians 15:33	To participate in activities which would cause personal loss to another person

Standing Alone in the Classroom

As our children progress through the educational system in your country they will eventually be faced with the non-Christian's naturalist world view that permeates our schools and universities. The pressure to conform and to embrace non-Christian thinking will become greater and greater.

A similar situation was facing a young man in the Old Testament whose name was Daniel. Of all the Old Testament characters held up before us as exemplary, Daniel is one of the most consistent in this regard. The prophet Ezekiel, a contemporary of Daniel, names him as one of three great men characterized by righteous living: Noah, Job, and Daniel (Ezek 14:14).

In some cultures, the children are targeted as a punishment to the parents. In Romania under communism in the 1980s, one sensitive young girl was brought to the front of the class and all the students were asked to ridicule her because of her belief in God. She had done nothing wrong, but it was a way to target her father who was a pastor. As result, this young girl had a nervous breakdown.

Daniel faced similar ridicule. The Babylonians changed his name, Daniel, which means "God is my judge," to Belteshazzar which means, "The treasure of Bel," a Babylonian deity. Hananiah's name, which meant in Hebrew, "The Lord has been gracious to me," was changed to Shadrach, which in Babylonian means "The Inspiration of the Sun God." Mishael, "He who comes from God," was renamed Meshach, "He who belongs to the goddess Sheshach." And, finally, Azariah, whose name in Hebrew meant, "the Lord is my Helper," was rendered into the Babylonian name, Abed-nego which means, "the Servant of Nego," a Babylonian deity.

Assignment

- Please read the following article:

Daniel at the "University of Babylon"

In the first chapter we meet the young Daniel, a teenager taken hostage by Nebuchadnezzar, king of Babylon. Upon arrival in this pagan city, he was promptly enrolled at the "University of Babylon," the king's training program to saturate Daniel and his friends with learning and world views of the Babylonians.

He was a boy among a captive people forced to live in a foreign land, yet his commitment to the Lord was already deep enough to enable him to stand firm in the face of the world's enticements.

The following study is designed for you to discuss with your child. The questions and insights which you acquire might be recorded in your Life Notebook so you can share these with you child.

Nebuchadnezzar ordered the chief of his officials to bring in some of the sons of Israel, including some of the sons of the royal family and of the nobility. Daniel was among this group.

For all practical purposes the training that Daniel and his friends received was meant to be a brainwashing, with the purpose of turning these young Jews into proper Chaldeans (Babylonians). The training consisted of a three-year intensive course in Chaldean literature and sciences, a course thorough enough to destroy everything that Daniel and his friends knew of God and of their spiritual heritage as God's chosen people. At the end of this time the young men were to enter the king's service.

Although this training was certainly far different from the godly upbringing that Daniel had had at home, Daniel and his friends were able to maintain their firm commitment to serve the one true God throughout this period of secular and occult influence.

Christian young people today may be forced to undergo training that is characterized by secular thinking and humanistic or even atheistic values. To come through such training with spiritual values intact, a child must know how to discern the good from the bad, the true from the false. We have no record of Daniel and his friends fighting against the educational process itself, but it seems apparent that these young men were already so grounded in the teachings of the Word of God that they could evaluate their education against what they knew to be true. All the years of brainwashing were not effective in swaying these young men from the truth.

Part of the brainwashing process was to make these young men feel an obligation, a sense of loyalty to their Babylonian captors. These young men were provided with special food from the king's table. As they became accustomed to this lavish provision, they would gradually become dependent upon the king and switch their primary allegiance to him. After eating the rich food available in the palace, it would be difficult to go back to the simple food and water to which a slave people were accustomed.

Daniel had every earthly reason to go along with the offer of a better way of life. Imagine all that he had endured: when he was a boy, he had been forcibly removed from his homeland in Judah, taken far from home and all that was familiar to him. Undoubtedly, he recognized that the king was offering him an opportunity to advance in the kingdom and that such an opportunity might not come again. Perhaps he considered the ways in which God could use him if he worked his way up in the king's good graces. But he also knew that to disobey the king's orders was to risk incurring royal wrath.

For Daniel to take the stand he did when he refused to eat the king's meat is quite remarkable for a young man. It reveals much about his character. Between the lines we can also speculate that Daniel's parents had done a remarkable job of raising this young man to stand firm when tested. We can speculate that Daniel's parents had provided him with a thorough education in obedience and allegiance to God. At some point in his young life Daniel had made a commitment to God that he would not defile himself. Even at that early age he carried through with this commitment in the face of incredible pressure to conform.

Discipline was an evident part of this young man's life. Not only did Daniel not accept the unclean food prohibited by the Lord, but he asked for only water to drink and vegetables to eat. This was a diet stricter than God required of His people in the Old Testament law. It appears that Daniel and his friends requested this diet as a direct statement of their implicit trust in God. The food provided by the king may have been a symbol of the attractions of the world offered by a pagan king. Choosing to subsist on vegetables and water may have been a choice that showed the young men's preference to live simply and allow God, rather than the king, to sustain them.

When it comes to our responsibility as parents, the principle here is clear. Daniel was prepared before he faced the situation that would test him. His commitment to the Lord was firm, and his knowledge of God's Word provided him with an anchor that would hold in the storms of life. To prepare our children to stand firm in this way, we must be involved with our child's education from his earliest days. No matter what society we live in, the world's contradictions of God's truth will inevitably be found in the pages of our child's textbooks and in the words of his teachers.

Children can never be totally isolated from the world, nor should we view isolation as the ultimate answer. Daniel, as a young man, had regular contact with secular authorities, yet he was able to remain faithful to the Lord because he was both spiritually prepared and committed to do so.

Children can be trained to evaluate what they hear according to the standard of God's Word. To instill this confidence in God and His Word, parents must begin early. They must be involved daily with their child's education, taking the time to explain both the truths and the falsehoods that he may be learning at school or in his contacts with those who hold other beliefs. The child's early values will be gleaned from you, and these can be strengthened as his discernment develops.

Daniel learned the language of the Chaldeans, he studied the literature and the sciences of these people, he would even be known by the heathen name of Belteshazzar, but it is clear that he never adopted the Chaldean religion or lifestyle. When our faith is strong, we hear what the world is saying and teaching, but that education is filtered through the sieve of the Word of God. Babylon could change a boy's name, but they could not alter his commitment to God.

QUESTION 2

According to Daniel 1:8-13 what decision did Daniel make?

- A. To pray to God
- B. To not eat the king's food
- C. To not bow to the king
- D. To serve the king

QUESTION 3

Read Daniel 1:8 again and then read Leviticus 11. Why do you think Daniel probably rejected the food from the king's table? Why was this issue so important to Daniel?

QUESTION 4

When Daniel was asked by the commander of the king's officials to eat the king's food, what characterized his response?

    A. He suggested a creative alternative.

    B. He steadfastly refused to obey.

    C. He told the official that what he was being asked to do was unbiblical.

    D. He quietly disobeyed, ignoring the instructions.

QUESTION 5

Think for a moment about "The Pillar of Wise Behavior." In your own words, summarize the three aspects of wise behavior.

Please read the following article, which is designed to give you a practical example of the Pillar of Wise Behavior and a project you could consider doing with your child.

How to Stand Alone in the Classroom

Remember that Wise Behavior involves being gracious and attractive as well as being in conformity to God's standards. It was said of the Lord Jesus that he was full of grace and truth (Jn 1:17). In teaching our children to stand alone in the classroom, it is important that both grace and truth be emphasized. Sometimes we are so truthful we unnecessarily offend, or we are so gracious that we compromise.

The following is a suggested way of teaching your children to stand alone in the classroom.

Have the right attitude in class

In order for a student to gain a good response from a professor who gives an assignment which the student cannot fulfill, he must have demonstrated a gracious and diligent attitude in class. Here are some important items:

- Be on time every day

- Sit up straight and don't slouch disrespectfully in the desk

- Lean forward during the lectures. This signals to the professor that you are paying attention.

- Always maintain a pleasant expression toward the teacher and class mates.

- Take thorough notes on the professor's lectures. Teachers see this and it shows them you are trying.

- Be neat in appearance. When a child comes to class looking like he is good for nothing, people notice. It communicates indifference to the professor.

- Participate frequently and respectfully in class discussions. Assume responsibility to help the professor in making the class a success.

- Occasionally, ask or inquire about extra credit work.

Remind your child that professors and teachers are people, they have feelings and they want to do a good job. It is a matter of love, respect, and graciousness to be on their team and help make the class a success.

If your child has followed the above suggestions, he is much more likely to receive a good response from the professor when it becomes necessary for him to disagree.

Never walk into class unprepared

Being prepared every day will signal to the professor that you are diligent and interested in his class.

Respond with Wise Behavior to a Morally Harmful Assignment
Discern the basic intent of the teacher

This is what Daniel did. Just as the king was not trying to get Daniel to violate his convictions by asking him to eat meat, in most cases teachers are not trying to get student to violate their moral convictions by giving them a morally harmful assignment.

Ask: What is the stated reason for the assignment?

Design a Creative Alternative

Because Daniel had correctly discerned the king's basic intent, he was now able to suggest an alternative which would achieve the same result without violating his personal convictions. Children can be trained to evaluate what they hear according to the standard of God's Word. To instill this confidence in God and His Word, parents must begin early.

For example, if an immoral book was chosen by the teacher for the purpose of illustrating a certain period of literature, then find another book written in the same period, by someone who had a positive influence.

Carefully Word your request

Your child should understand that a proper request should include:

- Respect for the teacher

- Appreciation for the class in general

- A desire to learn

- A non-condemning attitude

Here is an example:

> I have appreciated this class and your way of [include a positive quality] and I want to learn all I can from it, but this particular assignment creates a problem for me. To expose myself to this type of [book, activity, play, movie, etc.] would violate a personal moral conviction. Would you allow me to replace this assignment with the following one? [Explain your alternative.]

Respond Properly if Request is Refused

- Listen carefully for the teacher's reasons for refusal

- If you begin to doubt whether or not the assignment is really harmful, then offer to reconsider your stand.

- If you are still convinced that the assignment is harmful, then respectfully re-state your conviction and be prepared to take the consequences.

For example:

> I really don't want to cause any difficulty for you, but I'm just not able to do this assignment.

Respond Properly to a Resulting Hostile Teacher

Prepare your child for the worst. Read 1 Peter 2:20-21 together. Our children can view this hostility as a significant opportunity to reflect Christ-like qualities in return.

(Adapted from Gothard)

QUESTION 6

Sit down with your child and go through the article with him or her and then discuss a way of doing a project that he or she would be comfortable with. Record your child's responses in your Life Notebook.

Daniel learned the language, literature, and sciences of the Babylonians (Chaldeans), but it is clear that he never adopted the Chaldean religion or lifestyle. When our faith is strong, we hear what the world is saying and teaching, but that education is filtered through the sieve of the Word of God. Babylon could change a boy's name, but they could not alter his commitment to God.

Standing Alone in Dating Relationships

As young people mature and the hormone levels begin to rise, it is proper and natural that they are drawn to members of the opposite sex. This leads to the question of dating in some cultures. Under what conditions should a parent permit dating?

Obviously, parents in China, Burma, or the Middle East face different cultural ideas from those in the West. What do parents in cultures where arranged marriage is the norm need to think about? What about cultures where there is no history of dating, yet it is now an issue among the urban crowd—how do they guide their children through this?

We cannot anticipate all variations, however, what follows may help in many situations.

All parents know that this is an area where there are many traps that can snare our children and have lifelong consequences, such as pregnancy, abortions, wrong company, drugs, and failed marriages.

Just as it would be foolhardy to send a soldier into battle with absolutely no training, it is dangerous to send our children out into the world of relationships without some advance preparation.

In this section, we want to apply the Pillar of Prudence to help your child navigate this new world.

QUESTION 7

Discuss with your spouse your own agreed-on approach to allowing your children to date. While this is a good exercise, it only applies in some cultures. If this exercise is not applicable for your situation then think through issues that your daughters face, even if they are not in dating situations.

Fathers and Daughters

The impact that a father can have on his daughter's future is enormous. Many men have little awareness of the role they can have. Often a young woman has her father in mind subconsciously when she thinks about who her future mate may be. Her father's approval, affection, and involvement in her life is critical.

Toward the end of the Song of Solomon, the brothers of the young woman in the Song approach the king with a question.

QUESTION 8

Read Song of Solomon 8:8. As the brothers see that young men are coming around and want a relationship with their sister, they are concerned about what to do. Before reading further, take out your Life Notebook, sit down with your spouse and record what you would do when young men want a relationship with your own daughters.

QUESTION 9

According to Song of Solomon 8:9, on what does the answer to the question in Song of Solomon 8:8 depend? What does it mean to build on her ornaments of silver? What does it mean to barricade her with planks of cedar? What might happen if a daughter who is a "wall" was barricaded with planks of cedar? Record your thoughts in your Life Notebook.

The king's answer tells us that each child is different and as parents we must choose an approach which is appropriate for that particular child.

One father took his daughter out on a date and he challenged her to consider carefully the Pillar of Prudence and apply its wisdom in her courtship in regard to who she dated. Please read the following article. This article may not apply directly to your culture.

A Date with Your Daughter

Here is a project you might consider doing with your daughter.

Commitment to God's Best

Ask her out on a date. Perhaps, take her out to dinner with you.

Ask her what her goals in life are. After some discussion, challenge her to make a commitment to you that she will never settle for less than God's best in regard to whom she dates and whom she marries.

Have a discussion with her regarding the qualities she thinks would be essential in a young man that she would potentially have an interest in marrying. This is an opportunity to share qualities you think are important such as:

- A growing relationship with Jesus Christ
- A loving relationship with his parents
- A submissive spirit to authority
- A clear conscience
- A forgiving spirit
- A sense of purpose in life
- Responsibility with finances

Ask "Could we begin a section in your Life Journal dealing with essential qualities in a future husband if God should lead you to marry?"

Decisions for a Successful Life

Then say, "There are two very important decisions I would like you to make and your whole future may rest on whether or not you make them. Here is the first decision. I will tell you what the decision is, and then I will give you five reasons why it is to your benefit to make it."

First Decision

Decision: If any young man asks you for a date, I would like you to commit to me that you will give him this answer:

"I really appreciate your asking me but before I can say yes, we will need to check with my father. Could you come to my house to meet my father and ask his permission to date me?"

Five Reasons for this Decision

1. It will elevate the boy's respect for you. When he knows that he has to work for that date, he will respect you more.
2. It will illustrate for this boy how much your father loves you.
3. It will give me an opportunity to sense his character. A man can see through another man more quickly than a girl can.
4. It avoids the necessity of you having to say no. Many girls are afraid to say no because they think the young man will think she is arrogant.
5. It will establish a chain of counsel and authority with me over this young man.

Second Decision

There is one more essential decision you would like her to make. It is this.

Decision: The first time a young man talks to you about marriage, I want you to say, "If you are thinking about our getting married, my father would like to talk with you before we discuss this. Can you contact him and set up a time to talk?"

Why is this important? It allows me to evaluate this young man and see if he has the qualities we agreed upon for a successful marriage. When I talk with this young man, I'll ask him a series of questions that will determine how many of the essential qualities he has. I will share with you what he says.

QUESTION 10

Take some time to discuss this article with your spouse. Would this approach work well in your family? If not, how could you modify it to fit your particular situation?

Standing Alone in Friendships

Standing firm has to do with relationships. Another way parents can influence children is by helping them to choose friends wisely. We can start when our children are still small, by telling them what sort of boys and girls we hope they will choose as their friends. Encourage them to look for friends who exhibit kind actions, do not use vulgar language, and show respectful attitudes toward their teachers. There may not always be Christian peers in your neighborhood or school, but there may be some fine children who do not know the Lord yet. Be sure to emphasize the "yet."

Encourage your children to choose carefully, to take their time and not be so desperate for a friend that they make poor choices. Explain that cultivating wrong friendships is like playing with fire. Pray with your child about his choice of friends, starting on the first day of the school year. Read some verses together on the subject of friendship, or make a study of what the book of Proverbs says about the importance of having friends who encourage us to do right.

QUESTION 11

Read Psalm 1 and Proverbs 1. How could you use these passages to talk about choosing friends wisely? Draw up a little chart or diagram contrasting the two kinds of people described in Psalm 1.

While parents may not be able to choose their older child's friends, they can still do much to influence the group that their child chooses. Older children enjoy group activities much more than individual activities. Parents can plan games or parties for the whole group, which will give them opportunities to take a good look at their child's friends and to have some input as to the choice of the child's friends.

Another strategy for parents is to offer alternatives when we have to say no to our children. If we will not allow them to go to a friend's party where alcohol will be available or other inappropriate behavior will be encouraged, why not allow them to invite some friends over that evening for a party at home? Young people need to see that Christians are not a sad, sour-faced bunch of religious fanatics. They can have fun and still adhere to Christian principles.

The family should provide the greatest peer pressure of all—a positive support system to help face the negative onslaught from without. To develop such a support system, parents need to spend some time and effort planning family activities and developing a spirit of family camaraderie.

QUESTION 12

Discuss some of the peer pressures that teenagers in your society face. Can you think of any form of peer pressure that you yourself are experiencing at the moment? What lessons can you learn from this experience which you might apply with your children?

QUESTION 13

Think about ways that you can be a peer influence for others. What practical things could we ourselves do to be positive peers? What sort of things could we say to our children to encourage them to be positive peers? Write down several of your best ideas and identify ways you can apply your list to your life.

Topic 3: Projects for Mature Independence

In our discussion of the life journal in Topic 1, we mentioned that one thing a child would record in his life journal is his work on some projects for mature independence. These are practical projects a young person can implement that will lead toward a healthy departure from home and will increase our communication with our teens.

The Pillar of Discipline

In the sections to follow, we will suggest some projects you might consider proposing to the teenager in your house. You are the best judge of whether or not these particular suggestions would work and, of course, your child needs to agree.

One family successfully introduced the following project to their 15-year-old:

- Read through the New Testament this year
- Lose seven kilograms
- Run 1500 meters in 8 minutes and 30 seconds.

Simple, but it worked and the child developed a sense of self-discipline. Furthermore, dinnertime conversations often revolved around what he was reading and on many occasions, dad and mom went with him to the track to work out.

The Pillar of Discernment

When God visited this planet, He took on a human body. The Holy Spirit knows, even if we do not, that the best way to communicate spiritual truth is to clothe it in flesh and blood (Jn 1:14).

One of the best ways to challenge your children to commit to God's way of life is to expose them to godly examples.

Read some stories of great Christians or Bible stories. Ask your child, "What would you do in this situation?"

QUESTION 14

God has much to say about "wise men." Match the Scripture with the characteristic of God's wise men.

Scripture	A Wise Man
Proverbs 10:14	We are to associate with them.
Proverbs 13:20	They are able to reduce conflict and anger.
Proverbs 29:8	They have a storehouse full of knowledge.
Ecclesiastes 9:17	While their words are soft, it is better than the shouting of fools.

There are several ways to expose your children to God's wise men. For example:

1. Biblical biographies (a good place to begin is a Bible dictionary).

2. Historical Accounts (in English, see *Fox's Book of Martyrs*).

3. Personal experiences of how God has worked in your life.

4. Biographies of great Christians.

5. Invite to your home missionaries, church workers, other committed young adults, and people you want your children exposed to.

QUESTION 15

With your spouse, take some time to discuss a possible project for your child to implement and write out what you want her to do. Be sure to involve your child in this project and get her ideas as well. In this project you want her to talk to some mature adults. She can say, "My father asked me to choose someone I respect and you were the person who came to mind. I would like to ask you some questions about how you became who are today."

- How did you become a Christian?

- What are some of the difficulties you had in your Christian walk and how did you deal with them?

- What decisions did you make when you were in your twenties which have shaped who you are today?

- How did you find your life purpose and what counsel would you give?

The Pillar of Wise Behavior

The essence of wise behavior is the ability to deal wisely, fairly, and graciously in our relationships with others. Learning to deal with people in a wise biblical way is critical for maturity. Too many children never develop this skill.

QUESTION 16

With your spouse, read Philippians 2:1-5 and discuss what it means to see things from the other person's point of view. Think though some illustration in your child's life where this could be taught. Then read the passage as a family at dinnertime and propose this project. Ask your child to list the name of everyone in his class in his life journal and to record one positive quality about that person. Then, as the months progress, verbalize that quality to his or her classmate.

The Pillar of Prudence

QUESTION 17

Open your Life Notebook and with your spouse record the traps which your child seems to be susceptible to: appearance, sex, drugs, peer pressure, fame, the wrong kind of friends, etc. Pray about what God would have you do. Write it out. What Scripture applies? Review the pillar of prudence with your child and ask him to write out in his or her life journal the traps he faces. Ask him to record Scripture related to these traps. Ask, "Do you think there are any resolutions you need to record in your Life Notebook regarding these traps?'

The Pillar of Knowledge

True knowledge in the book of Proverbs involves both head knowledge and heart knowledge. It involves biblical knowledge that has been worked out in our lives.

QUESTION 18

Read each of the Scripture references below and then match each passage with the phrase describing an aspect of biblical knowledge that has been integrated into life.

Scripture	Aspect of True Knowledge
1 Timothy 1:5	Takes effort to obtain knowledge
2 Timothy 2:15	Knowledge is pure
2 Timothy 3:14-17	The goal of knowledge is love
1 Peter 2:1-3	Knowledge should affect how a believer lives

Here are some ideas which some families have successfully implemented with their young adults. These ideas may not work in your particular family but use your own creativity to develop projects of your own that you and your spouse want to try with your own children.

Dad's theology class. One father had a Bible study with his 10- and 12-year-old children called Dad's Theology Class. This particular father was good with PowerPoint software and always had a few slides prepared. It lasted about thirty minutes. In the first fifteen minutes he taught a concept and in the last fifteen they discussed what it might mean in their lives.

Categorize proverbs. Beginning at age ten to twelve you might consider challenging your child to categorize Proverbs. This is a project that might go on for six months to a year. You read through the book with him, and in his life journal he begins to classify various proverbs as they relate to the seven pillars, to friendship, to faith, to moral issues, etc.

One chapter a day in Proverbs. As a summer project, one mother had her children read one chapter of Proverbs every day. Their assignment was to come back to their mother with two things: (1) a question about something in the chapter and (2) which verse meant the most and why.

The Pillar of Discretion (Wise Planning)

As the article indicates, discretion is the ability to make wise plans, to formulate objectives and carry out a plan to achieve them.

A Christian teacher has suggested that parents try one creative means of encouraging responsibility in adolescents that she found helpful in her own family. Please read about her project, "The Teenage Challenge."

The Teenage Challenge
Approaching Adolescents with a Challenge

A mother we know has suggested that parents try one creative means of encouraging responsibility in adolescents that she found helpful in her own family. She calls this project the Teenage Challenge. It involves challenging a young adolescent to achieve something he can be proud of in four different areas: physical, intellectual, spiritual, and practical.

The parents had prepared the challenge in advance, so that when they approached their twelve-year-old son, they were able to explain their purpose and goals. Then they asked him to think about how he would like to grow in each of the four areas, considering his own strengths and weaknesses, and try to come up with a few specific and exciting projects he could do. Later, they sat down together with him and wrote a challenge, setting as a goal a specific reward if he completed these projects by his thirteenth birthday.

Along with this proposal went an important message: "We are excited! You are getting ready to enter a special time of life. You're on your way to adulthood. We want to help you be ready for this new phase of your life, and this challenge will help you prepare." Their enthusiasm was contagious, and their son Jonathan was eager to begin.

Below is an example of the Teenage Challenge similar to the one this teacher and her husband agreed upon with their son.

Teenage Challenge for Jonathan

    A. Physical Goals

        1. Run one kilometer in under four minutes.

        2. Do forty sit-ups in a row.

    B. Intellectual Goals

        1. Read one good book.

        2. Write about that book.

    C. Spiritual Goals

        1. Study Proverbs to see God's view of personal habits, such as laziness, pride, cheating, and lying.

2. Then work out your own standards and convictions for your teenage years, putting them down on paper.

3. Memorize Psalm 1.

D. Practical Goals

1. Save a certain amount of money before your birthday, and we will match what you have saved.

2. Plan and execute a hiking excursion with Dad.

This is strictly a sample of what you can do. Parents must be creative, establishing goals to fit their teenager's individual needs, abilities, and personality. One teenager may show financial irresponsibility, so the parent may suggest it would be good for him or her to learn to keep a budget. Another teenager may not need this challenge, having been a veritable accountant since age six. A third teen could benefit from working on her swimming skills, whereas her sister who is on the school swim team needs to be challenged in other areas. Of course, it can still be very productive to include an activity which is aimed at developing a child's already existing talent.

The point is to determine, along with your child, some realistic and specific goals, and then determine how he or she could accomplish them. Allowing a teenager to participate in establishing the challenge demonstrates to him that you want him to take increasing responsibility for his own life. While the time frame for such a challenge can be flexible, it is important that a child be given enough time. One mom gave her son his challenge two weeks before his birthday; their house was in chaos for the next fourteen days. A last-minute challenge is not likely to be very productive; planning is important for good results.

Some other parents did it differently. On their child's 13th, 14th, 15th, 16th, 17th, and 18th birthdays, they took him out to dinner and offered the challenge. Each time, they gave him a box with a birthday gift and a challenge and responsibility card. Each year, new challenges for that year were discussed, and also new freedoms and responsibilities were added. For example, on his 17th birthday (or 18th, whatever the parents decide) he could go on dates alone with girls. Each year his curfew was lengthened 30 minutes until at 18 there was no curfew. But along with these new freedoms, there were new responsibilities such as learning to balance a checkbook, becoming involved in a compassion ministry in the city, or offering to assist the pastor at the church in a new responsibility, etc.

QUESTION 19

Write a challenge for a young teenager. Are the goals measurable and attainable or unrealistic? Is it too simple and therefore not much of a challenge? Will your teen know when he has successfully met the requirements? Are the rewards clearly defined? Is there a reasonable time limit? When you have come up with what you believe is a reasonable challenge, review it again to be sure that it is practical.

Why undertake a project like this? Parents who challenge their children in a productive way are helping their child to begin his teenage years with a positive approach that can lead to a sense of accomplishment. In doing this, they are contributing to his self-esteem, as well as acknowledging that he or she is growing up. The challenge can also help to develop a sense of family camaraderie. When the kilometer has been run, the camping excursion is behind you, and every item checked off, both parents and teenager can lean back with a sigh and a sense of pride and achievement. Reward the child for what he has accomplished, perhaps in the form of a special certificate signed by you or in another tangible form. Celebrate with him, and let him know that you think he is a special gift to you from the Lord.

The Foundation: The Fear of the Lord

Probably one of the most important things you can do for your child is to help him get to know God personally by spending time with Jesus. Your child can be challenged to have his own personal devotions, particularly at a very early age. Many of us have started this practice with our children at age seven. If you do not start it early, it may not happen.

He must understand why he should do this. We have found it important to emphasize that this is not something our children do for us, but it is to help them to get to know God better. You are God's child and He wants to get to know you better.

How to train him to have a quiet time

First, we must model it. Initially we should have a quiet time with him. He learns to pray and to take things to God as he watches us do it.

Also, prayer must be a way of life, not just something we take to God in a quiet time. One mother remembers when she was out with her children on a rainy night, her husband was gone, and the car stopped dead in a large mud puddle. One of her daughters said, "That's it, God does not care about us, I am not going to pray to Him." The mother knew that this is real life and that we have to take things to God at all times. She told her daughter that they were going to pray anyway. They did, and eventually someone came and towed them to a garage and provided a place for them to spend the night. The point is, taking things to God is a way of life. If it is not a way of life, it will not work in a quiet time.

An excellent way to begin is to teach your child to journal. He can read a passage of Scripture he is interested in and then write a "Dear God" letter in his life journal.

Teach him to pray by praying with him

Let the child choose the time and place that is best for him. Show him how to begin the time with prayer, asking God to enable him both to understand and to obey what he reads in God's Word.

Encourage him to read his Bible at least five minutes daily (or longer, if he desires). Encourage him to begin reading in the gospel of Mark, followed by books such as Acts, John, Genesis, and Psalms.

As mentioned in Lesson 10, Topic 2, you might suggest that he read a short passage several times so that it may speak to him. Teach him to ask questions about the passage, learning to think about and reflect on the verses he has read. Five questions he can ask himself are:

- Is there a promise to claim?
- Is there a command to obey?
- Is there a warning to heed?
- Is there an example to follow?
- Is there a truth to learn about God or myself?

Help your child learn to find the promise, command, warning, or truth, and teach him to translate what he finds in a passage into a prayer to God.

Then challenge him to write down what God is saying in his life journal.

QUESTION 20

After reading the suggestions above, sit down with your spouse and record in your Life Notebook a plan to begin encouraging your child to get to know God by spending regular time with Him. What do you think would work with your children in your particular situation?

Lesson 11 Self Check

QUESTION 1

A life journal is a place for your child to record personal resolutions, insights from Scripture, experiences of biblical truth, and projects for mature independence *True or False?*

QUESTION 2

Daniel and his friends remained committed to God's ways even when they had to serve the king. *True or False?*

QUESTION 3

The Pillar of Prudence is the ability to avoid traps. *True or False?*

QUESTION 4

The Teenage Challenge is an effective

   A. Method of discipline
   B. Way of helping a child to begin his teenage years with a positive approach that can lead to a sense of accomplishment
   C. Challenge to set goals for your teenager that are slightly higher than he is able to achieve
   D. Challenge developed by the parents and given to the teenager to accomplish

QUESTION 5

It is dangerous to overemphasize the influence of peer pressure on your adolescent. *True or False?*

QUESTION 6

What should we do when we train our children to stand alone in the classroom?

   A. Show them how to verbally present Scripture passages to the class when the professor says something which contradicts the biblical worldview.
   B. Coach them how to tactfully present creative alternatives to fulfilling assignments they feel are inappropriate for a Christian.
   C. Explain the necessity of separating themselves from most of the activities that their non-believing classmates engage in.
   D. Identify a list of behaviors which they should avoid.

QUESTION 7

In the Song of Solomon, the brothers come to the king and say, "We have a little sister, the boys are interested in her. What shall we do?" What was Solomon's answer?

   A. Barricade her with planks of cedar.
   B. Honor and praise her for her virtue.
   C. Instruct her scripturally on the importance of avoiding non-believing boys.
   D. It all depends on what kind of person she is, strong or weak.

QUESTION 8

A good passage to use to discuss the impact of peer pressure on your child is Proverbs 1. *True or False?*

QUESTION 9

The best way to teach a child how to have a devotional time and how to pray is to model it before him. *True or False?*

QUESTION 10

When presenting a teenage challenge to your adolescent, it is important to involve him in the selection of projects he is expected to complete. *True or False?*

Lesson 11 Answers to Questions

QUESTION 1

Scripture	Life Situation
Proverbs 1:10-19	To participate in activities which would cause personal loss to another person
Daniel 1:8	Participation in activities which would cause us to violate our own moral convictions
Colossians 2:8	To fulfill sensual school assignments such as reading or watching impure books, movies, or plays
Romans 13:1-5; Ephesians 6:1	To defy authority in order to gain the approval of friends, e.g., curfew imposed by parents, regulations established by the school
Romans 12:2; 1 Peter 3:3-4	Desire to conform to indecent dress and fashion
2 Corinthians 6:14; Ephesians 5:11,12	To date someone who is not a growing Christian
1 Corinthians 15:33	To adopt as friends those not committed to God's way of life in order to be popular

QUESTION 2
B. To not eat the king's food

QUESTION 3: *Your answer*

QUESTION 4
A. He suggested a creative alternative.

QUESTION 5: *Your answer should be similar to the following:*
(1) conformity to God's will and standard; (2) dealing fairly and righteously with others; (3) gentleness and attractiveness

QUESTION 6: *Your answer*

QUESTION 7: *Your answer*

QUESTION 8: *Your answer*

QUESTION 9: *Your answer*

QUESTION 10: *Your answer*

QUESTION 11: *Your answer*

QUESTION 12: *Your answer*

QUESTION 13: *Your answer*

QUESTION 14

Scripture	A Wise Man
Proverbs 10:14	They have a storehouse full of knowledge.
Proverbs 13:20	We are to associate with them.
Proverbs 29:8	They are able to reduce conflict and anger.
Ecclesiastes 9:17	While their words are soft, it is better than the shouting of fools.

QUESTION 15: *Your answer*

QUESTION 16: *Your answer*

QUESTION 17: *Your answer*

QUESTION 18

Scripture	Aspect of True Knowledge
1 Timothy 1:5	The goal of knowledge is love
2 Timothy 2:15	Takes effort to obtain knowledge
2 Timothy 3:14-17	Knowledge should affect how a believer lives
1 Peter 2:1-3	Knowledge is pure

QUESTION 19: *Your answer*

QUESTION 20: *Your answer*

Lesson 11 Self Check Answers

QUESTION 1: True

QUESTION 2: True

QUESTION 3: True

QUESTION 4

    B. Way of helping a child to begin his teenage years with a positive approach that can lead to a sense of accomplishment

QUESTION 5: False

QUESTION 6

    B. Coach them how to tactfully present creative alternatives to fulfilling assignments they feel are inappropriate for a Christian.

QUESTION 7

    D. It all depends on what kind of person she is, strong or weak.

QUESTION 8: True

QUESTION 9: True

QUESTION 10: True

Lesson 12: Releasing Your Child to God

Lesson Introduction

Do you remember the day your first baby was born? Probably you still recall how you felt when you first held that tiny little form in your arms and gazed with wonder and pride at the miniature fingers and toes. Deep inside you determined to be the best mother or father in the whole world. You were committed to raising your child to be responsible, well-behaved, and happy. Perhaps you also had a desire to glorify God through your family so that others might see Christ in your home.

As the years passed, you became immersed in the task of parenting—training, teaching, and loving your child. You bore a great deal of responsibility for each of your children, and you made many decisions based on their well-being.

The years fly by so quickly. Eventually, there comes a time when your child becomes an adult, perhaps establishing his own family. Whether the adult child leaves the family home, or stays as an adult member

of the family, parents must release the child and realize the child is an adult. The thought of releasing a child is almost unbearable for some parents. They wonder whether the feeling of emptiness that occurs can ever be filled. Although this feeling is usually more intense if the child leaves home, parents may still feel as deep a sense of loss in the "graduation" of their child into adulthood even when they live under the same roof.

Learning to Release Your Child

Releasing a child to live as an adult is the culmination of all the careful training that has preceded this event. It should be a positive and even joyful experience, yet for some parents it is not. In this lesson we will explore the subject of releasing our children, discuss why it may be hard for some parents to release a child, and explore the sensitive area of relating to our grown children.

Lesson Outline

Topic 1: Learning to Release Our Children

    The Necessity of Releasing

    The Difficulty of Releasing

    The Method of Releasing

Topic 2: Learning to Relate to Our Grown Children

    Learn to Develop Open and Honest Communication

    Learn to Relate as a Friend

    Learn to Disagree Without Being Disagreeable

    Learn to Tear Down the Walls that Divide

    Learn to Support and Not Control Your Grown Child

Lesson Objectives

By the end of this lesson, you will be able to do the following:

- Explain the necessity of releasing your child and some practical steps to take to accomplish this
- List ways to develop good communication with your grown child and to relate to him or her as a friend
- Define some basic rules for living together in extended family situations
- Deepen your trust in the sovereign purpose of God for you and your family

Topic 1: Learning to Release Our Children

Our final task as mothers and fathers is that of releasing our grown children and launching them into the world of adulthood. For many parents it is one of the most difficult assignments to undertake. Parents who struggle to let go fully often lead to problems in the relationship between the parent and their grown child that can last the rest of their lives. In order for children to become true adults, parents must allow their child to live his own life, independent of his parents.

Parents must grasp that their child has grown from a dependent youngster into a capable and responsible adult. If they do not, they still tend to view their grown son or daughter as a child who needs continual advice and instruction if he or she is to do things properly. The grown child desperately wants to be granted adult status by their parents. They want to be loved and respected by their parents but freed from parental control. They are saying to their parents, "I still love you. I still need you. I still want you as my friend. But I no longer need you as the authority in my life." Somehow this message is not always received.

QUESTION 1

Do you know someone who is still treated as a child by his or her parents? What effect does this situation seem to have on that person? How has the person responded to his parents? Open your Life Notebook and record your thoughts. Come prepared to share at your accountability group.

The Necessity of Releasing

Assignment

- Please read the following article:

The Necessity of Releasing our Children to God

Releasing our children is a natural response to their increasing responsibility and maturity. As the child grows to adulthood, it is natural for him to desire to establish his own family. Genesis 2:24 says, "For this cause a man shall leave his father and his mother, and shall cleave to his wife; and they shall become one flesh." This verse indicates that it is both natural and desirable for a son or daughter to choose a partner with whom to spend the rest of his or her life.

In order for a couple to develop intimacy and trust and to become inseparably bonded, they must leave father and mother. That does not mean to abandon them or ignore them or neglect them but to move out from under their wing. There is to be a shift of authority as the new couple establishes their own home. Both sets of parents are to take their hands off the new couple.

It is hard for many parents to take their hands off their grown children and allow them to live their own lives. Release needs to be viewed as a process rather than a sudden event. This process should begin as soon as our children are old enough to make decisions of their own. The young child learns to choose what clothes he wants to wear or what game he wants to play or what color he will use to paint a picture. As parents we can either encourage a child's growth and enjoy his increasing maturity, or we can seek to stifle it. We can insist that he paint every picture using colors we find appropriate, but the result may be that he will not care to paint at all. We can demand strict, unquestioning adherence to our way of doing things and in so doing cripple our child's growth in creativity and responsibility.

If maturation is a process, so is release. Ultimate release of our child will be achieved gracefully only if we have fostered his gradual maturity, releasing him gradually to make his own decisions and to bear responsibility for his own actions. Wise, sensitive parents spend years helping their children learn to stand on their own and to reach their full potential.

Throughout this process the parents are accomplishing two things, both of which are healthy and wholesome. First, they are making it easier for themselves to loosen the ties. Year by year, as the child matures, the parents are gradually releasing their control of the child. As the child either verbally or nonverbally expresses his need for greater independence, sensitive parents interpret his needs correctly. They encourage the child to learn to act responsibly, and they give him increasing freedom. When the child reaches adulthood, they will be ready to release him because they view this release as a natural culmination of the years of child-rearing.

Second, the parents are preparing the child for the ultimate experience of adult independence. They are helping the youngster learn to stretch his wings, like a young bird preparing for flight. They are providing him with a loving context in which he can learn to exercise limited freedom and at the same time enjoy the security of reasonable limitations. Within this atmosphere the child knows he is both loved and respected. His parents love him enough to set some limits for him; they also respect him enough to expand the limits gradually. They trust him to make wise choices with the increasing freedom he enjoys.

Parents who do not respect their grown children or credit them with enough intelligence to take care of themselves often continue to treat their children like toddlers. Is it appropriate for a mother to remind her grown son about his table manners? The answer is no. If he has been inculcated with good habits from childhood, he will probably do these things without being told. If a grown son forgets to do something that he has been taught consistently, that is his problem. His forgetfulness may be a way of demonstrating his independence from parental authority, or it may simply reflect a set of values different from his parents'.

When our children reach adulthood, we no longer need to feel that it is our responsibility to remind them to pick up their clothes or pay their bills. It is no longer a part of our job. As a mature man or woman our child is now accountable for his own actions, as well as for the consequences of his actions. If we have trained him to make wise choices and allowed him to learn life's lessons through natural consequences, we have done our part.

Not all parents view ultimate release of the child as a desirable goal. On the contrary, some think only of keeping the child near them forever, and the results can be tragic. The parents of one twenty-three-year-old woman still tried to discipline her by spanking, using a belt. They insisted that she be home every evening by 10 p.m. They refused to consider the possibility of her moving away from home, although she had a good job, was very responsible, and had high moral standards as a Christian.

This young woman remained under her parents' authoritative umbrella too long. In a sense she was like an unborn baby in the tenth or eleventh month of pregnancy. Granted, the womb is a safe place to be, but only for nine months. After this, the placenta begins to break down, the proper nourishment of the baby may be prevented, and the baby's life is endangered. This young woman was overdue; she was never "delivered" into the opportunities and responsibilities of adulthood.

The process of childbirth is not without pain, but it is necessary to undergo this experience to bring a child into the world. The reward makes the pain worth enduring. So it is with releasing a grown child. Parents who release a child to adult independence reap the reward of watching their young man or woman function as an adult. Those who would keep a child in the "womb" of their protective care indefinitely may be forced to watch the child wither and die emotionally.

Some children are more willing than others to remain under the umbrella of parental authority as adults.

> It is the very compliant child who often yields to the tyranny of intimidation. Some remain closeted there for forty years or more. Even if they marry, their parents will not grant emancipation without a struggle, setting the stage for lifelong in-law problems (Dobson, *Parenting Isn't for Cowards*, 215-16).

Parents who refuse to let go often force their children to choose between two negative alternatives. The first alternative is acquiescing to parental domination and manipulation, and failing to accept responsibility. The result is immaturity.

The second alternative is for the son or daughter to engage in desperate means to throw off the yoke of parental control. The young person may respond like an erupting volcano. When the top of the volcano blows off, the hot lava of bitterness and resentment descends on everything in its path. Great anger and resentment may characterize the relationship of parent and child for years, leaving scars on both generations. Strong-willed individuals more frequently choose this response to parental domination. The result in cases like this is often alienation. In the process of breaking free, the young adult may sever himself from the support and fellowship of his own family.

QUESTION 2

After reading the article on releasing your child, review the two alternatives parents may force their children to choose if they refuse to release them. What are the potential results of each? Record your response in your Life Notebook.

Both of these alternatives are devastating and detrimental to the relationship between parent and child. The compliant child who accepts the domination of his parents may never grow up. This is a sad phenomenon—a physically mature but emotionally childish adult, incapable of making responsible decisions. On the other hand, the child who refuses to be dominated by his parents often chooses the path of alienation from them.

Are these the only alternatives? Thankfully, the answer is no. There is a better way to launch a son or daughter into adulthood. It involves gradually releasing the child until the fledgling adult is set free to fly on his own.

The Difficulty of Releasing

Why do some parents refuse to let go of their grown or nearly grown children? One reason is that children may have become an extension of the parents. Swindoll comments:

> The first reason for difficulty in releasing a child comes when parents built **themselves** into their children rather than developing the child according to how **God** designed him. When we do this either purposefully or inadvertently, we go through terrible feelings at the time of release. Why? Because a measure of our identity is being passed on. We are, in effect, losing something of ourselves. That's painful.
>
> The father who was not able to become an accomplished musician, for example, or attain other artistic achievements can suffer a lot of inner struggle when his musical son leaves the nest. Part of the father's desires have begun to be lived out in the boy. When release time comes, the father thinks, "I don't want to let him go."
>
> The mother who was terribly frustrated as a child sees in her child the opportunity to build those things she lacked. When it comes time for the daughter to leave on the day of her wedding, mom goes through definite withdrawal pains, because part of her goes that day too. . . .
>
> In other words, one of the most difficult things for a parent to do is to remain objective. Fight like an enemy this subjective tendency of pouring into your children the things you always wanted to become in life. (Swindoll, *You and Your Child,* 154)

A second cause for a difficult release is that the relationship between parent and child has become stronger than the marriage relationship.

QUESTION 3

Read Ephesians 5:22-33. What mention of children do you find in these verses? Can a home be complete without children?

Swindoll stresses that children are not intended to be the weld that holds the home together. Yet that is the case in some families. The marriage is held tenuously together by the glue of the children. When the parent-child relationship is stronger than the marriage relationship, the son or daughter is filling a role that he or she shouldn't. When the child needs to be released to marriage, the parents' use of the child to hold their marriage together is evident (Swindoll, 155).

Swindoll speculates that there may be a correlation between the national divorce rate in America and this tendency of parents to set children as their priority over their spouse. He says:

> The national divorce rate in America, if charted on a graph, resembles a "V" as far as time is concerned. Broken marriages hit a peak in the early years of marriage when the relationship is shaky. When children come along, the divorce rate drops down considerably. Responsibility brings the stark realization: "I have to raise these children, and it's impossible to do it alone." Often a couple will stay together for the sake of the children. The children become the glue that binds an otherwise tenuous relationship together.

Then, about the time the children leave home, the divorce rate soars again until it is almost off the top of the graph. With the release of the children, parents have lost the single thread that bound them together. Release of the child thus becomes cause for mourning. Parents who have built their lives around their child and neglected their relationship with their spouse have reason to mourn. Life suddenly seems so empty without the children when the love between husband and wife has not been adequately nurtured over the years.

It is not fair to you or your child to put him in the position of holding your home together. If parents have an abnormal, unhealthy need for the child, tremendous emotional damage may await the family when it comes time to release the child. Husbands and wives need to recognize if they are in such a pattern and make a commitment to rekindle their love relationship. (Swindoll, 155)

QUESTION 4

Review the two factors discussed thus far that make release difficult. Discuss these with your spouse, and try to ascertain if either of these factors applies to your family. If so, discuss what steps you can take to change the situation. Pray about nurturing your relationship with your spouse, and ask God to help you act on the steps you outline.

Another reason why release can be difficult concerns the immaturity of the child. Sadly, some young people are simply not ready for independence when it is time for them to stand on their own. This may be the result of poor training at home. If parents have not been gradually increasing responsibilities and privileges as the child grows, he or she may remain a child. The nest is too comfortable a place to leave. Mother or father sees that the child's food is prepared for him, his laundry done, his every need provided, and he has little or no responsibility at home. Why shouldn't he stay? There is no incentive for him to face the real world, nor does he know how.

On the other hand, poor training is not always to blame. Perhaps parents have assigned household chores and increased responsibilities with the increasing age of the child, yet the young man or woman appears lazy and lacking in motivation. How should loving parents respond when this is the case? Should they continue to provide for the grown child as they did when he or she was small?

QUESTION 5

Read 2 Thessalonians 3:6-13. What does this passage teach about a disciplined life and idleness? Do you think it is good to allow a grown child to pursue a path of idleness?

If independence and freedom must be granted to those who have passed through the far side of adolescence, it is not in the child's best interests for parents to allow him to pursue a path of laziness and continue to depend on them for all of his physical needs. The adult who continues to live with his parents should be required to carry a share of the household tasks and to make regular contributions to the costs of maintaining the household.

QUESTION 6

If you have grown children, evaluate whether they are still dependent on you to meet most of their physical and emotional needs. If they are, why do you think this is so? How can the situation be changed for the better to encourage more responsibility and independence? If you have no older children, observe a family that you know, and record your observations.

The Method of Releasing

You may be asking, "How is independence to be granted to those children who have passed through the far side of adolescence?" One religious group in America has a ritual concerning adolescence. This very conservative group, known as the Amish, keeps its children under the absolute authority of their parents for the first sixteen years, imposing both very strict standards of behavior and strict discipline. When the young person turns sixteen, however, he enters a period called "Rumspringa." Suddenly, all restrictions are lifted. He or she is free to do as he pleases, including leaving the Amish community.

This method of releasing a child seems to be too abrupt. It is very difficult for a child, who all his life has had his parents make every decision for him, to handle this much freedom all at once. He has not been trained to handle this much independence, and he does not know what to do with it. The process of release should begin much earlier, as parents gradually increase the child's privileges and responsibilities. Each year more and more freedom should be granted so that the final release in early adulthood is merely the final relaxation of authority.

One family developed a practical and fun idea aimed at increasing their child's responsibilities and privileges each successive year throughout the teenage years. On their child's thirteenth birthday they presented him with a small wooden box, a "birthday box," containing two slips of paper—one with new privileges and one with new responsibilities for the coming year. They had a special birthday celebration for their son.

At the conclusion of this family time the father said to his son, "John, I know that you are eager to grow up, and your mother and I are very excited about what lies ahead for you in the next few years. We want to see you become more independent too, and so we have devised the idea of giving you some new freedoms and new responsibilities each year for the next five years. We believe you can handle the new responsibility we have given you, and if you handle it well, you can look forward to further privileges next year on your fourteenth birthday. Whatever goes into next year's birthday box is completely dependent on how well you do with this year's responsibilities and privileges. If you fail in your responsibility, I'm sorry to say that you will not receive new privileges next year. But your mother and I are confident that you can handle these new privileges and responsibilities. We're excited about your growing up, son!"

John was encouraged by his parents' confidence and their desire to help him grow up. He was eager to take advantage of the new privileges they had granted him, of course, but he also wanted to make his parents proud of him by being conscientious in his new responsibilities. His teenage years began with a good attitude, with confidence and optimism, and most important, he felt that his parents were on the same team with him.

The idea of a birthday box can be adapted to each family situation. Parents can develop a plan by considering various areas to include in the privileges and responsibilities. For example, responsibilities can involve academics, household chores, spiritual life, and even personal grooming. Privileges may be added in areas such as curfew, allowances or use of personal money, or leisure activities. Parents can adapt the birthday box concept to the school year, presenting the child with the first box when he enters secondary school. It is also helpful for parents to have a periodic evaluation with their teenager to discuss his progress.

QUESTION 7

Spend some time with your spouse discussing how you might adapt the idea of the "birthday box" to use with your child. Write down any suggestions you have for new privileges and responsibilities that you think would be appropriate for your teenager or preadolescent. Develop a tentative plan of birthday box privileges and responsibilities.

If you do not have a teenager, try to recall your own teenage years. What are some of the new privileges you might have welcomed year by year? What new responsibilities do you think might have been appropriate?

As we plan and encourage our teenager toward the goal of independence, our relationship can grow in positive ways, so that we can look forward to a close and caring relationship with our grown children.

Topic 2: Learning to Relate to Our Grown Children

Parents are sometimes saddened when children reach young adulthood because they fear that the closeness that existed between parent and child will now be dissolved. As the child moves away from the control of his parents, they fear that they will also lose his love and have little involvement in his life.

The relationship between parent and child does change as the child reaches adulthood, but it need not deteriorate or dissolve. As parents learn to relate to their grown child, and as the young person discovers his parents as human beings and as friends, the relationship can deepen. We will look at several factors that are essential in learning to relate to our grown children.

Learn to Develop Open and Honest Communication

Earlier in this course we talked about the importance of knowing your child. We encouraged parents to study each of their children. The problem with making a study of your child is that children are not static. They grow and they change at an alarming rate—not only physically but in every other area, so our "research" must be ongoing if we are to know our child at each stage of his development. His abilities change, his interests change, and his opinions change. Parents of a young adult need to be open and available to communicate with their grown child if they really want to understand how he thinks.

To understand the young adult and to be able to relate to his world involves some effort on the part of parents. The gap between youth and age need not be so extreme, however, if parents make a real effort to understand how young people are thinking and if they recall that their own maturation was a gradual process.

Wisdom and maturity do not arrive overnight when a young person turns sixteen, eighteen, or twenty. They continue to develop. Parents sometimes make the mistake of expecting the young adult to have wisdom beyond his years, wisdom that they themselves have accumulated over the years. The young adult has to learn, as we did, from experience. We will have a better chance to communicate some of our accumulated wisdom if we learn not to push too hard and not to become overly critical of our child's differing opinions.

Learn to Relate as a Friend

When your child is grown, you relate to him differently—not so much as a parent but as a friend. Part of learning to communicate is learning how to relate more as a friend than as a parent. This is difficult for some parents, and some never achieve it.

What is the difference between relating to a young adult as a parent and as a friend? Let us imagine that your newly married daughter tells you that she has a problem with cockroaches in her kitchen. The "parent" in you is immediately prepared to give her advice—to tell her how to solve the problem. Instead, stop for a moment and think how you might respond to the same situation with a friend. You would likely say something like, "Oh, no!" and ask in an interested manner, "What have you done to get rid of them?" Eventually, you may tactfully suggest a way to deal with the pests, but it is best to do this in a nondirective manner. You may say, for example, "We had cockroaches a few years ago, and I tried several ways to get rid of them." Then your daughter is free to ask, "What worked?" In this way she is in the position of asking for your advice rather than receiving it unsolicited.

The wise parent learns to limit the giving of unsolicited advice and avoid lecturing or treating the young adult like a child. The young person who has reached adulthood desires above all to be treated like an adult. If you violate this principle, you will jeopardize your relationship with him. Your grown child generally is not seeking advice; he wants to talk to you on the level of one adult to another. He needs you to be a good listener and to convey your genuine interest in him. Open communication is vital to a close and loving relationship.

Learn to Disagree without Being Disagreeable

Must a parent sit and smile and agree with everything his child says in order to show him that he accepts him as an adult? No. As in a friendship, you can disagree, but learn to disagree without being disagreeable. Who of us likes to be around someone who censures all that we do? Just as in a friendship, you and your grown child will not always share the same opinion on things. Begin by accepting the fact that your opinion is just that—your opinion. You may not always be right. Some matters are not simply black or white, right or wrong. There can be more than one acceptable opinion on many matters.

Many of us are often prone to be too rigid, particularly in the areas where we feel we have some expertise. Think of the poor woman mentioned earlier, whose elderly mother believed there is only one proper way to peel a carrot. Since her daughter did not do it in this way, her mother banned her from peeling carrots in her kitchen. We can see the ridiculousness of this situation as uninvolved spectators, but if we are honest, there may be areas where we insist on doing things our own way or forcing our opinions on others.

QUESTION 8

Think about yourself for a few moments. Are you prone to be too opinionated, too sure that you are always right about things? Do you find it hard to be flexible? Does it bother you if others do things differently? Is your way usually the best one?

If you answer yes to these questions, ask yourself why you tend to be this way. Why is it important to you to always be right? What problems can this tendency create? What are some steps you might take to curb this tendency?

Learn to Tear Down the Walls that Divide

Many parents are overly critical of everything their child does. When their child reaches adulthood, such parents continue to criticize every decision their son or daughter makes. They cannot let their grown child accept the consequences of his own choices—they argue; they plead; they do everything to try to change their son's or daughter's mind.

By reacting negatively to their children's choices, whether it be the way they raise their children or the spouse they choose or how they spend their money, parents often build a wall between them and their children. Bitterness and resentment can grow in both child and parent. The Bible warns believers specifically about bitterness (Eph 4:31).

Bitterness can take hold in the soil of your heart or your child's heart and grow until it chokes the relationship between you and your adult child. Frequently this happens when a child makes a choice that the parents simply cannot accept. What do you do, for example, when your grown child chooses to join another church, one you know is not teaching the Word of God? One family was deeply hurt when their only child left their church and became involved in a non-Christian cult. Whenever the daughter came home to visit, she tried to convert her parents to this false belief. They were so uncomfortable that they thought it best not to see her at all.

Several years passed until the parents realized that they had allowed bitterness to choke out the joy they had previously had in their relationship with their grown daughter. They had grown apart from her, and they felt a real sense of loss. The parents were wise enough to open the door to a renewed relationship. They carefully explained to their daughter that, while they did not agree with her choice of a church, they loved her and would always love her.

Now they see each other and have warm personal contact with her and with their grandchildren again. The daughter has not left the sect yet, but the parents know that she loves them, respects them, and perhaps she will eventually see her error as they keep the door of communication open between them. They do not nag; they seldom discuss this touchy area. She knows how they feel, and the choice lies with her. For she is an adult; her parents are no longer responsible before the Lord for her actions.

As parents we must be willing to be flexible, to listen to the opinions of our grown child with an open mind, and to consider what he or she is feeling. We can be close to our adult child without having to agree on every issue. We are responsible to stand on our own convictions, to share our faith with our loved ones, to treat them with respect, and then to leave the results with God.

If you find yourself focusing only on the negative, it may help you to make a conscious effort to focus on the agreeable things, as Philippians 4:8 encourages us to do. Spend some time thinking about what you do like about your child, about the positive attributes in him or her. Ask God to help you accept your child the way he is now—a mixture of positive and negative things, just as God accepts that same unlikely mixture in you and goes on loving you and forgiving you and encouraging you to be more like Him.

If a critical spirit has built up a wall between you and your child, steps need to be taken to tear down the walls between you. The first step toward restoring a broken relationship is to forgive.

QUESTION 9

Read Matthew 6:14-15, Mark 11:25, Ephesians 4:32, and Colossians 3:13. What do these verses teach about forgiveness? Why do you think our heavenly Father cannot forgive us if we do not forgive others? Read Matthew 7:3-5. How do these verses apply to our need to ask forgiveness of our children? Do you think you need to ask forgiveness of your children for creating barriers between you? Ask God to make this clear to you, and then follow through on it.

Forgiveness is a prerequisite for restoring a broken relationship and tearing down the walls that exist between you and your child. Perhaps he or she has wronged you and never asked for forgiveness. Yet if you continue to hold onto your hurt and resentment, you can waste your life in bitterness. Ask God to help you let go of your anger or resentment and to help you forgive the one who has hurt you. If you need to, ask forgiveness of your child for holding a grudge against him or for rejecting him in anger.

Forgiveness Takes Down Barriers

Begin now to take down the wall between you and your child. If it was built brick by brick, it can be taken down brick by brick, and a new relationship of love, mutual respect, and trust can be built.

Learn to Support and Not Control Your Grown Child

The dictionary defines "control" as "to hold in restraint or check; to subject to authority; to direct; to regulate; to govern; to dominate."

Much of this definition describes the activities and responsibilities of a parent. As parents we hold our little ones in restraint; we do not let Junior hit his younger sister or throw his dinner against the wall. We "exercise control" over them until they have learned to exercise control over themselves. We "direct" them in personal hygiene and safety habits; we "regulate" their diet and bedtime; we "govern" their activities and see that they do their homework. This is all part of controlling our child.

But as a child gradually learns self-control, our role shifts increasingly to a support role. The definition of support is "to uphold by aid, encouragement, or countenance; to keep from shrinking, sinking, failing, or fainting."

This too is familiar to parents. From the time we hear that first cry, we are there to "uphold" our baby, pat his little back, rock him gently in the wee hours of the morning, and "aid" in any way we can to make our child comfortable and happy. We "encourage" him as he takes his first faltering steps. We lovingly take the hand of our kindergartner as he "shrinks" from entering the school room; we hold his slippery arms so he will not "sink" when he first ventures out into the water. We are also there through the teenage years helping our children so they will not "fail," and standing alongside so they will not "faint" when they are discouraged.

All of this we do to support our children physically and emotionally. Does this privilege end when our children are grown? No, the support system between parent and child becomes even stronger as the years progress. So while we are no longer responsible to control our grown children, we continue to support them, encourage them, and uphold them.

Unfortunately, it can be very difficult for parents who have been trying to control their grown children to cease controlling. We must cease control, however, and instead release our children as they mature so that they might become independent people.

But while control stops, the support of our children continues for a lifetime. We all appreciate it when someone encourages or uplifts us or keeps us from failing in our tasks. What a precious opportunity we have as parents to be able to support our own children. The world is a difficult place to live for a Christian, whose real citizenship is in heaven. Our grown children will always need our encouragement and our support!

QUESTION 10

Can you think of ways you may have been trying to control your grown child? List these in your Life Notebook, and spend some time in prayer before the Lord. Ask God to help you to undo any damage you may have caused by seeking to control rather than support your grown child.

QUESTION 11

Review the definition of the word "support." Discuss with your spouse some positive ways you can be a support to your children without having to be in control. Record the answers in your Life Notebook.

Topic 3: Learning to Relate When Parents and Grown Children Live Together

Whether a newlywed couple will live with their parents or live independently can be either a matter of culture or necessity. There can be many positive aspects of extended families living together, such as the additional support and physical help afforded by grandparents or other relatives. But under these living arrangements it is also common to experience added stress.

Develop Mutual Respect

In every family it is essential for each member to be willing to cooperate to make the family unit a healthy one. This is even more important when several family members of a wide age range must share a home. Physical and spatial arrangements can pose problems, of course, and we need to use God-given creativity to minimize these problems. But the most difficult part of living together is often meshing the various personalities so that each member will have his rightful place in the home and be free to live a happy and productive life.

When several families must live together, it is important to demonstrate mutual respect for one another's habits and ways of doing things. Every woman, for example, has her own particular way of doing things in the kitchen, often habits learned from her own mother. The mother or mother-in-law who insists that her way is the only way is inviting conflict or resentment.

Similarly, a father or father-in-law must recognize the varying gifts and abilities of his children or their spouses and refrain from having a critical spirit where they may not measure up to his standards. Criticism is always the beginning of an unhappy relationship within the extended family. Respect for other opinions and other ways of doing things is a basic requirement for healthy family living.

QUESTION 12

If you live in an extended family situation, do you think there is mutual respect for one another in this situation? How could such respect be cultivated?

Accept Your Child's Spouse

The child's choice of a spouse is frequently the subject of criticism from parents. Some parents would not be satisfied with anyone their son or daughter chose; others have a legitimate reason to disapprove, such as when a child chooses to marry an unbeliever. The time to express your reservations is definitely before the wedding plans are made. If you genuinely feel your child is making a big mistake, you should tell him so, but do it gently, lovingly, stating your reasons clearly when you are in a position to be calm and in control of your emotions. Ask your son or daughter to think about what you have shared and to pray over this decision again before finalizing it.

Once the child decides to go ahead with the decision, it is best if parents accept their child's selection and begin to cultivate the relationship with their new son- or daughter-in-law. If parents fail to do this, untold misery can result.

One woman described living with her husband's family for twenty-seven years. Her father-in-law made her life miserable. He did not believe she was good enough to marry his son, and he let her know that frequently during those years. In his later years he became an invalid, and it was his daughter-in-law who cared for him. One day she was shaving the old man, and he told her that she meant as much to him as his own children. Astonished, she replied, "But you didn't want me to marry Nicolas." He shrugged and said, "Oh, I didn't really know you then." Sadly, his praise came twenty-seven years too late for this woman. The pain and resentment this rejected daughter-in-law had experienced all those years were not swept aside so easily.

Sadly, her husband offered little emotional support to his wife throughout those years. Perhaps because of loyalty to parents, it is often difficult for a grown son or daughter to take a stand for his spouse if it means standing against a parent. Yet the Bible indicates that a man is to leave his father and mother in order to cleave to his wife, and this implies that the relationship with one's spouse should take precedence over previous family ties. If the parents reject their son's choice of a wife and refuse to change, then he must stand with his wife against his own parents and support her in the situation in which they are forced to live.

If Christian parents determine to accept their child's choice of a mate, much conflict can be avoided. Instead of seeking to prove that their child has indeed made a poor choice, parents can decide to make every effort to encourage and build up their child's spouse. The relationship can be fostered and nurtured to the point where genuine respect and love replace suspicion and dislike.

The relationship between a mother-in-law and daughter-in-law seems particularly prone to many problems. Many women seem to have a built-in distrust of their mother-in-law, perhaps fueled by the mother-in-law jokes and stories that are common in many cultures. Some younger women may feel a sense of rivalry toward their husband's mother, perhaps because in their mind he appears to be too attached to her. Some feel insecure in their new role as a wife and feel a need to prove that they are better cooks or housekeepers than their husband's mother. These feelings can create an awkward situation—a husband must walk a tightrope between trying to be a dutiful son and being emotionally supportive of his wife.

Young women need to remind themselves that their mother-in-law helped to shape this man they have come to love by her years of teaching and training. She should have a very special place in his heart and also in his wife's, and gratitude is due her for raising him. Whatever shortcomings she may have, it is best if the daughter-in-law refrains from criticizing her to her husband. To do so is to force him to make painful choices of loyalty and to attempt to divide him from one he is told to honor.

On the other hand, every mother-in-law would do well to recognize the difficult task facing her daughter-in-law, learning a new role as wife. If the young woman is living in her husband's parents' home, the situation may be even more difficult for her. She must interact in a setting that may be very different from what she has known in her own home. The ways of doing things are different.

As the more mature woman, it is the mother-in-law's responsibility to graciously help her daughter-in-law to feel at home. She needs to be sensitive and understanding if the younger woman asserts her will in some areas. Recognize that there are other ways of doing things; it will not hurt to let your daughter or daughter-in-law do things her way. As the young woman's confidence builds and her insecurity lessens, you may be rewarded with her deep respect and friendship.

Avoid Interfering in Child-Rearing

Another potential area of conflict when parents and grown children live together concerns child-rearing. Since the grandparents have had more experience, they are often eager to be helpful in the care and training of their grandchildren. Their advice is usually well-meant, and young parents should not feel threatened by it. The problem arises when grandparents become too helpful, when they cross the line from being helpful to interfering.

Interference can take many forms. Many parents find it especially distressing when grandparents interfere in the discipline of their children. Some grandparents attempt to shield their grandchild from parental discipline, to discredit the parents, or to win the love and loyalty of the grandchild by pampering him. Although they may have been strict with their own children, they recoil in shock when they see their precious grandchild being reproved or spanked.

Some ground rules regarding the children need to be established when two families live together. Ideally, parents should meet with the grandparents at the outset of the living arrangement to discuss their wishes regarding training and discipline, their philosophy of child-rearing, and to set up a few guidelines for working and living together. It would be wise to have periodic discussions to review the living situation in an effort to avoid misunderstandings that can easily grow out of proportion.

Parents need not insist that the grandparents have no right to discipline the child. Living in the same home makes it necessary for them to discipline at times, particularly if the grandparents help with childcare while the parents work.

Grandparents have rights also, especially in their own home, and the parents should recognize and honor their wishes as much as possible. But when it comes to child-rearing, the parents bear the ultimate responsibility. If grandparents disagree with the parents' handling of children, the matter should be discussed in private. Open disagreement about the means of discipline tends to undermine the parents' control and confuse the child. It might also give him the opportunity to manipulate his parents or grandparents.

Another important thing to remember is that, when there are more people living together, the result is inevitably less time for parents to spend with a child, giving him the undivided attention he needs. Parents need to be more aware of what a child is thinking and feeling, particularly the quiet child, who may not voice his hurts or frustrations. Make it a point to make time for each child individually. Plan some activities for parents and child alone—without the other family members.

QUESTION 13

Have you observed a situation where parents and grandparents disagree about the discipline and training of the children? What problems have you noted? What effect has this situation had on the children? What guidelines for living together would you suggest in this particular situation?

Establish Ground Rules for Living Together

One family faced a very painful experience when a mother moved into her daughter's home. Having been the boss in her own home, grandmother now determined to be the boss in her daughter's home. Although the family tried to make her happy, she became more and more demanding. She challenged everyone in every area, and each day brought new confrontations. She was determined to be in control: she countermanded the parents' instructions to the children; she interfered in their discipline and actually took over; she opened all mail, demanded to be told the details of every phone call, criticized the children excessively, and turned every meal into a confrontation. Life became unbearable, yet the parents did not know how to break the cycle.

Finally, after discovering their son in tears one day as a result of something grandmother said, this couple realized that their children were being adversely affected by the situation at home. After much prayer and discussion, the husband and wife recognized that it was necessary for the preservation of the family to set up some rules for grandmother to adhere to if she wished to live with them. They chose only the most important areas to set up rules, spelling out what would not be tolerated. Grandmother was not to interfere in the children's training: she was not to discipline them, and there were certain subjects that were no longer permitted at the dinner table. Grandmother was given the plan.

The grandchildren were also given a corresponding plan with rules for them to follow. For example, they would never be permitted to sass their grandmother but were expected to treat her with respect. But if she broke the rules regarding discipline, the children were free to leave the room.

The plan was strictly enforced. On nights when grandmother insisted on discussing forbidden topics at dinner, everyone else got up and left the table. Grandmother ate quite a few meals alone before she began to get the idea. At first the peace in the home was forced, but eventually genuine peace began to return. Grandmother lived with the family fifteen years after that and learned to adjust to family living in her

---

daughter's home. In her later years the grandson and granddaughter she had so often criticized became the source of great pride and joy to her.

This is one way a Christian family found to apply Christian principles to their living situation. Whatever the situation, there is a way to approach it that will honor God. Undoubtedly, multiple generations living together can present problems. Yet there are creative ways to make the best of an awkward situation and to bring peace and reconciliation to families, as we learn to respect and understand the other persons involved. Solutions that are based on biblical teaching and mutually agreed on will be most effective.

QUESTION 14

Think of an awkward family situation you know of. What do you believe is the major reason for the problem? Read Romans 12:9-21. What principles could you use from these verses that might be helpful in resolving the conflicts or easing the tensions of such a situation? How could you apply these verses to the situation?

Topic 4: Learning to Rest in God

The story does not end when the nest is empty of its baby birds. Being a parent is lasts for a lifetime. No matter how big our little ones have grown to be, they will always occupy a special place in our hearts, and we will continue to care very deeply about all that happens to them. The road now lies ahead of our children, and it may be a straight path or a crooked one.

If we have raised our children to love the Lord, if they know Him as their personal Savior, we can release our children with confidence that they are in His keeping. When we open our hand and let our child go, we have the assurance that our child is still in the hand of God. Jesus said of His sheep, "No one shall snatch them out of My hand," and He continued, "My Father, who has given them to Me, is greater than all; and no one is able to snatch them out of the Father's hand" (Jn 10:28-29).

Our children are safer in God's hands than they ever could be in our own tightly-closed fists. As we open our hands to release them, we do not release them to destruction or oblivion but to the care and the keeping of the loving Father in heaven, to the safety of the hollow of His hand. Where could a child go where God would not be? We looked at Psalm 139 early in this course, marveling at the gift God has placed in our hand. As we conclude this course, we return to Psalm 139. Like David, our child cannot flee from God's Spirit or from His presence. There is no place on earth he can run where God cannot find him. Though he makes his bed in the depths, God is there; though he settle on the far side of the sea, even there God's hand will guide him, and His right hand will hold him fast.

Resting in Crooked Times and Straight Times

Learning to trust God to work in the lives of our children is a lifelong process. Our grown children may make some painful mistakes. They may even choose a path that we feel sure will lead to destruction. There will be times when we may say to God, "Lord, where are You? Are You really working in my child's life?" Some parents may watch their child walk a pathway of suffering, illness, and even death. It is very natural that questions flood our mind when our children walk a crooked path or face a crooked world.

Our world is full of suffering that is often inexplicable. We can hardly experience life at all without running headlong into a brick wall, a problem or difficulty that we have no answer to. Life is full of puzzles and pain. Yet the Bible assures us that God is in control of history and of the circumstances of life. Ephesians 1:11 says, "In him we were also chosen, having been predestined according to the plan of him who works out everything in conformity with the purpose of his will" (NIV).

When problems arise, our tendency is often to question God, to wonder about the purpose of His will. We wonder where He is, if He cares, and why He does not change the situation if He is truly in control of the universe. Pain touches us most deeply, perhaps, in the deep recesses of our being, when it is our children who are suffering. When one of them is suffering or dying or walking far from the Lord, in the midst of our personal suffering we wonder, "Is God really in control? How can all things be working for good?"

As believers we need to remind ourselves that Scripture teaches that God is sovereign. As the supreme ruler of the heavens and earth, He is in control of all things (1 Chron 29:11; Ps 93:1). With the truth of God's sovereignty as his basis, Job proclaimed, "I know that Thou canst do all things, and that no purpose of Thine can be thwarted" (Job 42:2).

The God whose purposes cannot be thwarted—what kind of God is He? The Bible says His nature is love (1 Jn 4:7-8). The Bible says that He is good and that He withholds no good thing from His children (Ps 84:11; 86:5).

God reigns supreme. He is in control of all things, and He can never make a mistake. His way is perfect (Ps 18:30). He is in control when the path is straight and when it is crooked. "Consider the work of God; for who can make straight what He has made crooked? In the day of prosperity be joyful, but in the day of adversity consider: surely God has appointed the one as well as the other" (Eccl 7:13-14, NKJV).

When the path seems straight, when the day is one of prosperity for our family, we rejoice. When our children make right decisions, when they want to follow the Lord, we rejoice. We feel good about our parenting. We rejoice because it is a time to rejoice.

There will also be times, however, to mourn—crooked times. There will be times of adversity. And in these times, we must remember that God has made the one as well as the other and that during the crooked times God is still fitting together everything in our families, even though we cannot see it. When life is going smoothly, when everything seems to fall into place, we do not tend to question whether God is in control. But when things are crooked, when we face adversity, we wonder why God does not simply make the path straight.

The Bible indicates that there are several causes for crooked circumstances. Sometimes we create them ourselves and God allows us to live with the consequences. We think of the example of David, a man after God's own heart, who allowed lust to drive him to murder Uriah, the husband of the woman he desired. Although he sought forgiveness of the Lord and received it, he still suffered the consequences of his own sinful choices, including the death of the child born to Bathsheba. David brought grief to himself by his choice of a crooked path (see 2 Sam 11).

At other times a crooked path awaits us or our children for no apparent reason. We can only conclude that God has allowed this suffering in order to teach us some deep lessons about Him. Regardless of the cause of crooked circumstances, God can use them for His purposes.

When we sink in despair, believing that the pieces of our life will never fit together again, God says they already do. From the perspective of eternity God sees the whole plan of your life and your children's lives, and He sees how the pieces all fit together, the smooth ones and the crooked ones.

Romans 8:28 teaches that every event that befalls one who loves God, no matter how awful it may be in itself, will be taken captive by the hand of the Almighty and forced into bringing an ultimate blessing rather than a curse to the life it touches.

This confidence is fundamental to our spiritual, mental, and emotional health during times of crisis. The promise of Romans 8:28 is not given to everyone but to those who love God, those who are His redeemed children, who have repented of their sins and trusted in Jesus Christ for their salvation. As His children we can face even the hardest of circumstances with confidence that God is in control of our lives. Our loving Father has worked even our mistakes as parents into His plans for good.

God is supreme and sovereign, and God will never fail. Our children will fail and will disappoint us at times. We will be disappointed in ourselves at times. Our expectations will not always be fulfilled. We will have many opportunities to ask, "How can this be working for good, Lord?"

In her book *The Tapestry,* Edith Schaeffer conveys the idea that, though life may at times seem like a frayed and patternless mass of yarn, if we could but see it from God's viewpoint, we would see that all of the events of our life are being woven together into a beautiful tapestry that will one day declare the wisdom, love, and glory of God.

If we are confident that God is working out His purposes in our life, we can learn what it means to "be anxious for nothing" (Phil 4:6). We can relax and trust God to work in our children, to let Him remind them of what they have been taught, to convict them of sin, and to urge them to holy living. When we trust God, when we accept His will regarding our grown children, and when we release them into His hands, we know His peace. We know that He is weaving a beautiful tapestry of our lives.

He can use seemingly crooked thread at times. As we see our grown child make mistakes and as we grieve over our own sins as parents, we may be tempted to despair at times. But God can take these "crooked" threads that we have created and weave them together for good in our lives and in the lives of our children.

QUESTION 15

Rewrite Ecclesiastes 7:13-14 in your own words. What do these verses admonish you to do when things are going well? When there is adversity? How can you apply these verses to your own family life? Can you think of a "crooked" situation in your family life? Is it one God has created or one you have brought on yourself? How does Romans 8:28 relate to this crooked situation?

Deepening our Prayer Life

The natural outflow of trusting God is praying to Him. The natural outflow of prayer is trusting God. Prayer and faith and obedience form a cycle in the believer's life. We pray, and we are encouraged that God is a loving Father who hears us. Our faith is strengthened, and we desire to act out our faith in obedience. As we pray, our desires are brought more into line with the desires of God for us—so that we learn to desire His will and are content when He reveals it to us.

If we truly love our children, we should pray for them, entrusting them daily to the Lord's keeping, long after they are grown and living their own lives. As we pray for our children daily, we can learn to bring our desires concerning them into line with the desires of God, so that we truly seek His will for our children.

Job provides an example of a man who prayed faithfully for his children, offering daily sacrifices on their behalf. Job was a man of prayer, and his children's spiritual well-being was an important aspect of his prayer life.

In Philippians 4:6 we read, "Be anxious for nothing, but in everything by prayer and supplication with thanksgiving let your requests be made known to God" (NASB). We are not to be anxious in the crooked times but to bring our requests before the Lord. As parents it is often easier for us to be anxious than it is for us to pray. The natural thing is to be anxious. The supernatural thing is to pray—and to experience the peace of God even in the midst of crooked situations.

Since Paul admonishes us to "be anxious for nothing," it would seem that we can make a conscious choice not to be anxious. We are to choose not to be anxious but rather to give everything to God concerning our children. We are to let our requests be made known to Him, praying for our children from the time they are small until the time we release them. Then we need to pray some more—for our grown children.

According to Philippians 4:6-7, our part is not to be anxious but to give everything to God in prayer. We may ask, "What is God's part?" Verse 7 says, "And the peace of God, which surpasses all comprehension, shall guard your hearts and your minds in Christ Jesus."

God's part is to give us peace. God promises us that, as we choose not to be anxious about our children, as we choose to pray and bring our requests concerning our children to God, He will give us His peace. God promises that His peace will guard our hearts and our minds in Christ Jesus. Our heart, the seat of our emotions, needs to be guarded against those fears that all parents have at one time or another concerning their children. Our mind, the seat of our intellect, needs to be guarded against thinking and dwelling on all the negative things that can happen to our children. God promises that His peace is a peace that guards, so we might be free and be able to rest in Him regardless of the circumstances.

Engaging in the ministry of continual prayer, then, is a key step in the process of releasing our children to God. Indeed, to continue to pray regularly for our children throughout their lives may be our greatest ministry to them.

QUESTION 16

Have you chosen to pray concerning the things you are anxious about? This month record in your Life Notebook some particular areas in your child's life that God brings to your attention to pray about. Commit yourself to pray regularly for your child concerning these areas. Note any changes in yourself or your child you observe. If you do not already have one, begin keeping a prayer notebook for your children. Make it an ongoing habit to record answers to prayer in this notebook. Spend time praising God for answers to prayer regarding your children.

Trusting God in the Dark

How much easier it would be to trust God if we could just get a peek at the finished tapestry. If we could just see our child's whole life stretched out before us, if we could see that our child would receive Christ and would grow to become a godly man or woman, it would be so much easier to trust God. But that is not faith. Faith is the assurance of things hoped for, the conviction of things not seen. Faith is trusting God, even in the dark, when we do not know where the road leads or what the outcome will be.

We love our children so much that it is easy to become anxious, rather than to trust God for what we cannot see. God is sovereign, and He wants us parents to trust Him for what we cannot now see in the lives of our children. We are to trust our wonderful Father daily for wisdom to raise the children He has given us. We are to trust Him, too, for whatever the final outcome may be in the lives of our children.

QUESTION 17

In your Life Notebook, list the major areas of your child's life God still wants you to entrust to Him. If possible, attach key Scripture verses related to each area. As you pray for your child, commit these areas to Him, and trust Him for what you cannot see.

Answers to Questions

QUESTION 1: *Your answer*

QUESTION 2: *Your answer*

QUESTION 3: *Your answer*

QUESTION 4: *Your answer*

QUESTION 5: *Your answer*

QUESTION 6: *Your answer*

QUESTION 7: *Your answer*

QUESTION 8: *Your answer*

QUESTION 9: *Your answer*

QUESTION 10: *Your answer*

QUESTION 11: *Your answer*

QUESTION 12: *Your answer*

QUESTION 13: *Your answer*

QUESTION 14: *Your answer*

QUESTION 15: *Your answer*

QUESTION 16: *Your answer*

QUESTION 17: *Your answer*

Lesson 12 Self Check

QUESTION 1

The process of releasing a child begins at about age seventeen. *True or False?*

QUESTION 2

Most grown children are eager for advice from their parents. *True or False?*

QUESTION 3

By reacting negatively to our children's choices, we can build a wall between us. *True or False?*

QUESTION 4

The relationship with one's spouse should take precedence over previous family ties. *True or False?*

QUESTION 5

Some parents refuse to let go of their grown children because the children have become an extension of the parents. *True or False?*

QUESTION 6

Children are designed to be the weld that holds the home together. *True or False?*

QUESTION 7

Physical and spatial problems are usually the hardest ones to solve when families live together. *True or False?*

QUESTION 8

Once the decision is final, it is best if parents accept their child's choice of a spouse. *True or False?*

QUESTION 9

Grandparents have no right to discipline grandchildren. *True or False?*

QUESTION 10

God sometimes causes crooked circumstances. *True or False?*

Lesson 12 Self Check Answers

QUESTION 1: False
QUESTION 2: False
QUESTION 3: True
QUESTION 4: True
QUESTION 5: True
QUESTION 6: False
QUESTION 7: False
QUESTION 8: True
QUESTION 9: False
QUESTION 10: True

Made in the USA
Coppell, TX
27 October 2024

39226212R00164